"This book contains the most comprehensive study conducted so far on health innovation in developing countries. The author shows again her capacity to undertake empirical research with a solid theoretical background. This book is outstanding not only because of its academic value. The evidence presented and its rigorous analysis provides essential elements for policy makers in developing countries, and more broadly, for those seeking global solutions to the diseases that disproportionately affect the poor."

Carlos Correa, Director Centre for Law and Economics, University of Buenos Aires

"If you can read just one book on health, innovation and development, read this book. It is grounded on an enviable theoretical foundation and presents a set of new, fascinating evidence and case studies from latecomer countries. I recommend this book most highly."

Banji Oyeyinka, Director, UNHABITAT and Professorial Fellow, United Nations University-MERIT

"A most persuasive book that proposes a rethink on health issues and access to medicines in the context of development. The author builds a compelling case, based on evidence from several case studies, on how the health needs of the poorest can be met best."

Pedro Roffe, Senior Fellow, International Centre for Trade and Sustainable Development, Geneva

"Padmashree Gehl Sampath has an impressive record of researching global health and access to medicines. The innovation perspective on these issues presented in this book is of great interest to scholars and activists around the world."

Hans Lofgren, Deakin University, Australia

Reconfiguring Global Health Innovation

Reconfiguring Global Health Innovation presents the findings of multi-year research, contrasting experiences of different latecomer countries in building health innovation systems to cater to local needs. It analyses the emerging industrial structures in health innovation as more and more latecomer countries are foraying into what is a highly difficult and technologically intensive sector, with the aim of finding ways and means to balance these promising developments with public health needs worldwide.

The book presents empirical findings from six countries across Asia and Africa on health innovation, namely, India, Bangladesh, Vietnam, Kenya, Tanzania and Nigeria. The book concludes that the growth of knowledge and the accumulation of capabilities influence the ability of a country to cater to its health needs.

Comprehensive and wide ranging, the following issues are covered: the interplay between global "pull" institutions and local "push" institutions in building health innovation capacity, the role of states to provide supportive frameworks for the development of institutional capacity and, finally, the linkages between local health innovation, health systems efficiency and access to medicines. The author tackles these issues through a theoretical framework that links health innovation and technological learning with issues of late development. The theoretical analysis is substantiated with the empirical analysis using field data from the author's own work in six countries. This makes for a well-rounded study that will be of great value to academics and researchers alike.

Padmashree Gehl Sampath is Economic Affairs Officer at the United Nations Conference on Trade and Development (UNCTAD) and Research Fellow at the United Nations University-MERIT.

Routledge international studies in health economics
Edited by Charles Normand
Trinity College Dublin, Ireland
and
Richard M. Scheffler
School of Public Health, University of California, Berkeley, USA

Reconfiguring Global Health Innovation

Padmashree Gehl Sampath

Routledge
Taylor & Francis Group

LONDON AND NEW YORK

First published 2011
by Routledge
2 Park Square, Milton Park, Abingdon, Oxfordshire OX14 4RN

Simultaneously published in the USA and Canada
by Routledge
711 Third Avenue, New York, NY 10017

First issued in paperback 2014

Routledge is an imprint of the Taylor & Francis Group, an informa business

© 2011 Padmashree Gehl Sampath

Typeset in Times by Wearset Ltd, Boldon, Tyne and Wear

British Library Cataloguing in Publication Data
A catalogue record for this book is available from the British Library

Library of Congress Cataloging in Publication Data
Gehl Sampath, Padmashree.
Reconfiguring global health innovation/by Padmashree Gehl Sampath.
p. cm.
Includes index.

1. Medical innovations–Developing countries. 2. World health. I. Title.
RA418.5.M4S26 2010
362.109172′4–dc22

ISBN: 978-1-138-88079-5 (pbk)
ISBN: 978-0-415-58578-1 (hbk)

Contents

Figures

Tables

Boxes

Foreword

This book explores a fundamental question in international negotiations today: how do countries innovate in pharmaceuticals and health, and what factors distinguish those that succeed from others that fail? It focuses on the conditions and factors that are critical in enabling innovation in health technologies and related knowledge accumulation in the developing world. It seeks to understand the factors that explain the success of some countries over others in setting up health innovation systems *with a predominant emphasis on local health needs*. Through its title and its analysis, the book introduces a term – health innovation – that has been sparingly used in the literature on the topic and underscores the importance of viewing issues under such a classification. It provides a framework of health innovation systems to integrate issues of production, innovation, policy incentives and access to medicines – all of which, the book claims are intricately inter-connected in theory and practice.

The book and its analysis benefits from my extensive involvement in the field conducting wide area innovation surveys at the national and sectoral levels in pharmaceuticals and health in several countries over the past ten years, some of which have not been presented here because of space and other constraints. It is in fact the discrepancies between the policy negotiations and what one sees in the field, in different countries in Asia and Africa, working, interviewing and researching with all kinds of actors involved in pharmaceutical and health innovation that prompted me to write this book. Amongst the myriad concerns and perspectives being expressed on the broader thematic of pharmaceutical production, IPRs and access to medicines, an innovation perspective could help countries and policy makers prioritize and integrate the practical issues of technical change and knowledge accumulation for the sector.

Technological catch-up, especially in sectors that are of extreme importance to the social wellbeing of developing and least developed countries such as health, is rendered more complex and difficult by the range of international, regional and national factors that impinge on countries in the present landscape. Working together with governments and local actors to find solutions to these pressing issues of development calls forth newer perspectives on developmental issues; specifically those that are informed by ground realities of technological, social and organizational innovations in the sectors within countries.

The experiences lead us to two important sets of conclusions. There is no separation of issues in the creation, dissemination and use of innovations in health and pharmaceuticals according to popular notions of intellectual property, access to medicines, access to knowledge, drug quality and safety, and technological change. Access to knowledge does not automatically translate into technical change; access to medicines does not automatically guarantee better health care; and ensuring that countries have more TRIPS flexibilities does not automatically mean that they can and will use them to promote local industries. At the same time, promoting a country's local pharmaceutical capacity does not also mean that the people are assured cheaper and easily available medicines. These factors are all inter-linked in more ways that we had earlier imagined and operate within what can be called industrial or innovation policies of countries, at the sectoral and national levels. Central to the experiences of all countries that succeeded in building capacity in health innovation is a set of policies and institutions that today are lumped under industrial and innovation policies. State capacity to enact rules, provide institutional support and champion the cause of better health care and health access is critical to enable an actively engaged and functioning local innovation system that promotes access to medicines. Second, the weaker developing countries with low levels of capacity to perform health innovation today are faced with greater challenges that lay ahead of their predecessors – they have greater restrictions as part of the global multilateral regime and face greater competition within their local economies, while trying to resuscitate their weaker innovation environments that still suffer from the shortcomings of their colonial pasts and initial conditions. These countries need greater support from the international community, scholars and national actors alike in fostering and supporting technical change, especially in the health sector.

Such support is constantly undermined by two main assumptions. First, assertions that question the ability of low income countries or least developed countries to engage in health innovation, to provide for greater access to medicines only prejudice the discussions making it difficult for positive engagement and progress. Second, dividing issues under the easy-yet-increasing overlapping themes of health systems and technological innovation for pharmaceuticals is highly misleading.

The evidence and the theoretical framework presented in this book consciously takes on such and other prejudices against innovation in developing countries, while at the same time seeking to expand our knowledge of the ways and means in which technological change in pharmaceuticals and health occurs in different contexts. It also promotes the perspective that in the new industrial policy, at both the national and sectoral levels, the state is a key actor *facilitating* learning that leads to industrial and technological change. By doing so, it is my hope that this book will contribute in its own small way to a rethink on how and to what extent the international community needs to offer greater support to create supportive industrial policies that allow the state apparatus in latecomer countries to better support their health innovation systems.

Padmashree, 19 November 2009

Acknowledgements

The research project on which this book is based would not have been sanctioned if not for the support given by a colleague and dear friend, Banji Oyeyinka. I will remain deeply indebted to him for his support. This book has benefited from the support and intellectual discussions with a wide range of colleagues in the field. I begin with Lynn Mytelka (then the Director of UNU-INTECH), Professor Carlos Correa (Director, Centre for Law and Economics, University of Buenos Aires), Professor Richard Nelson (University of Columbia), Professor Hazel Johnson (Open University), Professor Rajah Rasiah (University of Malaya) and Pedro Roffe (Senior Fellow, ICTSD). I also thank Martin Bell (SPRU, Sussex), Charles Clift (DFID, UK), Cheri Grace (HLSP), Precious Matsoso (WHO), Charles Gardner (Global Forum for Health Research), Professor Luc Soete (Director, UNU-MERIT), Professor Joanna Chataway (Open University) for discussions on related issues and their encouragement. I am deeply indebted to the Rockefeller Foundation for the one month I spent in the Rockefeller Residency Centre in Bellagio in June 2009 (and the support of all the co-residents), which was critical to finish the manuscript.

Most of all, I wish to thank all my country teams and the people I interviewed in the various countries on issues of health innovation who have educated me in ways more than one, and increased my dedication to work in the field. I have published and presented several chapters of the book in various forums and am grateful for comments by fellow academics and researchers over time to various versions of the work. Lastly, and most importantly, I remain most thankful to my family for their support. Both Dirk and Nisha inspired me to get as fast as possible to the finish line.

Abbreviations

ACT	Artemesinin based combination therapy
AIIMS	All India Institute of Medical Sciences
ANDAs	Abbreviated New Drug Applications
APIs	active pharmaceutical ingredients
ARVs	anti-retroviral drugs
BAPI	Bangladesh Association of Pharmaceutical Industries
BCSIR	Centre for Industrial and Scientific Research Bangladesh
BIRDEM	Bangladesh Institute of Research on Diabetic and Metabolic Disorders
Cap Ex	Capital Expenditure
CDRI	Central Drug Research Institute (India)
CEOs	chief executive officers
CHAI	Clinton Foundation for HIV/AIDS
COMESA	Common Market for Eastern and Southern Africa
CNS	central nervous system
CRAM	contract research and manufacturing
CSIR	Centre for Science and Industrial Research (India)
CVS	cardiovascular system
DDA	Directorate of Drug Administration
DMFs	drug master files
DNDi	Drugs for Neglected Diseases Initiative
EIU	Economist Intelligence Unit
EMEA	European Agency for the Evaluation of Medicinal Products
EMR	exclusive marketing right
EU	European Union
FDA	US Food and Drug Administration
FDC	fixed dose combinations
FDI	foreign direct investment
GDP	gross domestic product
GFATM	Global Fund for AIDS, Malaria and Tuberculosis
GMP	good manufacturing practices
IAEA	International Atomic Energy Agency
IAVI	International AIDS Vaccine Initiative

ICDDRB	International Centre for Diarrhoeal Diseases Research, Bangladesh
ICTs	Information and communication technologies
IDCH	Institute of Diseases of the Chest and Hospital (Bangladesh)
IDH	Infectious Disease Hospital (Bangladesh)
IDMA	Indian Drug Manufacturers' Association
IDMR	Institute for Drug and Medical Research (India)
IFC	International Finance Corporation
IICT	Indian Institute of Chemical Technology
IISC	Indian Institute for Science
IP	intellectual property
IPA	Indian Pharmaceutical Alliance
IPH	Institute of Public Health (Bangladesh)
IPP	intellectual property protection
IPRs	intellectual property rights
ITNs	insecticide treated nets
KARI	Kenyan Agriculture Research Institute
KEMRI	Kenya Medical Research Institute
KIPI	Kenya Intellectual Property Institute
KIRDI	Kenya Industrial Research and Development Institute
LDCs	Least developed countries
LLINs	long-lasting insecticidal nets
MNCs	multinational companies
MeTA	Medicines Transparency Alliance
MHFW	Ministry of Health and Family Welfare (Bangladesh)
MOST	Ministry of Science and Technology (Vietnam)
MSF	Médicines Sans Frontières
NABDA	National Biotechnology Development Agency (Nigeria)
NACGRAB	National Centre for Genetic Resources and Biotechnology (Nigeria)
NACO	National AIDS Control Organization (India)
NAFDAC	Nigerian Agency for Food Administration and Drug Control
NCE	new chemical entity
NCSIR	National Council for Scientific and Industrial Research (Nigeria)
NCST	Nigeria Council of Science and Technology
NGOs	Non-governmental organizations
NICVD	National Institute for Cardiovascular Diseases (Bangladesh)
NIHE	National Institute for Hygiene and Epidemiology (Vietnam)
NIMR	National Institute for Medical Research (Nigeria)
NIPRID	National Institute for Pharmaceutical Research and Development (Nigeria)
NIPSOM	National Institute of Preventive and Social Medicine (Bangladesh)
NPPA	National Pharmaceutical Pricing Authority
NVRI	National Veterinary Research Institute (Nigeria)

OPPI	Organization of Pharmaceutical Producers of India
PDPs	Product development partnerships
PPPs	public–private partnerships
PRIs	public research institutes
R&D	research and development
S&E	science and engineering
SHESTCO	Sheda Science and Technology Complex (Nigeria)
SME	small and medium enterprises
SMI	small and medium industries
TB	Tuberculosis
TRIPS	Agreement on Trade Related Aspects of Intellectual Property Rights
UNCTAD	*United Nations Conference on Trade and Development*
WHO	World Health Organization
WIPO	World Intellectual Property Organization
WTO	World Trade Organization

Part I
The unhealthy divide

1   The global health imperative

1.1 Global health innovation, big pharma and emerging trends

The formidable health challenges facing over 90 per cent of global population embody a threefold divide in terms of diseases that specifically confront the poor, technological capabilities to devise solutions and, finally, the financial and human resources available both for health research and health delivery. Malaria, AIDS and Tuberculosis still account for over 20 per cent of the disease burden in the poorer countries worldwide and several other diseases like Sleeping Sickness, Schistosomiasis and Chagas disease continue to receive little focus in health research and innovation. Much as we witness a shift in discourses on the question of innovating health solutions for the poor with a surge in public private partnerships in both research and delivery of health, a greater paradigm shift is required.

Sustainable economic development amongst most developing countries (including least developed countries), which this book refers to jointly as latecomer countries, has been considerably delayed because of the misplaced emphasis on importing ideas, products and processes in the absence of autonomous local capacity to absorb, apply and adapt both techniques and the nature of products and processes to their advantage. This book focuses on what is perhaps the capstone of delivering health to the global poor: local capacity for health innovation. The book defines health innovation to include all forms of innovation – process, product and organizational – that are required to conduct basic research and development as well as ensure delivery of marketable drugs of importance to human health. Health innovation includes all forms of discovery, development and delivery (CIPIH, 2006) that may or may not be new at the frontier, but may be new to the firm, the local context or the country in question.[1] Within this spectrum of activities, drug research and development (R&D) is one. The book seeks to understand the factors that explain the success of some countries over others in setting up health innovation systems that address local needs. Clearly, knowledge and technologies that underlie health innovation are operated through organizations and institutional arrangements that are key to explaining its relative success or failure. A key issue therefore is whether there are lessons to be learnt in terms of duplicating success of some countries in building health innovation systems in those others trying to catch up? The analysis presented in this book is based on original empirical research conducted on sectoral systems of health innovation in six *latecomer* countries between 2005 and 2008. A total of 1500 organizations were covered by the country level surveys, of which approximately 500 were private sector firms involved in various aspects of health and pharmaceutical innovation, and the remaining 1000 were public sector based.

Global health innovation, which has for long been synonymous with the R&D models of multinational companies, is transforming in meaning and content. Increased competition, lack of multitudes of blockbuster drugs – and focus on incremental innovations worldwide – have led to large-scale mergers and acquisitions, and also called for cost-cutting modes that involve outsourcing of drug discovery and development opportunities to other parts of the world. The industry that was distinguished mainly by a "core" comprising a relatively small group of firms holding a dominant market position in the global market (Bottazzi *et al.*, 2000, p. 230), is being opened up to altered industry structures as a result of pressures on product pipelines, new technologies and the incumbent advantages of specialization.

At the same time, newer rules have emerged such as those on global trade and intellectual property sights (hereafter, IPRs) that prescribe the forms of protection affordable to technological innovations (patents, trade secrets and trade marks), and also challenge the ability of countries to provide institutional arrangements for the delivery of efficient public health, which includes new products, efficient organizational routines and delivery processes. Equally significant are other rules related to the governance of new emerging technologies such as synthetic biology and synthetic genomics, which in addition to already existing regulations on good manufacturing practices and regulatory approvals, are extremely influential in determining the pace and forms of products that are introduced worldwide.[2] These, as Tait *et al.* (2008) note, are becoming increasingly global with a "convergence of national regulatory systems, particularly those of the United States and the European Union, can be expected to be much more closely aligned by 2015". Therefore, catching up in health innovation is more likely to mean how countries attempt to reach where others have reached, rather than "copy" any particular path that today's frontier countries have taken, as Nelson (2007) notes in a more general context. Social capital of countries – in terms of attitudes, practices and informal codes of conduct that lead to inefficient institutional arrangements and mediate production processes in latecomer countries – will predetermine the potential of countries not only in terms of their endeavours to structure such strategies, but also to see them through (Abramowitz, 1986).[3]

1.2 Changing organizational structures: implications for innovation and public health

The global pharmaceutical sector, perhaps one of the earliest examples of organized exploitation of research and development activities (Dosi and

Mazzucato, 2006), was markedly different up until the 1980s due to its binary, vertical R&D structure. While the upstream open science was being conducted in public sector laboratories, research institutes, universities and teaching hospitals and commercial innovation was the domain of the "big pharma" (Cockburn, 2004). The innovation system worked primarily on a model where basic research of significance to commercial applications was conducted in the public sector institutions, which were funded through governmental programmes and grants. These were then shared with the "big pharma" that then developed commercial product and process innovations of importance to global health concerns. The global regulatory system has for long structured itself around the needs of the "big pharma", which followed the "blockbuster" drug model: drug discovery and development required large scale investments, uptake of enormous risks, time spans ranging between 10 and 15 years, but could be copied at marginal expense. Hence, there was a need to retain the incentives of the firms to continue investments by way of granting IPRs, as well as disabling regulatory hurdles to newer technologies that could help enhance product range and quality.[4] Pharmaceutical firms from latecomer developing countries were not significant players in this landscape.

Over time however, the "big pharma" and the blockbuster model has come under enormous pressure especially since the 1980s, since there have not been many blockbusters in recent times to justify the strong regulatory systems that have been put in place. Although this can quite logically be attributed to the fact that technologies that are invested in today only result in commercial entities after significant time lags, and thus the results may be some time away, global "big pharma" has been under immense pressure to produce results. This has catalysed the series of changes mentioned at the start of this chapter, including mergers and acquisitions within the big pharma to maintain productivity, cost-cutting measures such as outsourcing to firms, especially in India and China which are able to perform several stages of the R&D process at a fraction of the costs.

The pressure to deliver in the 1990s resulted in a series of global mergers and acquisitions amongst global pharmaceutical firms that focused exclusively on enhancing in-house productivity of R&D (CIPIH, 2006). At the same time, countries that housed frontier innovation capacity came up with regulatory measures that sought to ensure more commercial orientation of basic research within universities through the encouragement of university patenting through regulations such as the Bayh–Dole Act in the USA, and other incentives structured to further university–industry relations, in an effort to help boost product pipelines based on genomics and biotechnology (see Bartholomew, 1997; OECD, 2000).[5] These changes were accompanied by trends towards broader patent scopes[6] and lower novelty standards for pharmaceutical patents in individual countries justified usually on grounds of the peculiar features of life sciences research, and a move towards uniformly strong IPRs worldwide.[7]

The term "ever-greening" that came to being refers to the numerous ways in which pharmaceutical firms try (and succeed) to extend patent control over their molecules using various "life management techniques", such as patenting an analogue or crystalline or other version of the molecule whose patent is about to expire, or packaging two molecules whose patents are about to expire as a single new drug, or embedding drug brands in intricate clusters of patents that make patent disputes costly (Loefgren, 2007, p. 3). The Agreement on Trade Related Aspects of Intellectual Property Rights (the TRIPS Agreement) that is part of the World Trade Organization (WTO) set of Agreements incorporates higher standards of intellectual property (IP) protection for pharmaceutical products worldwide. These include extension of patent protection to 20 years, provision of both product and patent protection, restrictions on compulsory licensing of pharmaceutical products, among others (see Correa, 2002; Drahos, 1999, among many others). The move towards universal exclusive rights in terms of IP strengthens private sector based health innovation and tends to help "big pharma" in its efforts to replace "the magnitude of lost revenues as a result of patent expirations in a short period of time" (Kaplan, 2004, p. 42).

While these few realities explain where we are globally, these industrial and regulatory trends have profound implications for public health as well as the building of capabilities in other, not-so-advanced regions of the world. At the same time, the waning pipelines for health products to treat neglected diseases (type II) and very neglected diseases (type III)[8] such as HIV/AIDS, Malaria, Tuberculosis as well as more endemic illnesses such as Dengue, Leishmaniasis, Chagas disease and Schistosomiasis, calls forth alternate approaches.

1.3 IPRs, access to knowledge and access to medicines

At a broad level, there seems to be overwhelming consensus that extension of IPRs will entail costs of various kinds to latecomer countries, since considerable policy changes have to be made by these countries to conform to the TRIPS Agreement (Maskus, 2000, p. 6).[9] A good amount of theoretical work has gone in to show that a global IPR system will have adverse welfare effects on latecomer countries in the short or mid term (Deardorff, 1992; Helpman, 1993; Lai, 1998; Chin and Grossman, 1991, 1988; Glass and Saggi, 2002 and Lai, 2005, among others). For a latecomer country with certain levels of capabilities, the benefits of the TRIPS agreement in the long term could be threefold: (a) higher foreign direct investment and technology flows with potential positive implications for domestic learning, (b) greater innovative activities from access to patent disclosures and technologies and (c) competitive returns to innovative firms in latecomer countries from stronger IPRs and lesser legal uncertainty. Several studies have also tried to investigate the relationship between these factors, but empirical data is mixed and limited. It is also clear that in the short or mid term, universal IPR enforcement will entail costs in terms of reduced freedom to design and implement individual technology acquisition and use policies that is central to catch-up processes (Amsden and Chu, 2003; Chang, 2003). Innovation is continuously encouraged by wide accessibility of already produced knowledge to society at low costs (Nelson, 1990; Foray, 1995) and IPRs limit ways and means in which countries and firms access knowledge locally to generate newer knowledge which has played a key role in economic development since the eighteenth century (Mokyr, 2003).

Box 1.1 IPRs and the market for innovation

While much of economic discourse would lead us to believe that IPRs are a fundamental prerequisite for the market for innovation to work, three interesting caveats stand out. First, there is increasing evidence pointing towards the fact that stronger IPRs do not always translate into higher domestic innovation.[1] Second, it seems that IPRs do not assume equal importance as a tool to promote innovation in all areas of knowledge generation. Several factors seem to play a role, including the nature of technology and investments involved, on whether at all, and how firms use IP as a tool to protect innovation. A comparative survey that assessed the importance of patents in different industries showed that patents were most important for the development and introduction of products in two industries – the pharmaceutical and chemical industries – where they accounted for over 30 per cent of development activities (Mansfield, 1998, p. 174). Firms rely on a variety of appropriability mechanisms to protect their innovations, such as secrecy and first mover advantages, sometimes even much more than on patents (see Cohen *et al.*, 2000; Arundel, 2001). Finally, despite the obvious importance of IP, a range of firm level factors and institutional variables influences new product/process innovation at the firm level. This includes, but is not restricted to, availability of scientific/skilled manpower, the quality of local infrastructure services to new product and/or process development, the financial constraints and availability of venture capital, the collaboration with local universities, local R&D institutes, intellectual property protection (IPP), the participation in local SME development schemes, participation in government–firm–technology transfer coordination councils and the transfer of personnel between local firms or R&D institutions.

Source: author

Note
1 See Scherer and Weisburst (1995), Bessen and Maskin (2000), Sakakibara and Branstetter (2001) and Lerner (2002) among others. At least two other authors (Kanwar and Evenson, 2001 and Chen and Puttitanum, 2005) find a positive correlation, but these are attributable to the second point made in the box, which relates to the variegated impact of IPRs in different sectors.

Mainly due to these reasons, the TRIPS Agreement has sparked off an intense scrutiny of the ways and means technologically backward countries can still build capabilities for health innovation. The Agreement is now in force in all member countries of the WTO, except the so-called least developed countries, where the Doha Declaration on TRIPS and Public Health grants an extension until 2016.[10] Despite this, a large number of least developed countries have already complied with levels of IPP as required by the TRIPS Agreement due to obligations agreed under bilateral free trade agreements with the USA, EU and other developed countries (Fink and Reichenmiller, 2005; Roffe, 2004). While the TRIPS Agreement contains some flexibilities on how countries can balance intellectual property protection (IPP) with their public health needs,[11] latecomers need to think strategically on how to use these flexibilities to not grant or grant weak intellectual property protection (the former is an option for least developed countries whereas the latter is for other developing countries) or for that matter even using compulsory licensing to promote domestic production and domestic innovation. Countries that are not at the frontier of health innovation will have to revisit their own catch-up strategies in terms of what is permissible under the new multilateral trade regime.

The proliferation of stronger intellectual property protection on pharmaceutical products conflict with global access to medicines on various fronts, most of which have been clearly elucidated in the literature on this point. IPRs accentuate the already dominant tendency amongst firms to focus on diseases of rich countries where the consumers have the ability to pay for the products as opposed to the poor in the latecomer countries who need drugs at lower affordable prices. Drugs, vaccines and diagnostics for global public health causes therefore constitute what has been termed "global public goods". A global public good is defined as a good where no one *should* be excluded from its consumption (due to its non-excludable nature) and no one can be excluded (Stiglitz, 1999, p. 309).[12] Stronger IPRs also conflict with goals of making medicines available to the poor at cheaper prices, as demonstrated by international disputes over drug prices and availability for HIV/AIDS in South Africa (2000), Brazil (2002) and Thailand (2007), where national governments have had to resort to difficult options to leverage public health concerns.

However, despite these broader conclusions on the impact of IPRs on access to knowledge and access to medicines, quantifying the impact of IPRs on international trade is very difficult due to many reasons (Maskus, 2000, p. 111). First, the strengths leveraged through patents are incorporated into the price of the goods and this cannot be separated from other factors that dictate pricing behaviour. Second, decisions of firms that own new products or processes on how they decide to export, enter new markets or sell these through licences are affected by a variety of strategic motives, such as the use of IPRs in joint ventures (Merges, 1994; Grandstrand, 2000), as negotiating levers (Dumont and Holmes, 2002) or merely as tools to leverage market power (Barton, 1998; Kanwar and Evenson, 2001, among others). Such behaviour is common to sectors wherein IPRs play an important role in promoting R&D like chemicals and pharmaceuticals. However, it tends towards inequities because of the public significance of the products in the pharmaceutical sector (Mansfield, 1998).[13]

And herein lies the problem: despite the obvious impacts of IPRs on global health innovation, the question of access to health is not just limited to stronger IPR protection (see Box 1.2). If this was the case, then merely relaxing some of the limitations of the TRIPS Agreement, or even the provisions of the Doha Declaration and Public Health, that allow for local production of drugs in countries with public health crises, would suffice to solve the gigantic issues of global public health. The tendency to focus primarily on the inequities of the TRIPS Agreement takes away critical resources from the discourse on health innovation and development. While IPRs will form an important part of this discourse, the question of enabling health innovation requires us to look at how health innovation occurs in different contexts and what the linkages between health innovation and health systems in latecomer countries are, including newer ways to organize health delivery, which is currently highly inefficient or non-existent in most latecomer countries (Attaran, 2004).

Box 1.2 Other hindrances to accessing health in latecomer countries

Human resources for health are perhaps the biggest challenge that faces latecomer countries in making access to health care a reality. For instance, the World Health Report 2006 stated, "A shortage of human resources has replaced financial issues as the most serious obstacle to implementing national HIV treatment plans." Lack of clinical staff and loss of health care workers on a regular basis is a crippling reality in latecomer countries. Research in several countries indicates that apart from financial rewards, non-financial incentives such as career development and management training and positive work environments plays a critical role in retaining workforce.

Socio-economic inequities are other major determinants of access and health care outcomes across latecomer countries. In 2004, the World Health Organization (WHO) established a Task Force to identify research priorities that followed from an emerging concern with health equity (www.who.int/entity/bulletin/volumes/83/12/948.pdf). Subsequently, WHO established the Commission on Social Determinants of Health whose final report, in 2008, entitled "Closing the gap in a generation: Health Equity through action on the social determinants of health" adopted health equity as a central organizing concept: it concluded not only that "social injustice is killing people on a grand scale", but also that implementing its ambitious goals for reducing health inequity "is critically dependent upon changes in the functioning of the global economy".

Underutilization of health care services itself is another major hindrance that prevents several public health interventions from having their intended impact. Causation factors include distance to health care providers, lack of information about health aspects, stigma associated with particular forms of health care access, social, economic and political motivations and perceptions of health technologies by the society among many others.

Source: author

Per capita government expenditure on health in most latecomer countries is extremely small and distortions caused by out-of-pocket expenditures to fund health needs[14] skew incentives of actors in the health system and impact upon how drugs are accessed by those who need it most. Health care expenditure was still less than US$10 per person per year in most African countries in 2008, despite projections that over the next one decade Sub-Saharan Africa will require between US$25 and 30 billion as health care expenditure to meet the growing health care demands (IFC, 2008). Only 31 per cent of all those infected with HIV/AIDS had access to treatments largely due to the idiosyncratic nature of health care access and delivery in latecomer countries (Dionisio *et al.*, 2008), and similar figures exist for Malaria, TB and other such diseases. At the same time, newer health technologies are influencing the organization of medical science and treatment (in ways that were earlier unfathomable) and challenging the distinction between innovation and delivery in health (Fennell, 2008). For example, systems biology and biologics allow for therapies that are oriented towards smaller groups and even individuals, thus linking issues of innovation, development and delivery of health products in an unconventional way. All these crucial inter-linkages call for a rethink on how health per se will be funded, and not just health research that can deliver diagnostics, vaccines and drugs of importance to latecomer countries.

1.4 Global health innovation and the expanding role of latecomer countries

Although the technology clubs of the world have remained almost unchanged from the 1980s until now (Oyeyinka and Gehl Sampath, 2009a; Castellacci and Archibugi, 2008), there is clear evidence of a gradual reconfiguration of innovation activities at the global level (Chesbrough, 2003, 2006) where several developing countries are beginning to play a critical role. In 2007, the Chinese economy accounted for 36 per cent of all manufacturing value added goods produced worldwide (UNCTAD, 2007), recording a steady increase of R&D expenditure in China by approximately 24 per cent per annum since 1999, with the R&D/GDP ratio having more than doubled in a decade in China, reaching 1.34 per cent in 2005 (UNCTAD, 2006a). Similarly, India comes immediately after the USA as the second-most favoured location to offshore R&D globally (Economist Intelligence Unit, 2007).

In health innovation, the increasing capability of firms in other parts of the world that could help cut costs at various stages of the drug discovery and development processes have lent an urgency to global redistribution of innovation activities. India and China are the two foremost outsourcing destinations and account for the largest number of US Food and Drug Administration (FDA) approved manufacturing plants outside the USA (Bain and Co., 2008). While China is ahead of India in stem cell and biology based research, India is far stronger than China in active pharmaceutical ingredients (API) engineering (Loefgren, 2007; Bain and Co., 2008). More significantly, emerging technologies like genomics and life sciences research have increased the innovation complexity of drugs, both generic and new chemical entities, thereby blurring the boundaries between generic firms and pure innovators. Indian and Chinese firms, for example, compete with international firms in generic categories that require significant innovation ability, such as new drug delivery systems or even bio-generics. Indian firms offer stiff competition to the global "big pharma" despite India's full scale compliance with the TRIPS Agreement in 2005, aggressively expanding their operations globally and even venturing into new drug discovery (Gehl Sampath, 2008).

In addition to India and China, there are several other countries that are emerging to be important, such as Cuba, South Africa, Kenya and Bangladesh. Firms from South Africa, Kenya and Bangladesh supply to global consortia that seek to address public health concerns, such as the GFATM and UNITAID.[15]

These developments constitute a new hope in an otherwise troubling situation as far as global burden of disease and access to medicines are concerned. Ninety per cent of global disease burden is unduly concentrated in developing countries, which gets all the more disturbing when viewed through a regional lens. Sub-Saharan Africa houses only 11 per cent of the global population but accounts for 24 per cent of total global disease burden despite which it commands less than 1 per cent of total global health expenditure (IFC, 2008, p. 1). Growing innovation capacity in latecomer countries has infused fresh enthusiasm into initiatives that seek to organize the production of drugs and vaccines that have the character-istics of global public goods.

A range of innovative push and pull mechanisms have emerged over the past decade that seek to focus on rectifying the divide in provision of "global public goods" (Maskus and Reichman, 2004). Push mechanisms typically seek to induce investments by reducing the firm's private cost of undertaking a particu-lar form of research, and generally include R&D grants, tax subsidies and access to public resources for firms to engage in particular forms of R&D (see Hollis, 2008). Pull mechanisms create incentives through the promise of enhanced profits, and consist of patent extensions, prize funds, *ex ante* assurances to buy bulk amounts of the end product (Kremer, 2000) and market exclusivity arrange-ments. Simultaneously, calls for creating institutional capacity at the global level to help better coordinate such efforts have borne fruit in the form of organiza-tions such as UNITAID.[16] Although unresolved issues persist[17] they are being employed in various combinations and indicate huge leaps in promoting health innovation of relevance to developing countries.

Product Development Public–Private Partnerships (PPPs) deserve a specific mention in this regard, and are collaborative push and pull hybrids with both not-for-profit and for-profit organizations that pool together R&D capacity, skills and resources either at the national or the international level. PPPs are usually focused around a particular disease (such as the International AIDS Vaccine Initiative and Medicines for Malaria Venture)[18] or a particular form of inter-vention (for example, vaccines) or even both (Orbinski and Burciul, 2006). Although the Drugs for Neglected Diseases Initiative (DNDi)[19] has set an example of success amongst PPPs by recently coming up with an anti-malarial that will be produced in Morocco, PPPs are generally coming under immense pressure in the present environment. There is a large emphasis on value for money, and the emphasis is shifting from vertical PPPs to horizontal PPPs that seek to integrate the results with the health system (Chataway and Hanlin, 2008).

On the health side, innovative mechanisms that pool in multi-stakeholder views and forces to improve health delivery systems and enhance health equity have emerged. MeTA (Medicines Transparency Alliance) for example, now operates in seven countries and brings together stakeholders from governments, civil society and business with the aim of enhancing transparency, accountability and access to information around medicines.

At the same time, newer opportunities for building capacity are beginning to emerge with south–south cooperation models, and with a new emphasis on knowledge sharing and technology transfer. Several countries have begun to look inwards into how they can jump-start local capabilities in health innovation, through various means, at least to promote local production of products that are of immense local significance.[20] Some of these initiatives are the result of sporadic successes in the field of health innovation, as in the case of Nigeria, whereas many other national initiatives have been triggered off by the new opportunities presented through south–south cooperation, for example, Uganda. In Nigeria, for instance, the development of a typhoid vaccine and two sickle cell drugs, NIPRISAN and NICOSAN, by local public research institutes, began to focus attention on the capabilities of local organizations to engage in health innovation (Oyeyinka and Gehl Sampath, 2007).[21] The Ministry of Health in Uganda has recently set up a plant in alliance with Cipla Pharmaceuticals of India, for the manufacture of anti-retroviral and anti-malarial drugs in the country. The Cipla–Ministry of Uganda alliance is the first of its kind, between an Indian firm and an African government, aimed at building local capacity to produce drugs of critical relevance to the country's health care system.

What this brings forth is the very important question: how can these emerging industrial structures and newer models of collaboration be studied and understood to reveal ways and means of balancing them with public health needs worldwide? While there are reasons to hope for better solutions for tomorrow, the danger of replicating incentives that may pit us farther away from public health concerns looms large.[22] The answer to this question lies in intensified social science research on the sectoral determinants underlying the emergent restructuring of health innovation systems to allow more informed policy formulation to foster dynamic growth of capabilities in developing countries and construct optimum configurations of policies and institutions that are currently feasible.

This book is rooted in the understanding that the knowledge and technologies that create capacity for health innovation are especially difficult to catch up with, since they involve establishing synergy between a range of disciplines such as chemistry, biotechnology, genomics, pharmaceutical sciences, health sciences and the like. The inter-disciplinary nature of health innovation is such that it necessarily requires capabilities in aspects of pharmaceutical sciences (as required for conventional pharmaceutical research) and newer technologies such as genomics, systems biology and biotechnology (as required for life sciences research) that add to innovative strengths of firms/sectors and countries.

1.5 Innovation policy, the innovation systems framework and institutional economics

Innovation from the viewpoint of the firm essentially comprises the practice and production of all product and process technologies that are new to them and their context and not necessarily to the universe (Nelson and Rosenberg, 1993). All activities at the firm level that enhance learning skills, expand the knowledge base and increase competitiveness both locally and globally, are innovative activities. R&D is one form of knowledge production, but such a definition of innovation includes also all other forms of activities through which firms access knowledge and technologies in order to progress along the learning curve. The information and knowledge that form the primary inputs to technological learning and innovative capacity in firms, originate from within the firm and from outside (the knowledge system).

However, the learning and knowledge accumulation relies on availability of human skills, technologies and infrastructure all of which are shaped by institutions and policies that can be broadly called *innovation policy.* Innovation policy is therefore much more wider a framework than science and technology policy and R&D, and encompasses a wide array of policies that seek to bring together actors to create "systems of innovation". It includes science and technology policy, industrial development policy, education policy, SME policies and other sectoral policies as may seem important. Viewing sectors or countries through innovation policy lens lends acknowledgement to a long-overdue fact that without considering all the key aspects of capacity, including education and skills building, knowledge-led development will remain a myth. In the innovation policy framework, the broader so-called "framework" policies of industrial development, education and enterprise growth are augmented through a range of incentives to foster collaborative linkages between all actors especially the private sector, universities and public research institutes.

This book employs the innovation systems framework and institutional economics as the main analytical tools to analyse sectoral systems for health innovation. The systems of innovation framework emerged as a response to conventional economic analyses of technological change, which underplayed the role of institutions as well as the evolutionary nature of technological change, stressing mainly upon the role of market incentives for the allocation of information in society. While there are a wide variety of definitions of the national systems of innovation (Freeman, 1987; Lundvall, 1992; Nelson and Rosenberg, 1993; Metcalfe, 1994),[23] there is also a fairly good convergence of the key ideas at the heart of the systems of innovation framework. One of these ideas is the persistent but uneven distribution of the capabilities of firms to innovate across sectors, countries and regions. This skewed effect of innovation performance is a function of specific national or sectoral factors and as such the competitive advantage of sectors and nations depends greatly on how advanced the systems of innovation is, and how well it has generated coherence and interactions.

Critiquing the notions of conventional economics, two fundamental assumptions form the core of the systems approach. First, innovation (as opposed to information or even knowledge) is the result of the interactions between firms and other organizations within a system, shaped by social, economic, political and historical dimensions. The inclusion of contextual, social and historical factors helps to understand innovation and its determinants as it is and as it occurs in most contexts: incremental in nature and boosted from within the system. Within the innovation systems approach, interactions are central; the nature and extent of interactions accounting for the ways and means learning occurs and knowledge is put to use. Interactive learning is a process through which different agents within the system communicate and collaborate for the creation, use and dissemination of new economic knowledge (Johnson and Lundvall, 2003, p. 159). Within a given system, it is assumed that the learning capacity and the actions of any set/sets of actors affects the way other actors make decisions, and even learn and perform (Lundvall, 1992). Thus the concept of learning is collective and has social and context specific connotations to it (McKelvey, 1997). Technological capability derives from both internal and external knowledge sources and while firms themselves do have internal R&D facilities, external knowledge sources are an invaluable source of firm capability. In other words, one of the reasons for the persistent differences in the innovative capacities of sectors and industries is the gap in the knowledge bases. Organizations and individual capabilities differ in their scientific and technological skills and experiences. Firms, however, require the absorptive capacity – defined by Cohen and Levinthal (1990, p. 128) as the ability of a firm to recognize new information, assimilate it and apply it for commercializing inventions – which relies on the localized knowledge parameters, such as the availability of human skills, infrastructural elements that helps firms avail and recognize knowledge, collaborative aspects of applying it to production. Second, institutional factors play a central role in fostering linkages in innovation systems to boost effective performance. The behavioural norms of actors regarding how and what they learn for instance, diversification into new peripherals clones and services is intricately bound to the institutional framework that fosters innovation.

Technological knowledge that underlies innovation capacity exhibits certain attributes that are localized – this includes the ways and means through which tacit knowledge is created and dispersed, the cumulativeness of knowledge systems and the path dependence of institutions in shaping knowledge patterns of countries. At the same time, increased specialization of products and services within sectors and the increasing complexity of knowledge accumulation are globalizing factors. This interplay between local and global factors is clearly evident in the case of health innovation where constant advances in science are altering industry structures and global demand constantly. The role of local public research is in this wise pivotal to the advances made in industry as shown by the experience of the United States. For instance in the 1993–1994 period alone, 73 per cent of scientific papers cited by US industrial patents originated from public science, while the remaining 27 per cent came from industrial sources. Sales of inventive products from academic research that were licensed to industry was over US$20 billion in 1996, further underlying the importance of localized academic science institutions (McMillan and Hamilton, 2000). Other factors that reinforce the localization of innovation capabilities in health innovation are technologies such as biotechnology and genomics that rely on university strongholds and university–industry interactions (Bühler *et al.*, 2007; Champenois, 2008).

In contrast, the global "pull" factors that constantly interact with localized health innovation strengths have received relatively less attention. These global factors regularly impact on the external knowledge sources that local firms can access and tap into, the collaborations they can form, the synergies that can be reaped from such collaborations and the markets they can expect for their products. What really informs health innovation capacity is in fact the interactive linkages between the local "push" factors and the global "pull" factors that firms and organizations constantly have to cope with (see Table 1.1), thus calling attention to the innovation systems framework as an appropriate tool to analyse issues of health innovation.

The analysis conducted in the book augments the innovation systems approach with relevant insights from institutional economics in order to understand the institutional bases that promote capabilities formation in health innovation.

1.6 The "why" and "what" of successful health innovation systems

The novelty of a health innovation approach as opposed to narrower perceptions of pharmaceutical innovation or health systems based approaches is that a broader health innovation framework views both technological innovations that lead to the creation of health technologies and products *and* social and institutional innovations that impact upon the quick absorption of these on the user side as equally critical. Health innovation depends on the constant interplay between the technological, social and institutional innovations and the user–producer feedbacks that enable these. Smits and Boon (2008) summarize the advantages of including users in the health innovation process to be fivefold:

a   users make it possible to view market failure in health innovation (neglected diseases research) more holistically and help to put these issues on the innovation agenda;
b   user feedback is critical in ensuring the absorption of health products;
c   public and patient involvement can increase the cost-effectiveness of R&D processes, for example, disease advocacy groups helped raise US$3 billion for stem cell research in the USA;
d   introduction of new technologies can be met with social resistance – user involvement tends to iron out these differences at early stages by eliminating information asymmetries; and
e   innovation in health impacts on the users' lives and life opportunities pervasively and they have a moral right to be a part of the processes.

In addition to these five, another one deserves mention here: an impact on health outcomes and health equity of health products will ultimately depend on the empowerment of the beneficiaries.

Table 1.1 Push and pull factors for health innovation capacity in latecomers

Local "push" factors		Global "pull" factors	
1	Consistent investment in knowledge infrastructure, mainly scientific infrastructure and education institutions.	1	Intellectual property rights protection and the TRIPS Agreement.
2	Availability of physical infrastructure, for example, roads, Internet, electricity and water.	2	Other international regulatory measures, such as data protection regimes.
3	Incentives for interactive learning and collaboration amongst local agents.	3	International R&D collaborations with universities and centres of excellence in frontier countries.
4	Favourable institutional incentives for innovation, especially translation of R&D into marketable products. Policy vision to achieve self-sufficiency in health care (production of drugs, provision or both).	4	Emerging models of south–south cooperation.
5	Significant local demand for particular forms of health innovation, for example, public health crisis.	5	International R&D and marketing alliances with private sector firms in frontier countries.
		6	International acquisitions and international patenting.
		7	Integration into global value chains.

Source: author.

The present times are extra-ordinary because despite the 10/90 gap in health research, we have the thickest innovation pipeline (Elias, 2006) of health products that are in demand in latecomer countries and in the absence of substantial coordination between technological innovation and health care institutions, we risk not being able to devise timely, efficient and sustainable initiatives that promote our ability to deliver the innovations to those who need it most, given the momentous health systems issues in latecomer contexts. Failure to view issues along the technological and social innovations continuum that a health innovation perspective offers also puts at risk the ability of the international, donor and national communities to sustain the interest in this growing pipeline for health products for latecomers, and to integrate further local demand functions into such future ventures. Finally, to be able to understand the ramifications of how national capacity that is already present amongst latecomers, such as India, Brazil, China can be pooled to better address the 10/90 gap for the future, we need to build further on a framework that accounts for all health innovation interactions, helps us to gather evidence systematically to map the capabilities building processes and their determinants, and assists the discussion on the impact of global rules on local innovation to proceed in an evidence-informed environment. On the user side, international agencies involved in global health are beginning to move their focus away from funding individual programmes, such as HIV prevention, to strengthening health systems as a whole. The data and analysis presented in this book will be a highly important policy input to both these issues.

1.7 Central hypothesis and propositions

Health innovation capacity of countries builds expensively on four main components: availability of physical infrastructure, knowledge infrastructure, collaboration and policy support. *Physical infrastructure* includes local infrastructure in terms of electricity, fresh water, roads and railways, as well as technological infrastructure, such as regular Internet access, phones and mobile networks that speed up the pace of communication and foster collaboration. *Knowledge infrastructure* is composed of science infrastructure and human skills, and refers to the quality and quantity of human skills as well as the availability of scientific infrastructure within the country. Good human skills are a product of quality academic institutions within a country at the secondary and tertiary levels that offer academic education that suits the needs of the sectors at large. Knowledge infrastructure also includes the availability and quality of good public sector research institutions, research publications in science journals (as evidence of ability to create new knowledge locally) and percentage of manufactured exports.

Collaboration remains central for innovation capacity specifically due to the highly inter-disciplinary nature of health innovation that mandates not just the presence of a strong knowledge base, but efficient exchanges between institutions. Three features of the innovation process make collaboration imperative, namely, the increasing costs of doing innovation, the increasing multidisciplinary of health innovation and the ever narrowing gap between basic research and industrial application (Kaiser and Prange, 2004). Efficient exchange and collaboration however rests on institutional coherence – systems with weak institutional basis give rise to transaction costs that accrue from institutional heterogeneity and conflicting agendas of the different agents (Eisenberg, 2001).

Institutions and policy support and diversity therein account for observed differences in economic performance of countries (North, 1996). Institutions and organizations are routinely involved in the creation and dissemination of useful tacit and codified knowledge that needs to be applied to the production process and in creating an enabling learning environment. Institutional efficiency, defined as how effectively access to knowledge for local firms can be achieved at minimal transaction costs, is critical in explaining the process of knowledge sharing that underlines interactive learning and innovative success. Institutions are essential at each stage of the innovation process: to grant incentives to actors to innovate and collaborate at the individual level, to enable knowledge flows and interactive learning between the different components of the system at the organizational level and to create networks between the more localized "push" factors and the global "pull" factors to promote knowledge formation.

The term "institutions" is defined variedly in the literature. This book uses the term "institutions" as the "rules of the game" (North, 1993), essentially denoting formal or informal frameworks that structure interaction amongst actors. Formal institutions include technology policies, patent systems, industrial policy or other rules and prevailing legal frameworks. Informal institutions are the unofficial attitudes of actors in a system, their established practices of interactions that have been conditioned by local social and cultural contexts. "Organizations" are actors in the innovation process, and include agencies that are set up to carry out the various institutional mandates, such as enterprises, professional associations non-governmental agencies, R&D laboratories and governmental agencies, standard setting bodies and extension services, among others.

In analysing ways and means in which these four components interact for building health innovation, two sets of issues arise. A first set of issues is more innovation related and can be framed thus:

a   What factors promote the formation of health innovation capabilities within countries, and how can we best understand them?
b   How do firms learn which systemic components play a critical role in enabling such learning, and how can successful learning experiences be replicated in other countries?

The fundamental question of whether these experiences can be duplicated is not a unique one in innovation studies. It also does not presume that one or the same set of institutions and policies can render results in different contexts. It has rather sought to ascertain whether one can identify certain elements of policy that "can take on different forms in different countries in different eras, and seem to provide the key" (Nelson, 2007, p. 5).

A second set of issues, however, is specific to health innovation only and emerge from the reorganization and global decomposition of innovation activities in this sector and the observed inequality of access to health worldwide. These can be framed thus:

a   Who is gaining from emerging global collaborations and strategic alliances in terms of innovation capabilities (Ohba and Figueredo, 2007), and are there reasons for concern from the perspective of increased global competition for health innovation products and reasonable pricing?
b   How are global regulatory measures, especially those related to trade, IPRs and regulatory approvals, impacting upon the entire structure of health innovation and how can we best understand and mitigate them?
c   How can we harness the opportunities presented by south–south cooperation for health innovation, and also promote more broader and inclusive mechanisms for knowledge and technology sharing in this sector between latecomers?

In recent years, although there have been several accounts of individual issues raised here (especially, the impact of IPRs on health), an integrated approach to innovation and development as applicable to health is only beginning to emerge now. This book, by creating such a holistic framework for health innovation and development, furthers our understanding of these issues. It advances three sets of hypothesis. First, the way physical infrastructure, knowledge infrastructure and collaborative linkages are structured to build localized innovation capacity depend on a range of local institutional factors that account for the inner dynamism of sectoral innovation systems.[24] Institutions, both formal and informal (in terms of cultural and social attitudes), permeate not only the process of how physical and knowledge infrastructure is built, but also how collaborative linkages take shape within the system thus lending strength to the gradual expansion of learning activities. Local factors – in terms of disease trends, level of country's development, social and cultural attributes – profanely shape health innovation capacity. To understand how the institutional framework structures ways in which knowledge is created, used, absorbed and transformed from global/ codified to local use and possibly recreated, we need to get into the micro-economic processes of learning through different kinds of interactions in health innovation in latecomer countries. Such a framework should be one that calibrates the innovation systems framework as well as insights from institutional economics according to different levels of development. Second, in the present globalized context of knowledge activities, a large variety of externally imposed factors, such as the multilateral trade regime, IPR protection and newer modes of technology transfer and acquisition, all determine the ways and means in which countries can design catch-up strategies to access knowledge and build innovative capacity for health innovation. These need to be mapped and understood in a more systematic way. Finally, and perhaps most importantly, health innovation capabilities are formed, remain unformed or are formed incompletely in countries owing to the interplay between local "push" and global "pull" institutions. It is the constant interplay between global pull and local push institutional rules that structure knowledge flows, actor configurations, capital formation, manpower accumulation as well as inform collaborations. These include those that are purely industry or technology oriented and some others that are more health care oriented. While all the local "push" institutions listed out in Table 1.1 and elaborated on in the previous section give the much-needed impetus to the innovation environment, the *emergence and dynamic evolution of health innovation capabilities squarely rests on its institutional capacity.*

Institutional capacity, which is central to the analysis of this book is defined to include:

a   the ability of the country in question to set up institutions and policies that eliminate all physical and knowledge infrastructure related and collaboration oriented costs to health innovation;
b   the ability to envisage the threat or opportunities presented by the global pull institutions on the local agenda for health innovation; and
c   the ability to set into motion appropriate incentives, rules and institutional changes as maybe required to offset the negative impacts of global push institutions to achieve dynamic growth and competitiveness of the sector.

Not all global pull institutions are negative and undesirable, and, in fact, each one of them represents an opportunity as much as a threat to the growth of local innovation capacity in health. However, the burden of ensuring that global "pull" factors impact upon the local innovation system in the form of "institutional instruments" to attenuate the weak knowledge (Gerschenkron, 1962) environment of the latecomer countries is an enormous one. Countries that succeed in building significant health innovation capacity demonstrate extensive policy competence in balancing local and international convergent factors that shape systemic learning.

Box 1.3 Emergence of policies and capabilities in latecomers

Policies and capabilities can emerge from very different origins, such as major political strategies and visions of industrialization, local needs or sometimes are even purely accidental. But comparing lessons from countries that managed to leapfrog and catch up with those others that stagnated at some interim stage of industrialization shows that the former countries learnt from their failures as much from their successes. Policy learning, in other words, is as continuous a process as the accumulation of capabilities themselves, that accrues either by *leaning inwards* and revising existing policy frameworks to correct their ineffectiveness constantly or by *leaning outwards* to learn lessons from success of other countries and ways and means in which they can be replicated in the local context. Whether countries planned thoroughly or not, it is imperative that they put physical and knowledge capacity in place, constantly invest in furthering them and support incentives that promote collaboration. The distinction between the countries that catch up and those that do not reflects in the differences in their national institutions, technological capabilities and infrastructure all of which are underlined by, political, legal and socio-economic choices made over time.

Numerous, country level, comparative studies on health innovation support these observations, by pointing to the relevance of the following factors:

a   well-formulated innovation policies and strategies;
b   well-endowed institutional frameworks that promote collaboration and networking amongst various organizations in the innovation processes;
c   support infrastructure for the development of a private sector, such as finance (OECD, 2006);
d   enforceable incentives that foster cooperation and mobility of skilled labour, such as property rights, IPRs (or the converse thereof), research grants, memberships in professional organizations, tax and export credits, among others;
e   regulatory frameworks that promote access to knowledge at several levels: within firms, within the sector, from outside the sector and outside the country;
f   well-functioning public sector institutions for education and applied research.

Source: author

This book is not a prescription on what latecomer countries should do to build health innovation capabilities. It is a sketch of the complex canvas of the technological, social and institutional and policy factors that impact upon the process of building health innovation, so that latecomer countries can make informed choices.

1.8 Methodology and data collection

The case studies presented in this book are some of the first efforts that systematically gather quantitative and qualitative data for health innovation through innovation surveys that were designed to capture the features of innovation in latecomer contexts.[25]

Data were collected through a three-stage approach, namely:

a   *Descriptive analysis.* Each country level sectoral survey was aided by a report on the sectoral system for health innovation that was put together in conjunction with a local team. The reports in question mapped out the main actors and interactions in the sectoral system, in addition to shedding light on the country specific innovation parameters that could account for the performance. These reports also formed the basis for running pilot surveys with local experts to test the semi-structured questionnaires that were administered as the next step.
b   *Sectoral surveys of health innovation systems.* Based on the characteristics of the sectoral innovation system for health, and the specifics of latecomer innovation, semi-structured questionnaires were designed to capture aspects

of innovation and the main factors that contributed to/impeded sectoral performance. For purposes of the analysis, a sectoral system for health innovation is construed to include all private and public sector actors involved in various aspects of the health innovation process. As a result, the sectoral surveys in all five countries covered private firms (both local and multinational), universities (and university centres of excellence) and public research institutes, teaching hospitals, governmental agencies involved in policy formation for health innovation and delivery, traditional medicinal practitioners and health dispensaries. For purposes of the surveys, innovation was defined from the viewpoint of the firm to essentially comprise the practice and production of all product and process technologies that are new to them and their context and not necessarily to the universe (Nelson and Rosenberg, 1993). All activities at the firm level that enhance learning skills, expand the knowledge base and increase competitiveness both locally and globally are innovative activities.

c   *Face-to-face interviews.* As a final stage, a wide cross-section of actors were interviewed in face-to-face interviews to gather additional information on various aspects of health innovation that are relevant to local contexts. These actors included CEOs and directors of R&D and marketing of large, medium and small pharmaceutical and biotechnology firms, directors of large public sector institutes and centres of excellence that specialize on various aspects of health innovation, Drug directorates and senior officials of ministries of health, IP offices, directors and heads of departments in teaching hospitals and traditional medicinal healers.

On the whole, over 1000 actors in sectoral systems of health innovation in the various countries were surveyed and over 400 actors were interviewed for the analysis carried out in this book. In addition, the analysis benefited from numerous other projects (international, regional and national) that the author has been involved in the field of health innovation over the past few years.

1.9 Book structure and organization of chapters

The analysis is organized into three main parts. In the first part of the book (Chapters 1 and 2), a detailed overview of what constitutes health innovation is provided and a sectoral system of health innovation framework is developed. This framework builds further on the hypothesis identified in section 1.6, and establishes the actors, boundaries and interactions of successful health innovation systems as applicable particularly to latecomers in Chapter 2. In the framework developed, four levels of health innovation capacity are set out and distinguished upon: frontier R&D capacity, capacity to incrementally innovate and manufacture, capacity to manufacture and no capacity at all. It is shown how differences in institutional factors between the frontier countries, fast followers, latecomers and very latecomers account for the four levels of capabilities found in health innovation, building further on a general classification arrived upon by the author elsewhere (Oyeyinka and Gehl Sampath, 2009a). The key differences in institutional frameworks that impact upon physical and knowledge infrastructure building as well as collaboration between system actors thus impeding the catch-up process are articulated.

In Part II of the book, empirical evidence gathered at the sectoral level in six different latecomer countries – India, Bangladesh, Vietnam, Nigeria, Kenya and Tanzania – is presented (Chapters 3 to 6). This is the first book of its kind to apply a rigorous methodology that combines both field survey and case study techniques to health innovation in latecomer countries in both Asia and Africa. A central message of this part of the book is that irrespective of the variables employed, national differences in innovation and technological capabilities could be traced to the distinctiveness of national, regional or sectoral institutions and *local factors matter in the way actors respond to both internal "push" incentives and external "pull" factors*. These six countries have been thoughtfully chosen for the diverse experiences they present in health innovation.

Using the new empirical data generated by the sector surveys, factors that underlie new process/product innovation are analysed by employing first an econometric analysis and supplemented by a number of case studies. By providing empirical and econometric analysis, one is able to draw general conclusions, which are not otherwise possible with case studies. The aim is to arrive at a broad understanding of what factors determine the present state of the countries' innovation capacity rather than attempt some form of "ranking".

The country level analysis presented in Part II of the book thus seeks to present as holistic a picture of innovation capacity as defined here and factors that impact upon it from a latecomer country perspective, not restricting itself to conventional indicators of capacity such as patent data. Patents are only one indicator of innovation, and pose shortcomings in providing a holistic picture because not all new innovations get patented (Pakes and Griliches, 1984) and patents are not equally important to promote innovation across all sectors (see also, Thumm, 2000, pp. 90–94). Patent statistics can also suffer from quality problems across countries, depending on standards of patentability and details of patent enforcement (ibid.). Even apart from all this, the most important problem in using patent proxies for measuring innovation in the context of latecomer countries stems from the fact that frontier level technological activities in these countries are mostly conducted by foreign firms, who protect it through local patents, and not by the local firms themselves. Therefore, measuring innovation through patents granted in such countries will present a very skewed picture of reality, in which local firms and their innovative capacity may not figure at all. For example, as of 2006, 162 patents were granted by the Patent Office in Bangladesh, of which only 16 were granted to local firms (Gehl Sampath, 2007b). This reality can be easily extended to most least developed countries (see UNCTAD, 2007) and these divergences between local and foreign capacities to patent only strengthen the case for reconceptualizing innovation capacity using variables other than patents in the case of latecomer countries. Following the success stories such as China and India, what seems more important to analyse are the individual forms of institutional innovations for transition that were unique to each country but succeeded in linking knowledge domains in academia and private sectors to promote growth. Yet, several of these aspects remain insufficiently corroborated and analysed in the literature because of the limitations of the techniques used.

Part III of the book (Chapters 7 and 8) analyse the extremely important issue of how lessons from building national capabilities in health innovation can be used to find solutions to the global access to medicines debate and public health issues of drug delivery that need to be included in the discussions both globally and nationally (Chapter 7). Chapter 8 presents the comparative insights for policies and institutions that promote learning and health innovation.

2 Sectoral systems for health innovation and development

This chapter analyses the main characteristics of sectoral innovation systems for health in latecomer countries and advances two main propositions. First, while a sectoral innovation system has several components, its success depends on institutions that help coordinate efforts of all actors in the system. Institutions, defined as the "rules of the game" and institutional capacity defined as "the capacity of the state to provide the basic rules for actor interaction and coordination", lie at the heart of the issue. While institutional and innovation economics have addressed issues of institutional variances and their impact on innovative performance, there is a need to view these in conjunction with developmental concerns that confront the latecomers specifically. Second, health innovation is a much broader and more complex sector than pharmaceuticals or biotechnology. It not only has a broader technological base and a wider range of actors, but it spans well beyond the realm of mere technological innovation to include social and institutional innovations. It therefore calls for rigorous framework that could help analyse the issues in building capacity.

This chapter begins with a discussion of the triangulated relationship between innovation, knowledge and development, and maps out the main characteristics of innovation in resource-constrained environments. Whereas knowledge, skills and experience are key in building technological capabilities, modes of learning as promoted through institutional coordination are the precursors of innovation capacity. This section will show how innovation capacity holds the key to how countries master the knowledge they have, and how learning process conditions the accumulation of technological capabilities for actors to innovate, access new forms of knowledge to move into higher domains towards the global frontier. The analysis makes a distinction between information and knowledge and the means by which they are created, thereby moving the discussion away from the lure of simple, magic-bullet incentives like IPRs, to holistic perceptions based on innovation policy. Section 2.2 elaborates the salient features of sectoral systems of innovation in the latecomer context. Health innovation as a sectoral system has its own knowledge bases, actor configurations and boundaries and these are analysed in Section 2.3. In keeping with the fundamental hypotheses that inform this book, Section 2.4 discusses the importance of sector specific "push" institutions in building local health innovation capacity. The changing regulatory landscape, the newly emerging global "push" institutions and their impact on health innovation is then discussed to show the wide divergences these might have on country specific capacity to perform health innovation. The analysis in Section 2.4 onwards brings out two important results. First, integrating the local push institutions and global pull institutions to build capacity for health innovation calls for extensive and advanced policy formulation skills within countries, which itself is a public good. A state's own capacity to formulate policy vision and sustain it through appropriate implementation strategies for health innovation relies on the availability of good human skills and accountable and transparent governance processes, and it is institutions that facilitate their presence and functioning. Second, it is the ability of states to identify local priorities, build local institutions accordingly and leverage the global "pull" factors to local needs that determines the ability to succeed. In other words, the various global institutional changes that impinge upon the sectoral system's ability to respond need to be mitigated and structured through state action. State actions manifest in the capability to identify market failures and opportunities, strategic choices that are made in the form of policies and the apparatus put in place to implement such policies. State's capacity to influence the technology choices of actors and sectors and its ability to enforce them through relevant organizations lies at the heart of building capacity in health innovation in latecomer countries. The analysis conducted in this chapter is furthered through the evidence in the country specific chapters that follows from Chapters 3 to 7 on precisely these issues.

2.1 Innovation systems and capabilities building for economic catch-up

Effecting innovation requires a concerted effort involving several agents within the economic and non-economic system. On the supply side, we have the provision of physical infrastructure (roads, communication and electricity), scientific infrastructure (technological equipments and laboratories), human skills (universities, public research institutes and other tertiary education institutions) and financing (venture capital, loans, tax cuts or subsidies), among others. On the demand side, the requirement of each one of the agents involved in innovation differs from one another. A firm seeking to innovate has the demand for access to knowledge both from sources within the economy and outside such as universities, public sector institutes in areas relevant to its expertise, to have access to competent human skills, to get information on consumer needs and preferences and to gain efficient access to finance sources. The university departments and public research institutes that perform basic and applied research have a demand for adequate financing and collaboration possibilities with firms in the same fields of technology so that their research results can feed into product development. Universities require adequate information on the state-of-the-art developments in each discipline, so that courses and research programmes can be structured/updated accordingly, to meet industry needs.

The sheer complexity of dealing with the processes involved explains why the results of neoclassical economics and information economics on the one hand (the market failure theory), and evolutionary economics on the other (the systems failure approach), fall short of a comprehensive theory that explains innovation and institutions that promote it.

2.1.1 Market failure and systems failure as competing explanations

Arrow (1962) was amongst the first economists to identify the problem of creating technological knowledge (narrowly framed as information) in a perfectly competitive market: indivisibilities, inappropriability and uncertainty (ibid.). The use of knowledge and its demand are both indivisible in the absence of some form of property right to the creator. Inappropriability is a problem created by the non-exclusive and non-rivalrous nature of knowledge. Uncertainty denotes the situation where people have to make decisions without knowing for certain what the consequences of their decisions will be (see Katz and Rosen, 1998). Because of uncertainty, agents are not aware at the time of their decisions how to invest into any particular inventive activity, not only as to in how many states of the world the said event/result will materialize, but they are also not aware of the contingencies that may prevent the desirable state of the world from materializing. These three factors lead to sub-optimal allocation of resources/or underinvestment in R&D (from the viewpoint of societal welfare) in perfectly competitive markets.

Arrow himself suggested two ways to resolve the divergence between individual and social gains from the creation of technological knowledge: grant of some form of incentives (although he did not suggest any himself), and direct public intervention by the state as some form of primary financer of scientific research (see Archibugi and Bizzari, 2004). Arrow's (1962) and Nelson's (1959) work pioneered the subsequent literature that started "treating information itself as a resource", which need to be allocated through the market. The work laid the foundations for two different strands of research: one that dealt with problems of allocating resources to the creation of knowledge characterized as a public good, and another that looks at the economics of technological change. Subsequent work on economics of technological change brought to the fore the fact that Arrow's assumptions do not necessarily hold in the case of technological and scientific knowledge which rely extensively on tacit skills for application and duplication and hence cannot be diffused at marginal costs (Pavitt, 1987; Arora and Merges, 2004).[1]

Ways and means in which knowledge is perceived, applied and transformed are all limited through human perceptions and notions that are socially and historically conditioned. This makes innovation as much a social and cultural process as it is a scientific and technological one. As Nelson (1986) rightly notes, no technology, no matter how simple or complex, can be fully expressed in terms of its material value and the components that it is made up of. The unwritten, tacit, not easily embodied knowledge of applications accounts for the fact that when two producers in different parts of the world use the same technologies, there is always a discrete set of possibilities that they may branch out into, thereby producing completely different results.

Economics of technological change also points out that technological change is evolutionary in character and a firm's capacity to innovate relies essentially on its absorptive capacity (Cohen and Levinthal, 1990),[2] wherein the external environments within which firms operate play a central enabling role. A firm's absorptive capacity lies is its ability to identify important sources of knowledge and technological change, route it into its internal learning processes and utilize it to build its own competitive advantage and this is an ongoing process. Systems within which firms are located dictate the process through which firms accumulate absorptive capacity, and follow dynamic paths themselves.

The systems failure approach is centred on these assumptions and emerged in the works of Freeman (1987, 1988), Lundvall (1985, 1992) and Nelson (1993). Originating primarily as a tool to help explain the performance of country specific factors that contributed to its innovative performance and economic growth,[3] it focused initially on the impact of improved coordination between R&D institutes and other secondary research units with the production system in its initial stages (Lundvall, 1985). The approach largely relies on evolutionary economics (Edquist, 1997; Carlsson, 1995; Oyeyinka, 2006), although some scholars emphasize other theories such as the theory of interactive learning (Lundvall, 1992) and Schumpeterian economics. A basic premise in the systems conception of innovation is that firms operate, grow and innovate within a network of other firms and actors; and do so through interactive learning, which is essentially incremental and cumulative, leading in turn to the accumulation of new in-house capabilities. Both market and non-market mechanisms mediate interactive learning and innovation, and hence market failure is only one component of the system that can be rectified by altering the cost and benefits or payoffs of R&D to firms. As opposed to this, a system failure occurs when market and non-market organizations interact in sub-optimal ways or do not interact at all, that is when critical actors within an innovation system do not promote innovation (OECD, 1998). Systems failure requires broader market and non-market coordinative intervention since its causation is rooted in structural and institutional inadequacies. The existence of systemic failure provides an economic justification for policy to intervene in order to correct the underlying causes.

Various features of innovation processes do not fit into the neat modelling techniques of traditional economic theory thereby strengthening the case for using the systems framework to analyse innovation. A good example is the notion that institutions that promote innovation are path-dependent. If a country invests in rich secondary and tertiary educational institutions today, its benefits will be felt at least one generation later, and perhaps even more time is required to fully analyse its implications on innovation capacity, depending on various factors such as technological opportunities, among others.[4] The same is true of provision of public goods that are essential to build innovation capacity within countries and sectors. Predominant focus of the systems of innovation analysis remains on institutions and goods that operate in the public sector. Whereas producing skilled students (and related human resources) is not a public good, *establishing the capacity to produce good students* is a public good. Although people can be excluded from universities and tertiary educational institutions (on grounds such as merit) and the consumption is also rivalrous (due to capacity constraints), the social benefits of provision of capacity through such institutions outweighs individual gains such that no single individual/groups of individuals have adequate incentives to provide for them. *Research outputs* are also public goods, although they could be converted into private goods (through patents, gains related to publications, among others). As opposed to the market failure approach that lends strength to a set of policy actions that have guided decisions about the role of government technology policy in industrial countries, which are mainly market based, the systems failure approach relies on both market and non-market elements. The market based elements include patents, tax incentives and subsidies while the latter includes all actions to promote the generation, validation and sharing of knowledge within a collaborative learning environment.

The approach does not focus on information, but rather on knowledge, whose access, creation and use are central to innovation capacity of countries at all levels of development. Innovation signifies the capability of actors to use knowledge to create newly marketable products, irrespective of whether they are new to the local market, the country, the region or the world at large. Continuous innovation is the basis of technology-led development, therefore feeds off persistent knowledge access, generation and use of previously accumulated knowledge (Oyeyinka and Gehl Sampath, 2009a).

2.1.2 Knowledge, learning and technological capabilities[5]

Learning processes through which firms/actors tap into knowledge sources to acquire, assimilate, use, adapt, change and create innovative products, leads to accumulation of technological capabilities (Bell and Pavitt, 1993; Pavitt, 1992). From a dynamic perspective, availability of knowledge infrastructure and human skills predetermine how actors can scale up the knowledge-intensity of their activities in the process accumulating greater technological capabilities.[6]

Innovation systems are made up of different knowledge domains that are progressively ordered: a country/national innovation system moves from the lowest (informal sector activities) to the top-most domain (R&D based domain) depending on its stage of development (and technological capabilities) in a seemingly monolithic fashion. These are contained in Box 2.1. When a country gets more technologically advanced, its mix of activities in the knowledge domains shifts drastically upwards to concentrate on the first, second and third domains, whereas a latecomer will largely be stuck in the third and the fourth domains.

Box 2.1 Knowledge domains as the basis of innovative activities

New knowledge creation through laboratory based R&D activities constitutes but one dimension of the science, engineering and technology domain that makes up a large part of the national innovation systems. A more holistic perspective arrives upon four such knowledge domains that coexist within a national innovation system:

1   The largely science based domain with scientists and engineering R&D as the dominant activity. The actors are mainly research scientists and engineers working in these private and government research laboratories. Contrary to what conventional wisdom and popular indicators suggest, this knowledge domain employs only 10 per cent of science and engineering (S&E) manpower even in the most research intensive country of the world, USA (NSF, 2006).
2   The second domain is the design and engineering based one, which involves systematic engineering and scientific specification of products, processes, systems including computer hardware and software. This component is linked more directly to domain (3), which is the manufacturing and production component rather than R&D, although outputs of applied research and development feed into this sub-system.
3   The third domain is the modern production and manufacturing based domain with engineers as well as skilled technicians but less so scientists as the dominant actors. The locus of activity here is the factory and manufacturing centres.
4   The fourth knowledge domain is the informal or traditional sector, which characterizes developing environments. The main actors are artisans, crafts persons and technicians. The locus of activity is the diverse but structurally homogeneous maintenance and repair garages, clusters of low technology, traditional products and production processes such as indigenous knitwear, leather and footwear making. The mode of knowledge is largely skill based tacit and experiential. There are three characteristics of this knowledge base. First, the actors are largely low level skilled workers and apply low level technologies based on a mix of modern and traditional methods to manufacture. Second, it is largely disconnected from component (3) (of modern manufacture and production) although it is not unusual that it draws raw materials, such as for instance scrap metals, manufacturing rejects and so forth as inputs. Third, its disembodied (human) knowledge is equally disconnected from formal educational centres and laboratories although it is a large part of the economies of developing countries.

Source: Oyeyinka and Gehl Sampath, 2009a

Moving up into more demanding knowledge domains depends on the availability of knowledge infrastructure and human skills and the learning processes that are fostered by local institutions. These factors predetermine how firms build on stocks of existing knowledge to acquire greater technological capabilities. Three reasons stress further the importance of the local institutions to promote learning based on local knowledge infrastructure and human skills (Archibugi and Pietrobelli, 2003):

a   whereas the codified components of knowledge can be transferred easily, and at negligible costs, it is the local capabilities that determine its potential for use;

b   the tacit component of knowledge continues to be elusive, less easy to transfer and replicate in a different context;

c   the innovative core of firms worldwide is moving from trading in embodied innovations to disembodied ones; where the technological expertise is coded in terms of managerial and organizational specializations, or technological ones that are fortified through IPRs and trademarks. In this context, merely locating production within a country might not really lead to significant knowledge "spillovers".

Various modes of learning condition the transition of firms and organizations from one knowledge domain to another, as presented in Table 2.1.

Experiences of the latecomers and the technologically advanced countries point to a common pattern of capabilities accumulation, wherein learning trajectories of firms and other actors in the innovation system almost always proceed in a progression from reverse engineering and adaptation to incremental innovation to an R&D based approach. Budworth (1996) similarly classifies innovation into several degrees, predicting that incremental innovations are most likely to be prevalent in latecomer countries. Incremental innovations can range from small changes in process technologies that lead to significant improvements in production methods or organizational techniques that lead to delivery efficiency of existing products or they may also lead to the production of new technologically improved products (OECD, 1997). In the early literature, however, incremental innovation is not usually recognized as being part of the R&D process, because it may overlap with development and is not formalized as a clear category of activity (see Rosenberg, 1982). Despite this, incremental innovation is a very important stage in capacity building processes at the firm level, thus affirming the ability of the enterprise to adapt existing knowledge and create commercially viable products. Such a product, although not new to the world or science at large, is a significant step towards the creation of independent local enterprise in latecomer countries: a backbone of industrial activity.

Scholars, who have analysed the process through which latecomers compete in world markets at a stage in their economic development where their industry is neither "infant" nor at the "frontier", have also arrived at similar conclusions (Amsden, 1989). Maintaining sustained competitiveness has much to do with upgrading technological bases or moving from low-tech to mid-tech to high-tech industries (Amsden and Chu, 2003).

However, in any given state of knowledge, it is assumed that greater innovative efforts (read inputs) by actors results in greater innovation results (read outputs) as measured by products, processes, organizational outcomes (Archibugi and Michie, 1997) Institutions are ubiquitous to this process and hold the key to how actors

Table 2.1 Modes of learning as they correspond to different knowledge domains

Knowledge domain	Learning mode
1 Science based domain	R&D based activities.
2 Design and engineering domain	Incremental innovation based on large-scale reverse engineering skills, evidence of clear strengths in certain sectors over others with perhaps a few R&D based activities.
3 Modern production and manufacturing domain	Learning mainly through reverse engineering activities, with a focus on increasing efficiency of existing activities but also on diversifying the structure of their economic activities (see Bell, 2006) to expand to newer industrial sectors.
4 Informal or traditional activities domain	Traditional technologies with the emergence of low-scale, reverse engineering, but generally a heavy focus on narrow specialization of economic activities.

Source: author.

master the knowledge they have, access new forms of knowledge, build technological capabilities through learning processes to move into higher domains.

2.1.3 Designing and implementing innovation policies

Following from Chapter 1, the range of policies that go under the umbrella term "innovation policy" are extensive. They range from those that promote human capital formation to science and technology (S&T) policies to industrial policies to general infrastructure policies. Incentives for institutional coordination amongst the organizations set up to fulfil these mandates form an equally critical part of an enabling innovation environment. Domestic agents need appropriate incentives to interact optimally in order to translate research/incremental innovation efforts into entrepreneurial ventures that are constantly transgressing public and private sector boundaries. Incentives and policies that enhance coordination include policies that focus both on primary research as well as extension services that will help to build up/foster the enterprise sector to collaborate with public sector institutions to commercialize products based on ongoing inventive activities. It also encompasses a range of policy efforts specifically aimed at enhancing collaborative research, through subsidies, joint research programmes, product development initiatives and IPP or sharing schemes, within the framework of a national innovation policy.

Institutions for physical and knowledge infrastructure come generally under what are termed horizontal policies for innovation, meaning they are directed to stimulate technological development irrespective of specific technological area or industry (Teubal, 1999). Horizontal science and technology policy often include policies for:

- R&D investment (government funding of research);
- government technology procurement;
- standard setting – which often requires the public and private sectors to interact;
- training and education policies;
- collaboration oriented policies, which generally target collaboration between the various actors, including but not limited to:
  - supplier–producer (university–industry programmes),
  - user–producer (pharmaceutical firms–biotechnology firms and other agencies articulating demand such as hospitals, dispensaries or even intermediary agencies),
  - producer–producer (firms),
  - among university schools and departments – licences, sponsored research, university–industry technology transfer offices, consulting guidelines and codes of ethics,
  - interface organizations (e.g. research technology organizations) making a bridge between science based organizations and industrial practices (User–producer–supplier (interfaces)).

As opposed to such framework policies, innovation policies can often comprise dedicated policies such as those employed in biotechnology and these are discussed later on in this chapter.

2.2 Sectoral innovation systems and development

The observed differences in patterns of technological change and productivity growth across sectors have pioneered applied research to analyse technological regimes and firm level activities on a sectoral basis (Pavitt, 1984; Castellacci, 2008). A wide range of investigations have been conducted at least over the past decade at the sectoral level to understand the kinds of opportunities – technological and market related – that configure firm level actions and decisions in particular ways towards capabilities build-up, thus accounting for the variable performances across sectors in the technologically advanced countries (Archibugi, 2001; Malerba, 2002, 2004). Such studies have primarily sought to ascertain the factors that demarcate sectoral systems of innovation (as opposed to national systems) with a focus on explaining the sector characteristics that account for the innovation and industrial activity patterns (see for example, Marsili and Verspagen, 2002; Malerba, 2002; Dosi *et al.*, 2007). This literature defines a sectoral system of innovation as centred around four aspects (Breschi and Malerba, 1997; Malerba, 2002, 2005, 2006):

- the nature of the knowledge base (that is, the characteristics of the knowledge and technologies that the innovative activities in the sector are based, see Malerba *et al.*, 2001);
- the conditions of appropriability (being, possibilities to appropriate rents from innovative activities in the sector, through patents, trade secrets or other means);
- the relevance of sector specific institutions;
- the technological opportunities peculiar to the sector (that is, the likelihood of innovation outcomes in return for investment).

2.2.1 Firms, networks and boundaries of the system

In the sectoral systems framework, which has mainly been validated by evidence from the technologically advanced countries with a few exceptions, firms are the main actors.[7] Capabilities and learning processes are the major drivers of innovation and growth; and competitive relationships among firms proceed through the selection environment in which they operate. Systems are delineated by endogenous boundaries because they are defined by the knowledge and technological domain of a given sector.

The essence – and main advantage – of the sectoral systems framework lies in identifying the boundary of a system so that appropriate policy interventions that could help firms upgrade their industrial capacity and competitiveness can be devised. The boundary of any particular system is in turn determined largely by its knowledge base and technologies. Even when disaggregated at the sectoral level, the knowledge base, skills and experience that firms can draw upon are the building blocks of technological capacity and are associated with different modes of learning, as elaborated in the previous section. The capacity of the firms in a sector to move up different learning modes and acquire higher levels of technological capacity therefore falls back on the sector specific institutions that enable innovation. Analysing sectoral systems of innovation helps to understand the dynamics of the various sectors that contribute to the domestic economy, at the same time providing clues as to how international competitiveness of a sector within a country/set of countries can be enhanced through targeted interventions at the sectoral level (Castellacci, 2008).

2.2.2 Sectoral innovation systems in latecomer countries

Sectoral innovation systems in developing countries reveal specific characteristics that are non-trivial in terms of their implications for development:[8]

a   *Lack of access to knowledge in key areas*, which is often mistaken with access to information. Access to knowledge is contextual for each sector and country and refers to the requisite knowledge sources that are key to their technological capabilities building process at a particular point of time.
b   *Lack of local capacity to absorb and use knowledge* primarily determined by the availability of human skills locally and the institutional capacity of the system to provide the basis for innovative activity within any of the four knowledge domains identified in the previous section. In the absence of this, *access to knowledge remains, at best, access to information* since the actors lack the capacity to build further upon it.
c   *Lack of well-developed institutional frameworks to forge second-best responses to innovation issues* manifests in the form of high transaction costs to conduct innovation activities. Incomplete institutional frameworks or institutional frameworks that do not prescribe the roles of responsibilities of various actors in an adequate way often result in organizations[9] being set up with overlapping competencies and duplication of roles and responsibilities or, at the other extreme, may be missing altogether.
d   *Lack of resources in the general innovation environment*, which includes missing physical and knowledge infrastructure, as well as financial instruments that attenuate innovation risks. Innovation processes are associated with their own range of technological and market related uncertainties, but, at the same time, there are differences in innovation outcomes when the same activities are conducted by different groups of individuals in different contexts, with different levels of "imagination and accuracy", which goes a long way to explain the divergent performances of firms and sectors (Archibugi and Michie, 1997, p. 277). Institutions that attenuate risk – especially of the latter form – are missing to promote innovative conduct in resource-constrained environments.

e   *Lack of a good public sector* that has the human and financial capacity to conduct relevant basic and applied research and industrial R&D can, once again, have very different consequences for different sectors. In sectors that require public science, such as pharmaceuticals, agriculture and new technologies, efficient and well-endowed public sector is a precondition for innovation.

f   *Lack of a thriving private sector* that can uptake results of industrial R&D conducted in public sector organizations is a very general characteristic of innovation environments in latecomer countries.

g   *Lack of collaborative linkages* that allow for mobility of ideas and human capital between firms and organizations alike. Competing agendas of organizations for science, technology and innovation, lack of a collaborative culture amongst academics and industry practitioners, lack of incentives that reward modes of collaborative conduct, lack of discernable benefits within the system for indulging in collaborative linkages, all contribute to the lack of collaborations that impacts upon the process of interactive learning.

h   *Lack of policy competence* in latecomer countries is perhaps as complex a phenomenon as the lack of innovation capacity itself. States, by their actions as well as their inactions, make technology choices for development within their boundaries. State actions manifests in the capability to identify market failures and opportunities, strategic choices that are made in the form of policies and the apparatus put in place to implement such policies.

These characteristics differ in their severity and can often times be totally absent, depending on the level of development, thereby impacting upon the growth of sectors in highly idiosyncratic ways. We need not belabour the importance of having the basic components in place – the essential building blocks for industrial development – because their absence either in part or *in toto* signifies innovation systems that are highly embryonic or truncated (Bell, 2006). In order to create a simplistic dichotomy of how innovation systems differ between technologically advanced countries and latecomer countries, Table 2.2 maps the main differences on a one-on-one basis.

Sectoral systems of innovation in latecomer countries demonstrate, as Metcalfe *et al.* (2005) state, emergent properties due to the transient nature of innovation systems; wherein the loci of innovative activity may in most cases not be the firm but rather other organizations that operate in the public sector. This may not only be true in the case of sectors where public science plays a critical role, such as pharmaceuticals or biotechnology, but may be applicable across the board in late development. As a result of this shift in focus, the *system boundaries will be determined not only by the technology and knowledge base of the sector, but also by the capacity of the state to provide public goods through various organizations* set up for this purpose within the sectoral systems of innovations. This dual boundary-setting is a shift from the sectoral systems approach as applied to technologically advanced countries and is developed and elaborated in detail in the next section. Second, given that latecomer countries are at different

Table 2.2 Differences in sectoral innovation systems between technologically advanced and latecomer countries

	Basic characteristics	Technologically advanced countries	Latecomer countries
1	Knowledge bases that underlie innovative activity	Easily available	Difficult to assemble, may be available in parts or even wholly absent
2	Institutions to promote innovation based activities	Well developed	May or may not exist
3	Organizations to fulfil various institutional mandates	Well mapped out	Missing altogether, or may have overlapping competencies that thwart efforts
4	Presence of human skills to deploy for innovative activities	Well developed and available	May not exist or may exist only to a partial extent
5	Enterprise sector	Well developed	Entirely missing or largely stunted with the presence of large state-owned enterprises (in a dysfunctional state) and dominance of small and medium enterprises
5	Feedback loops between demand and supply	Well developed	Does not exist
6	Financial instruments to reduce risk and uncertainty	Attuned to innovation needs, and possible to develop sector-specific interventions	Largely absent, with little or no means to focus on sector-specific interventions
7	Incentives for collaboration variables	Well developed	Hardly exist
8	Public science to support innovation	Well developed, moving away from increased public science to more efficient private sector based research	Hardly existent or dysfunctional, operating with incoherent and insufficient mandate and funds
9	Co-evolution of policies with the emergence of new technologies	Usually the case, see for example, Malerba (2006), Nightingale and Mahdi (2006)	Institutional inertia and rigidity prevent this form of co-evolution in most latecomer contexts

Source: author.

stages of technological capabilities, *the knowledge bases required to promote innovative activity even within established sectors could vary from what we assume them to be while analysing technological change at the frontier.* These distinctions will necessarily matter, especially in formulating sector specific policies, which is the ultimate goal of sectoral analysis of innovation activities. This aspect deserves greater emphasis also because with the gradual decomposition of innovation activities in the sector, there is a range of opportunities for other latecomer countries to specialize in particular sub-disciplines of health innovation. Third, studies of sectoral systems of innovation have tended to focus on how various systemic imperfections can be improved mainly because the approach has focused on countries that have a well-informed basis for innovation. It is but natural within such contexts that the inquiry is restricted to how certain systemic imperfections that manifest for a sector specific activity due to its distinct characteristics need to be remedied. This inquiry, however, needs to be broadened while considering sectoral systems of innovation in latecomer countries to include the question of how to provide entire missing components of systems, such as the private sector enterprise or science community, when they are absent. Fourth, formal and informal institutions that are centrepiece of a sector's innovative performance differ in latecomer countries in their scope, content and extent of embeddedness (Evans, 1995). Accounts that rely on replication of institutional frameworks from one successful context to others are not only heretical, but also misleading on empirical grounds. The issues that impact on exchange, namely, institutional inertia, rigidity and organizational heterogeneity are all sources of transaction costs in latecomer institutional frameworks and need to be addressed in a framework that also takes into account the informal attitudes of actors. A final point relates to the co-evolution of policies and institutions along with technological advances in the sector; which demonstrates the partnership between state and enterprise sector to move towards more productive frontiers.

2.2.3 Institutional issues in latecomers: inertia, rigidity and effecting change at the margin

Institutions, defined simply as the "rules of the game" (North, 1993) matters for economic performance (North, 1996), and while small reforms may suffice to jump-start industrial activity, rigorous institutional support is required to cushion innovation systems from the long-term shocks of economic activity (Rodrik, 2004; Metcalfe *et al.*, 2006). Institutional capacity alone enables firms to follow dynamic trajectories in industrial sectors "whose knowledge base and capabilities are closely related to the constellation of emerging radical innovations", by enabling them to avail the broader set of opportunities and giving support against the risks related to these activities (Castellacci, 2008, p. 980). How much and how fast firms in any sector transition to build technological capabilities to compete at the frontier depends on how well the institutional framework is geared towards promoting coordination within the various parts of the domestic knowledge system.

Informal institutions, understood as attitudes and established social and cultural norms of actors in society, are in a state of constant give-and-take with formal institutional rules. While on the one hand, the moral and cultural underpinnings of a society tend to get codified in the form of rules that determine accepted conduct and modes of interaction, formal rules get institutionalized over time to create informal attitudes that govern the behaviour of actors within systems of innovation. These can often times be more daunting a challenge than simply reforming inefficient formal rules for innovation. Latecomer countries possess varying levels of institutional capacity to promote development, which explain to a large extent the difficulties they face in transforming knowledge through learning activities to technological capabilities and innovative performance. Why is access to knowledge not sufficient to promote the use of knowledge? Why is technology transfer not a necessary precondition for technology absorption? Why is public sector research not sufficient to promote product development through the private sector? The answer to most of these very basic, often-assumed-to-be-given, constraints lies in the formal and informal institutions that underlie innovation in latecomer countries. Latecomer institutions and organizations that have been set up to perform specific mandates exhibit substantial inertia to change. *Institutional inertia* manifests in resistance both to changes that are imposed from inside (through newer policy emphasis) and outside (as a result of global rules, emerging technologies, market opportunities and competitive pressures).

Institutional inertia develops over time mainly because innovation systems in latecomer development are not fully operational and comprise institutional frameworks that are largely, if not mostly, incomplete. Ill-defined and unenforceable property rights structures, lack of contractual laws and other enforcement mechanisms not only create scope for legal uncertainty, but also prevents the demand for knowledge from occurring in the first place (since parties are unable to transact to implement institutional agendas in the absence of coherent property rights). Theoretically, in the absence of formal institutional setups to guide collaborative behaviour, positive informal institutions could emerge to mitigate transaction costs and facilitate exchange in certain instances (Williamson, 1979; Milgrom and Roberts, 1996), *or* the system could get captured by negative informal institutions.[10] Economic literature has keenly studied the cases where positive informal rules emerge as a response to opportunistic behaviour to enable actors to contract. As opposed to this, limitations in the formal institutional framework can lead to the emergence of "negative" informal institutions simply because agents, who gradually internalize these formal institutional constraints, evolve payoff mechanisms that accrue from patterns of low level of transactions with simple contracts instead of high level of transactions with complex contracts, indicating the lost potential of beneficial exchange. Agents in the system, who have to repeatedly transact with one another for the provision of various services and goods for innovation, devise strategies (and "co-learn") to focus on the maximization of their immediate, individual payoffs (Kreps, 1995). They learn adaptively in this context to unlearn all the norms and habits that lead to maximized collective payoffs, to create the way for norms and habits that will ensure maximum individual payoffs. Over time, the incentives in both the formal and informal institutions evolve in ways geared to exploit the weaknesses of the innovation system as created by the incomplete formal institutional framework. Individual/group rents begin to depend on the existence of already created organizations for their profitability, and this produces lock-in outcomes for institutional change, as pointed out by North (1990) and other scholars. For example, academic researchers tend to focus mainly on extracting rents from collaboration with international researchers in terms of foreign exchange visits, and other such perks in kind. Similarly, researchers in public sector institutions perform few, unsystematic services for the private sector, often in a haphazard environment where firms are chosen for exchange of such services through personal contacts and not performance indicators.

These incentives can take various forms. For example, the lack of well-defined property rights is one such incentive that produces lock-in effects that are resistant to newer institutions that promote efficient allocation of property rights. Incentives for academic researchers in latecomer countries that allow for promotions without substantial collaborative credentials create resistance for newer forms of organization that seek to create accountability. Similarly, mistrust between actors, unhealthy competition for resources and other such aspects get entrenched into social values, habits and practices of people and organizations in the form of informal institutions to such an extent that they even undercut/resist new changes in the formal institutional frameworks that seek to channel the system towards producing collective gains.

As a result, innovation that is meant to be for the progress of the society can be turned into a process for the advantage of a few incumbent groups that manage to capture the rents, as a result of the incomplete institutional framework. These "unexpected winners" perpetuate individual gains at the expense of the progress of the rest of the society. The state, which is ill equipped to provide and enforce a coherent innovation policy in the first place, is even more at a loss to tackle the unwanted distribution effects of this process on social inequality. These failures are non-trivial and even competitive market pressures and market incentives under the present multilateral trade regime fail to enhance patterns of interaction and learning needed for innovation. Even when sectors do learn and move upwards in terms of their technological capabilities, these negative institutions come in the way of forging distribution of innovation returns in an equitable way.

This calls for a more nuanced understanding of the institutions for innovation in a latecomer context with a *greater focus on the informal domain*. In other words, often times, governments in latecomer countries fail to realize and boost the right forms of support structures required for economic growth and innovation within sectors. These incomplete formal institutional structures may lead to the creation of inefficient "lock-in" situation by firms, since once the sector is on a particular path, actors evolve second-best solutions to missing institutions that may not be suited for the collective gains of the system as a whole. Once on a "wrong" path (read inefficient from a social welfare point of view), innovation systems in late development tend to get captured by incumbent groups that thrive on the rents that accrue by way of inefficient informal rules internalized into the system over time and show tremendous resistance to change.

While most latecomer countries are only beginning to view these issues in innovation terms and moving away from the dominant S&T emphasis that governed their perspectives on technology-led development, merely enacting organizations that succeeded in enabling innovation in other countries is unlikely to achieve the required emphasis. The imperative is on initiatives that understand the local barriers to innovation capacity and enact incentives that seek to change entrenched modes of socially disruptive behaviour into more collectively efficient patterns. Such change, by nature, can only be induced at the margin and will require sustained efforts to bear results. Moreover, it calls for rigorous stock-taking of the nature of innovation in any latecomer context including empirical studies that inform patterns of actor behaviour over time.

2.3 Health innovation systems: boundaries, knowledge base and actors

Health innovation includes all forms of innovation – process, product and organizational – that are required to conduct basic research and development as well as ensure delivery of marketable drugs of importance to human health. Thus defined, drug R&D at the frontier is one aspect of health innovation, thus defined. Health innovation includes all forms of discovery, development and delivery (CIPIH, 2006) that may or may not be new at the frontier, but may be new to the firm, the local context or the country in question.[11] Organizational and institutional innovations in service delivery that are based on application of knowledge to new contexts, or new ways of conducting activities in an age-old setting addressing the concerns of local implementing actors are an integral part of health innovation.

Whereas much of the sectoral systems of innovation studies have focused on pharmaceuticals or biotechnology as a sector (see for example, Malerba, 2004; Tait, 2007b), health innovation is a relatively newer concept (Mahoney and Morel, 2006). Health innovation weds the technological innovation process of producing new drugs, vaccines and diagnostic tools with the health system aspects of countries, thereby bringing to the fore issues of access and delivery that hitherto did not figure. Conceptualizing issues of innovation, production and delivery jointly in the frame of health innovation systems allows the analysis to capture the increasing overlap between innovations and applications in the sector which is increasingly the case as newer health technologies challenge the distinction between innovation and delivery in health (Fennell, 2008), and also points attention to the sensitivity of innovations to rules and regulations at each and every level of the process.

Box 2.2 The imperative of health innovation

Pharmaceutical innovation is intricately connected to health systems in which they are embedded. Even at a cursory first glance, the linkages are compelling. The most pertinent question in the debate on how firms can focus on local demand itself centres around issues of demand not only for products in the conventional sense, but also diagnostic tools and services and delivery mechanisms that were hitherto in the realm of health systems. Even ignoring this convergence caused by technological developments, there are several other areas where aspects related to innovation have a pervasive impact on health equity. Notable amongst these are:

a   regulations on quality of marketable drugs and practices followed for good manufacture determine the quality of health care products available to the local population;

b   accepted norms on how drugs can be marketed (including mechanisms that check doctor practices for prescribing drugs, especially patented versions over generic brands) play a crucial role in ensuring affordable access to medicines;

c   the ways in which medicines/health services are prescribed and distributed have, in turn, innate connections with how local demand finds its way into firm level decision making based on future markets; and

d   innovations in products, diagnostic services and other modes of treatment rely increasingly on the level of organization, training of personnel and efficacy of health systems delivery.

e   Health systems restructuring in latecomers is increasingly beginning to rely on the role that the private sector can play, thus enmeshing issues further. Some good examples include the National Rural Health Mission launched by the government of India in 2005 to bring about "architectural correction" in the basic health care delivery system, which adopted partnerships with the private sector as a strategy for expanding and rationalizing affordable health services for the poor in rural areas.

f   Including users in the innovation process is important because they help pinpoint market failure, facilitate absorption of marketable products, increase cost effectiveness of R&D efforts and reduce social resistance to new technologies (Smits and Boon, 2008).

g   There is a need to ensure that the new health innovation products that seek to address the 10/90 gap do indeed reach those who need it most in latecomer contexts, through sustainable health systems interventions that match the technological products and their characteristics.

h   International agencies involved in global health are beginning to move their focus away from funding individual programmes, such as HIV prevention, to strengthening health systems as a whole.

As a result, effectiveness of health innovation for any given local context depends on issues such as availability, effectiveness and levels of centralization (or decentralization) of public service delivery by asking whether and how national governments should have incentives to invest in capital assets that improve the quality of health services. A health innovation perspective also enables one to take into account factors that influence how health care and health systems innovations are perceived and implemented in practice, in different countries across the globe and includes institutional and organizational innovations that are essential to counter the effects of imposing global innovations to health systems at national or local levels.

Source: author

In short, the concept of health innovation captures the ongoing *quid pro quo* between technological, organizational and social innovation in creation and dissemination of new knowledge in health on a routine basis. Gradual recognition of these interfaces is triggering off several initiatives that seek to integrate health research and health care initiatives such as the recent "shared management in health" programme in Brazil. As mentioned in Chapter 1, this book mainly views the health innovation process from the technological innovation perspective, with some reference to the social and organizational aspects of health systems delivery and associated equity issues.

2.3.1 *Knowledge base for health innovation*

The knowledge base for health innovation is embedded in the stocks of human capital that the sector can draw upon (both for innovation activities and health sector delivery activities), the state of public science that is a prerequisite for good innovation capacity and the presence of private enterprise sector. Health innovation capability is inter-disciplinary and relies heavily upon integration of traditional strengths in established science based disciplines like chemistry, biology and pharmaceutical sciences with newer knowledge bases such as biotechnology and systems biology.[12]

Although most of the focus in health innovation is on the technological innovation aspects, the main technologies are as follows:

1   *Pharmaceuticals and vaccines.* Pharmaceutical innovation for drugs and vaccines includes the much R&D intensive new chemical entities (NCEs) and the production of "me too" drugs that include a variety of imitative activities including generics production. There is a wide literature that stresses on the nature of pharmaceutical innovation for the production of new chemical entities, and the analysis will not aim to reproduce it here. In sum, it is not just a matter of R&D capabilities; it involves extensive risk-taking, since the result is erratic and outcomes highly unpredictable. The difficulties inherent are evidenced by the results: only 154 new chemical entities have been introduced between 1975 and 1994 worldwide, and although the search for blockbuster drugs is what drives the R&D process in pharmaceuticals (Grabowski, 2002), much of pharmaceutical innovation centres around the second category due to reasons of diversification of risk portfolios for the larger firms, and the lack of risk-taking abilities for most

of the other firms worldwide. This second category, also called imitative R&D for the production of "me too" drugs ranges from inventing around existing molecules, to creating new combinations of existing molecules, to discovering new ways of drug delivery as well as more direct generic drugs production (Bottazzi *et al.*, 2000).

Generic manufacturing of pharmaceutical drugs can be further broken up into two forms of technological capabilities: the production of active pharmaceutical ingredients (APIs), which requires chemical synthesis skills and is commonly referred to as "reverse-engineering" capabilities, and final formulations, which is a purely manufacturing activity and involves the mixing of active pharmaceutical ingredients with other non-active ingredients into pills, tablets or other forms of administration.

2   *Biotechnology.* Biotechnology is a core component of biopharmaceutical and biomedical research due to its ability to help elucidate the physiological mechanisms of disease causation and response (pharmacogenetics). It is also used extensively in development of biopharmaceuticals, diagnostics (immunodiagnostics and DNS diagnostics) and vaccines (OECD, 2006, p. 25). Of the two, its role in drug and vaccine R&D is of far greater significance. There have been several efforts to map out the top ten biotechnologies for latecomers (Singer *et al.*, 2007; Chataway *et al.*, 2007), which include molecular diagnostic tools, recombinant vaccines, recombinant technology for therapeutic products and combinatorial chemistry for drug discovery.

3   *Genomics based technologies, synthetic biology and other emerging techniques.* Genomics technologies are pioneering newer techniques for drug discovery, including small chemical pharmaceuticals. Biologics are protein based medicines, the production of which involves large-scale cultures of living cells. Similarly, synthetic biology comprises the design (or redesign of existing) and assembly of new biological parts or systems for purposes of treatment delivery makes it possible to match disease profiles and treatments on a one-to-one basis.

4   *Health care technologies.* This broadly includes technologies required to conduct health technology assessments,[13] diagnostic and laboratory technologies that are important to ensure delivery of health care to the masses.

This list is not exhaustive. Global patterns of knowledge change are becoming increasingly convergent across different areas of science and technology (Oyeyinka and Gehl Sampath, 2009a), developments in health innovation being no stranger to this. For example, newer technologies as represented by genetic engineering, material science technologies as combined with computer science technologies have carved out new applications of importance to both health care delivery and pharmaceuticals innovation including bioinformatics, which though not listed above is nevertheless important (Srinivasan, 2008).

Economics of innovation studies offers a set of conventional indicators to measure knowledge infrastructure in all sectors, including health innovation and this consists of R&D investments as percentage of GDP, centres of excellence for basic and applied research in both the public and private sectors of the economy, and scientists and researchers per million of the population, patents granted and number of new drugs/vaccines introduced. While these remain important as variables that offer us some sort of criteria for comparability primarily as a result of their extensive application in technologically advanced countries as innovation variables, knowledge infrastructure to conduct health innovation in latecomer countries is best understood in terms of other forms of knowledge interactions critical to competence building at the sectoral level, including:

- knowledge interaction between university departments, centres of excellence and public research institutes;
- knowledge interaction between traditional knowledge holders (local and indigenous communities) and other more research based and product development actors;
- knowledge interaction between local and foreign firms and universities;
- knowledge interactions between local and foreign firms and public research institutes (PRIs);
- knowledge interactions between local and foreign firms;
- interactions between farmers, consumers, seed banks and other intermediary organizations that help gauge local demand and issues imminent to the agricultural system;
- interactions between various governmental agencies responsible to promote these competencies locally;
- types of interactions, and within what disciplines of science; and
- the determinants and variety of knowledge interactions.

Such knowledge interactions are difficult to measure, and can be done through a composite of factors that includes:

a   the percentage of monetary allocations devoted to research;
b   the percentage of research contracted to and from outside organizations;
c   the level of joint research with other organizations (basic, applied or product development initiatives);
d   the number of scientific publications jointly written with other institutions;
e   the level of co-authorship based on joint research;
f   the exchange of key technical and scientific personnel (numbers and levels of qualification);
g   the involvement in joint R&D programmes organized by the government at the sectoral level;
h   the consultancy research carried out for other organizations, both local and foreign.

The health innovation surveys presented in this book were aimed particularly to capture these forms of interactions, and have been used in the context of other sectors and countries over the past few years.

2.3.2 Actors and networks

The key actors in health innovation include universities and public research institutions, firms, teaching hospitals that mediate demand and supply in a variety of specialized ways, governmental agencies and policy institutions.

2.3.2.1 University education and human capital formation

Whereas other fields of social science (such as human capital theories) viewed schooling as a factor that enhances productivity of workers, recent innovation studies have begun to unravel the extent to which schooling, higher education and industrial productivity correlate with one another. It is still difficult to map the impact of certain kinds of education investments made by countries on their technological trajectories on a one-to-one basis simply because opportunities are driven through technological breakthroughs, markets, customer-preferences and, most importantly, the ability of the innovation system in a country to rapidly respond to such stimuli. But clearly *ex ante* decisions on various aspects of innovation capacity, such as a country's schooling system, its preferences for secondary and tertiary education (whether there should be greater emphasis on natural sciences or other disciplines, whether there should be centres of excellence for tertiary education), investment into public sector research – all impact upon the generation of human skills and availability of knowledge infrastructure to build technological capabilities.

Three critical components make universities a successful centre of innovation especially in sectors that are knowledge intensive and inter-disciplinary in nature:

1   level and quality of human skills (amount and quality of researchers) available to train new manpower, and to conduct research;
2   laboratory technology and equipment to train students in inter-disciplinary areas of research;
3   human interaction and coordination between researchers in various departments and universities and good channels of dissemination of research results with both national and international agencies.

In health innovation, it is precisely these factors that have ensured that innovations that have greater value originate from small academic laboratories that focus on inter-disciplinary applied research or research intensive firms (Gambardella, 1995). University education of relevance to health innovation spans across three fields: medical education (for doctors, nurses and health service personnel), education in traditional science disciplines (including chemistry, biochemistry, pharmaceutical sciences, pharmacology and biology) and disciplines related to emerging technologies (such as biotechnology, molecular biology and genetic engineering). The knowledge dependent nature of innovation has two major implications for the provision of human capital. First, the dynamically evolving state of technology calls for constant revisions of academic curricula that incorporate the newest scientific insights to produce highly skilled human capital. Second, the fact that health innovation capabilities exhibit technological overlap with advances in other sectors (some of which are not predictable *ex ante*) implies that provision of skilled personnel depends on quality education across the board. Innovation in health presupposes that states will have good, if not excellent, tertiary education institutions in several science intensive fields.

2.3.2.2 PRIs, university centres of excellence and public science

The complementarity between science and technology clearly varies between sectors, especially when measured in terms of direct usefulness of results of scientific research in technological advances (see Dosi *et al.*, 2007). In health innovation, public science is a major source of new knowledge and has played a critical role in the emergence of several new technologies that are of increasing importance to the sector, including biotechnology. In addition to producing skilled manpower, much of the knowledge that forms the basis of innovation emerges as part of applied research carried out at universities and public research institutes, and there is a positive relationship between university research and innovativeness (see for example, Andersson and Ejermo, 2004). Innovation studies continue to shed light on how the state of research in public research institutions acts as a precursor to a range of health innovation skills in both technologically advanced and latecomer countries alike.

Public research institutes play two main functions in the development and maintenance of competencies in health innovation. First, they act as primary centres of interactive learning and innovation in early periods of various technical disciplines such as biotechnology. They foster interactive learning between public and private institutions by promoting product/market focus in innovation efforts in public sector institutions which tend often to be very disjoint from product development, by increasing mobility of skills and personnel between the public and private sector institutions, and by attracting funding from the private sector for important research venues. Even when the health innovation system is sufficiently developed, PRIs continue to perform a supportive role at two critical stages of research and patenting. In research, they collaborate with the smaller firms engaged in niche areas to provide the requisite knowledge base and help to promote the growth of these enterprises in the economy. PRIs also provide substantial support services to universities due to their specialized focus and advanced laboratory and human facilities, and thus continue to act as coordinating centres for interaction between universities and industry in several instances.

2.3.2.3 Firms

Emergence of new firms to jump-start sectors or entire sub-sectors is symptomatic of a vibrant region or economy where new knowledge drives differentiation and division of labour (Oyeyinka and Rasiah, 2009). Theory informs us that

Schumpeterian innovation is ideally induced by competition, the process of doing which creates "winners" and "losers". Innovative firms have a negative externality on firms who do not innovate and thus lag behind the "state-of-the-art" innovators in any field of technology. Such an externality gets internalized through the market mechanism, since innovation induces changes of production functions that result in newer sets of production prices, and firms that do not upgrade accordingly fail to compete.[14] The process of innovation based on constant competition promotes social welfare, and therefore the primary aim of policies should be to promote competitive environments for firms to thrive within sectors, health innovation being no exception to this general rule.

Sectoral systems literature has repeatedly found evidence for varying firm characteristics across technologies. In health innovation, in addition to the usual market and technical uncertainties that affect capabilities formation (Freeman, 1982), firms and organizations are faced with an added technological uncertainty that is caused by the constant influx of newer technologies that not only affect products and innovation cycles, but also consumer behaviour and reallocate strategic advantages of firms on a constant basis. This accentuates the two-way relationship between firms and the underlying technological base of a sector that is well acknowledged in economic literature. On the one hand, the changes in firms' organizational arrangements affect their technological opportunities and outcomes (e.g. Robertson and Langlois 1995; Brusoni and Principe, 2001; Ernst 2005), and on the other, technological sophistication of the production/delivery process often substantially impacts upon the firms' accepted and time-tested notions of organizing innovative activity. Firms constantly compete and reorganize their internal strengths to make their realignment with new technological opportunities possible.

The degree of vertical integration in any sector is related to its technological regimes (Ciarli *et al.*, 2008; Dosi *et al.*, 2002).[15] The dominant technology in health innovation has maintained a private sector enterprise that is globally split between the large multinational companies that continue to perform a large part of the new drug discovery activities, with smaller, knowledge intensive firms emerging to cater to other niche areas, as is the case in biotechnology. Although the dominant model remains pharmaceutical innovation as led by the global big pharma, innovation processes are characterized by inter-dependent tasks, split normally between firms operating in other areas that have emerged to be important such as biotechnology and systems biology.

Apart from firms that can be categorized into neat categories such as pharmaceuticals, biotechnology and so on, other forms of business enterprises performing a wide variety of activities that can be clubbed as "knowledge intensive business services" in this sector (Chiaroni *et al.*, 2008). Such firms are critical because of their ability to perform:

a   knowledge intensive work
b   consulting services – in the legal, marketing or other domains and
c   client related services.

The emergence and performance of these firms has had large ramifications of the performance of the sector as a whole in the industrialized countries with frontier capacity in health innovation.

2.3.2.4 Institutions and organizations that structure networks and provide collaboration incentives

Cross-fertilization across the various disciplines required for innovative prowess not only calls for a broad range of human skills that are required within firms and other organizations based on relative specialization of innovative activities. Despite the dominant pharmaceutical technology that runs through the sector, collaborative networks ensure that knowledge is constantly accumulated and used through a combination of tacit human skills and codified information produced in innovation processes between the public and private sector institutions through a dynamic, self-reinforcing process of capabilities formation.

The reasons for intensifying networking vary from access to new forms of knowledge, shared risks as a result of escalating cost of innovation[16] and the leveraging of market and skills opportunities in the sector. Inter-firm and inter-organizational flows of knowledge and skills in a user–producer type relationship, could take the form of the movement of skilled staff from one firm to another, sub-contracting (manufacturing), licensing and joint ventures, franchises and collaborative agreements for marketing of health products and supplier–customer relations. Most importantly, asset pooling, be it human, finance or machine, provides an important basis for collaboration.

A range of institutional interventions provide ancillary mechanisms for learning to proceed, both in the form of generic national innovation policy instruments, and in the form of dedicated policy instruments. While the notion of dedicated instruments emerged mainly in the context of enabling biotechnology (see Oyeyinka and Gehl Sampath, 2009b), they are as relevant to health innovation. Dedicated policies primarily target attenuation of financial and collaboration constraints, but rely on the pre-existence of a strong science base, which is in itself a questionable attribute of latecomer development. They need to be preceded by generic innovation policies at the national level that clearly promote the science base, including (Enzing *et al.*, 2008):

- policies that fund basic research (to promote high level biotechnology and other relevant research in universities and PRIs);
- policies that fund applied and industrial research (to promote industry oriented work in PRIs);
- policies that make available human resources (for the development of the sector);
- policies that enable collaboration between private and public sector actors.

Three forms of dedicated policy instruments build further on this (Enzing *et al.*, 2006):

a   Those that support the commercialization of university research and "spin off" scientists. Given the science intensive nature of the sector, these are often extremely essential both in promoting mobility of scientific labour between university and industry and also ensuring that university research is more outcome oriented. Policies that promote this include grant of IPRs to universities, geographical clustering policies that locate biotech clusters around science based universities, technology link foundations, biotechnology exploitation platforms.

b   Those that reduce risk of innovative activities through finance. Finance, given the uncertainty of the outcome of translating R&D efforts and inventive activities into successful commercial ventures, is central to product development initiatives. Support models to help agents overcome financial constraints and engage in innovation include government-support soft-loans, R&D subsidies, public risk capital funds, public support for private enterprise through grants, subsidies, private equity, venture capital and buy-out investments. Policies that could promote these (from a review of literature) include: seed-financing programmes, business angels networks, enterprise subsidy programmes (for setting up new biotechnology start-ups), common placement funds for innovation and research tax credit programmes.

c   Those that provide other forms of business support to fledgling ventures. Emerging biotechnology entrepreneurs require a range of specialized skills that are very important during their early stages of growth (ibid.). They battle with issues related to IPP (what is protected, what not, how to obtain licences), marketing and demand assessment, advertising and reaching consumers, among many others. These call for policies that provide technology incubation facilities, science and technology parks, competence centres that provide expertise such as legal affairs and marketing.

Organizations that perform tasks set out by such policies fall mainly into five different categories:

a   Knowledge based. These primarily involve formal research organizations that produce codified knowledge in the public sector, including training organizations.

b   Enterprise based. These are agencies set up to enable the private sector, such as those for SME development, technology incubators.

c   Demand based. These agencies are important to gauge local and international demand for innovation products based on a sector or even generally. They need not be consumer based, but rather those that have the responsibility to gather information of relevance to producers and firm strategy development. These also include technology foresight agencies.

d   Support-systems oriented. Such organizations are different from the knowledge based ones, in the sense that these are responsible for ensuring knowledge flows between different system actors, such as technology transfer offices, or others that facilitate access to knowledge and technologies in one form or the other.

e   Political, legal and regulation based. These are organizations that enforce
    the basic regulatory framework or collect opinions of system actors and
    provide for lobbying activities. These include IP agencies, courts of law and
    industry associations.

2.4 Institutional capacity and sector specific "push" institutions for health innovation

Institutions and policy frameworks are the a priori element of systems that give
shape and form all the other components, namely, knowledge bases and infrastructure, physical infrastructure, collaborative agreements and networks. Institutions set out the formal rules for education, human capital formation and
scientific infrastructure on the one hand, and physical infrastructure amenities on
the other. Sectoral performance is securely tied to the institutional framework
that firms and organizations operate in: its absence not only means that firms and
organizations fail to progress through successive stages of capabilities to innovate at the frontier, but firms and organizations that have the appropriate institutional support sometimes manage to succeed even without the best of the
innovative capabilities, and often do so at the cost of innovative firms that lack
them (Chesbrough and Teece, 1996). Institutional efficiency can thus be defined
as how effectively access to knowledge for local firms can be achieved at
minimal transaction costs, and is critical in explaining the process of knowledge-
sharing that underlines interactive learning and innovative success. The country
specific institutional framework as shaped by laws, rules and regulations, and
propped up through social and cultural aspects and level of human skills, determines the institutional efficiency of organizational coordination.

As mentioned in Chapter 1 briefly, health innovation capabilities are formed,
remain unformed or are formed incompletely owing to the interplay between
local and global institutions. The constant interplay between global and local
institutional rules that structure knowledge flows, actor configurations, capital
and manpower accumulation and collaborations, are structured through the local
push and global institutions. These include those that are purely industry oriented and some others that are more health care oriented. Table 1.1 presented an
overview of the global pull institutions and local push institutions for health
innovation.

Domestic agents need appropriate institutions to interact optimally in order to
translate research/incremental innovation efforts into entrepreneurial ventures;
several of which are constantly transgressing public and private sector boundaries. The failure of markets to provide knowledge inputs such as extension services for standards setting, testing,[17] metrology, quality and information, IP,
vocational, technical and skill training, and scientific and technological laboratories that could be private or public research organizations all need to be augmented through institutional mechanisms created to bridge these gaps. The work
of Stiglitz and Greenwald (1986) demonstrates that whenever markets are
incomplete and/or whenever information is imperfect (which is literally the case

in almost all latecomer economies), governments are required to intervene to enhance the efficiency of markets through various institutional interventions.

This brings us to the issue of institutional capacity, which is central to the framework elaborated in this chapter as well as the analysis that follows in the rest of the book. *Institutional capacity* is not just the capacity of the sector to borrow rules and regulations, but it is the capacity of the sector to respond – to both external (global rules, IPRs, new markets) and internal stimuli (local diseases and availability of local knowledge infrastructure). Institutional capacity therefore is determined by: (a) the ability of the country to deal with a sector's potential by providing physical and knowledge infrastructure at the basic level, but also by providing rules that diminish information asymmetry and promote mutually beneficial exchange (local push institutions), (b) the ability of the country to balance the local "push" with the global "pull" in a way that the local interests prevail and, finally, (c) state capacity to enact institutions that achieve this balance and change inefficient rules at the margin.[18] The first point is dealt with in detail in this section, whereas the other two points form the core of the analysis in Section 2.5, which deals with the capacity of the state to balance internal needs with external pressures and challenges.

Latecomer countries are by no standards a homogeneous set, and exhibit extreme variations in innovative capacities owing to differential institutional and human endowments. Several countries such as India, China, Brazil, South Africa, Thailand, Indonesia and Argentina have now come to be classified as "innovative" developing countries, which have demonstrated significant promise in carrying out innovative activities (Morel *et al.*, 2005). Such countries are diametrically opposed to several others who demonstrate low institutional endowments to support innovative capacities not only in new technologies but also in the so-called traditional sectors of the economy. Investment into both R&D and other forms of learning that lead to innovation are also unevenly spread out: there are several countries like India and China which although poor invest large amounts into R&D (Lederman and Saenz, 2005, p. 24) when compared to others.

On this spectrum, health innovation capacity ranges between being non-existent to capacity to perform simple manufacturing activities (formulating tablets, capsules and other simple products not involving extensive skills), to other higher domains, depending on the sector specific "push" institutions available locally. Latecomer countries are a heterogeneous nomenclature that can be distinguished into fast following countries (those that are dynamic and moving ahead to catch up with other countries at the frontier, such as India, China and Brazil), latecomers (those that remain relatively slow in economic catch-up but have significant institutional basis for technology-led development) and very latecomers (those that provide very weak institutional and political stability for economic development).[19] This applies to health innovation as much as it does generally and Table 2.3 maps the typology of capabilities with the dominant institutions as observed across latecomer countries at different stages of development.

Table 2.3 A typology of health innovation capabilities

	Capabilities	Institutional basis for learning and innovation	Latecomer examples
1	No skills	Fragmented basis for innovation, lacking human skills and knowledge infrastructure, lack of policy focus on health innovation.	
2	Manufacturing activities	Incremental innovation based on large-scale reverse engineering skills, evidence of clear strengths in either API formulations or assembling medicines in pills, tablets or other dosage forms by importing the APIs required, commensurate human skills, policy emphasis on local production.	Kenya, Uganda, Tanzania, Nigeria.
3	Reverse engineering for APIs, incremental innovations in generics, some drug R&D	Learning mainly through reverse engineering activities, persistence of at least some international collaborations, a resilient local generics sector and presence of local demand to sustain production activities, policy vision/emphasis to promote local production.	South Africa, Bangladesh.
4	Drug and vaccine R&D, niche specializations in biotechnology, biologics, clinical work, etc.	Gradual technological upgrading visible across the sector, capacity to perform R&D in both private and public sector institutions, availability of competent human skills and knowledge infrastructure, policy emphasis on knowledge creation and presence of secondary instruments such as IPRs, venture capital and other dedicated measures.	India, China, Brazil.

Source: author.

2.4.1 *Physical infrastructure, knowledge infrastructure and learning*

Roads, telephone and Internet facilities, electricity, water and transportation facilities are important physical infrastructure elements that determine the efficiency of innovative activities in health, both on the technological innovation front and on the health care and services delivery front. The absence of these facilities increases costs of conducting good teaching and research work for universities and public research institutes enhances production and networking costs for firms. It makes access to knowledge and collaborative arrangements an uphill exercise wherein getting to know and linking up with similar programmes with other universities and institutions within the sector/country/international partners and retaining these contacts becomes a primary research challenge. It makes the design of health care interventions formidable, and latecomer countries where critical shortage of power, water and other infrastructure facilities is common calls into question the commitment of governments into facilitating both research investments and innovation activities on the one side, and health care facilities on the other.

Ex ante decisions on various aspects of innovation capacity, such as a country's schooling system, its preferences for secondary and tertiary education (whether there should be greater emphasis on natural sciences or other disciplines, whether there should be centres of excellence for tertiary education), investment into public sector research – all impact upon the generation of human skills and availability of knowledge infrastructure to build technological capabilities. On the technological side of health innovation, the gradual transition from being a no-skills sector, to a purely manufacturing oriented one to a knowledge intensive one, where reverse engineering skills for APIs' development, speciality generics and vaccine production are all available is based on the availability of human skills through appropriate university education. The story on the services and delivery side is a similar one indeed: it calls for management personnel, doctors, midwives and health care practitioners all of whom require training and vocational opportunities within the system. Latecomer countries demonstrate varying levels of weak knowledge infrastructure, in terms of secondary and tertiary enrolments, R&D investments and scientists per million of the population, when measured in terms of conventional knowledge indicators (see for example, Oyeyinka and Gehl Sampath, 2009a). Education related to disciplines based on newer technologies, such as biotechnology is conspicuously absent, or taught at levels that do not prepare students for laboratory based specialized work of the kind that is needed for the local industry to emerge competitively. Furthermore, the tendency to focus merely on the science and technology aspects of biotechnology neglects the importance of social science specializations – such as law, management and marketing skills required to commercialize and market the innovations based on such technologies (Eicher *et al.*, 2006).

Box 2.3 Policies for human capital formation in latecomer countries

At a broad level, two forms of policies seem to impact human capital formation in latecomer countries: those that determine the distribution of primary, to secondary to tertiary education schemes and options and those that set criteria for schooling quality across the country in question. Latecomer countries exhibit two interesting features that duplicate in different combinations across the spectrum: there is a critical drop of enrolment from primary to secondary education, which dips even further in the case of tertiary education. Second, the low quality of schooling leads to large drop out rates and "the widespread failure to take advantage from the apparently high returns available from education" (Hanushek, 1995; p. 235). The quality of schools and educational institutions differs and these differences matter for the emergence of human capital that can sustain knowledge-driven innovation. Whereas generally, schooling issues are measured by variables such as teacher–pupil ratios, teachers' education level, expenditure per student, school quality is better measured by factors that look deeper – such as, curriculum differences between schools, personality development schemes for teachers and students, social factors that promote education trends amongst societies, class sizes. Hanushek (1995) succinctly notes in this context that the discussions on quality of schools and quantity of schools in latecomer countries are not mutually exclusive (that is, the argument that governments have limited resources and hence they have to forego quality in order to ensure maximum number of schools in the country). It is rather that quality and quantity are intricately connected, and countries with better schooling quality have larger school enrolments and more steady progression from primary to secondary and tertiary education. Such factors are non-trivial simply because they not only determine how many people in a given context avail education up to secondary or tertiary levels, but they also dictate the various disciplines that they choose to study, thereby the mix of skills available to conduct innovative activities. For example, several African countries, like Kenya, demonstrate a very clear preference amongst parents and students for social science disciplines which then manifests strongly in a lack of science based human capital. Why do we observe these trends and what factors motivate these to replicate themselves needs further research. The poor schooling quality observed in latecomer countries brings to the forefront another stark feature of innovation systems: the organization building competence of latecomers, that is, the inability of relevant and competent human power in organizations to steer processes to their legitimate ends.[1]

Source: author

Note
1   This issue has been dealt with by the author in depth in another book, see Oyeyinka and Gehl Sampath (2009a).

2.4.2 Information asymmetries and incentives for collaboration

There is a self-reinforcing relationship between how universities and public research institutes evolve to become centres of knowledge generation and collaborative networks in health innovation. On the one hand, research excellence makes the institutions promising partners for collaborative ventures with industry, whereas on the other, collaborations reinforce the strengths of universities in achieving research excellence.

University behaviour is conditioned by socially accepted norms, organizational structures and incentives related to promotions, tenure and commercialization of research. Gittelman (2006), for example, argues that institutions governing scientific careers, which shape the professional identities and boundary-spanning activities of research scientists, critically affect national technological performance in biotechnology. University relationships with industrial counterparts are formed through sponsored research, licences of university-held IP, spin-off firms, labour mobility (hiring of students and sabbaticals for staff in universities to pursue entrepreneurial interests, among others (Mowery and Ziedonis, 1998; Siegel *et al.*, 1999). Sponsored research may take different forms with individual firms making strategic decisions to sponsor research of immediate relevance to them and the ability of university scientists to participate in such research endeavours, their individual incentives and their behavioural norms are all predetermined by the innovation system (Bercowitz and Feldman, 2003). In health and biomedical innovation, research indicates that firms are more inclined to support sponsored research (Cohen *et al.*, 1998) and technology transfer offices to facilitate university–industry technology alliances are very useful tools in facilitating such exchange (see Seigel *et al.*, 2003, 2004). Policies that promote this include grant of IPRs to universities, geographical clustering policies that locate biotech clusters around science based universities, technology link foundations and biotechnology exploitation platforms.

However, most such interventions are sector specific and sectoral innovation policies are harder to enact and enforce than broader national innovation policies in latecomer contexts and these have tended to be fewer and far between. Two further reasons amplify the failure of design and/or success of sectoral policies amongst latecomers. First, sectoral policies require a capable and sometimes sophisticated S&T bureaucratic mechanism for enforcement (especially for sectors that employ new technologies), an institution that is unfortunately quite weak in latecomer countries. Second, sectoral policies, despite their individual focus, function within the larger innovation context of the country and tend to build upon existing strengths in traditional sectors. If the larger context for innovation is constrained, the impact of sectoral initiatives will be marginal.

2.4.3 Translating health R&D into marketable products

A further striking point of departure between latecomer countries themselves, when those that have performing health innovation sectors are compared with those that do not, is the absence of private sector enterprise. Vibrant private sector enterprise is a reflex that depends on relatively stable political and economic environments that offer business support through risk attenuating mechanisms. There are a variety of ways in which financial instruments can be provided for technological innovations in health such as:

a   *Small-firm financing/risk-sharing financing schemes*. Several countries have initiated financing schemes that bolster small enterprise development through innovative finance schemes, especially in biotechnology. Risk-sharing finance schemes envisage a state investment that matches the private sector in order to make more resources available for innovative activities. For example, as part of the EU's framework 7 research programme, the European Investment Bank will match up to €1 billion for biotechnology enterprise within the EU with its own resources (Huggett, 2008).

b   *Venture capital*. Venture capital, a time-tested means that provided the basis for thriving biotechnological start-ups in the USA and European economies has come under much pressure in recent times. However, over time, the investment has been shifting from the more risky initial phases to other opportunities in biotech that "offer better returns and less risk" (Huggett, 2008). Although the year 2006 witnessed US$47 billion into global biotechnology, biotech firms are struggling with scenarios of product pipeline failures and withdrawal of funding from their pharmaceutical partners at advanced stages. As of 2007 several prominent biotechnology firms experienced drop in their value after promising drugs failed to deliver (Raffetry, 2007).

c   *Government owned private enterprise*. This is a common initiative meant to jump-start private sector activity, especially for the production of pharmaceuticals. As part of this, the government undertakes to enact policies and institutions for the accumulation of technologies, set up government owned enterprises that produce drugs locally, ensure the emergence of adequate human skills that are required for the enterprises to function and also deploy policy interventions that limits foreign enterprise activity in the country to ensure low cost medicines for its population. India, Bangladesh and several other countries have used such techniques to empower local production and China still continues to do so (see Chapter 3).

d   *Other incentives*: such as clauses that allow for scientists to take time off and venture off into entrepreneurial domains.

The constant influx of new technologies and the dynamism induced thereby is very specific to the nature of innovation in health and this further challenges the extant institutions for innovation in latecomer countries. There is a well-acknowledged discussion in the literature on how firm organization and technology runs in both directions: i.e. changes in firms' organizational arrangements affect their technological opportunities and outcomes (e.g. Robertson and Langlois, 1995) and vice versa. For example, when firms are faced with rapidly evolving markets, their suppliers may lose track of the technological evolution of the product's characteristics in the final market and, in the case of a highly integrated good, of the whole product architecture: economies of specialization are then offset by "dynamic transaction costs" (Langlois, 1992). At the same time, technological sophistication of the production/delivery process may substantially impact upon the firms' accepted and time-tested notions of organizing innovative activity. These are challenges that call upon ability of system actors to constantly adapt, realign interests and co-evolve – all of which are harder to imagine in the context of institutional inertia and rigidities observed in the context of low and middle income countries.

Acknowledging the fact that latecomers face extreme hurdles in enabling private sector enterprise in health innovation, newer models are emerging, which include donor participation in funding for biotechnology start-ups. One of these is the "research in-situ" model, wherein multilateral funding agencies can work with indigenous for-profit biotechnology start-up companies to deliver change (Agbo *et al.*, 2008). There are also additional models emerging from the frontier countries, such as a new one in the USA, wherein a new scheme that takes 2.5 per cent of the extra-mural budget of every state agency is dedicated to fund SMEs in high technology areas, including those for health innovation. While these are mostly aimed at the technological side of health innovation, innovative financing for health that caters to the delivery and supply side is summarized in Box 2.4.

Box 2.4 Innovative financing for health

The interesting initiatives on this front include:

a   *Low cost insurance/community based health insurance schemes.* These schemes seek to pool risk across a wider base (community membership, generally) wherein the issue of low utilization of health care services is combated through improved financial access to health services.

b   *User fees in public health facilities to cover running costs.* These schemes aim to fund the running expenses of otherwise defunct state provided health care facilities by charging nominal user fees. User fees are an instrument through which the quality of heath care available can be improved. However, this option is in practice difficult due to waning governmental investments and an acute surge in demand for health care in most latecomer countries.

c   *Fiscal decentralization.* Such initiatives aim at transforming health facilities into autonomous entities so that they can manage their fiscal and human resources according to local needs. Fiscal decentralization presupposes the presence of extensive management skills and availability of human resources at the local levels.

d   *Performance based financing.* This mechanism shifts onus from input based financing to output and performance oriented one, wherein the Ministry of Health (or international and donor agencies working with the Ministry of Health) purchase outputs based on the functioning of individual facilities for health care services within the country. This promotes intra-facility competition and delivery of better health services within the country.

e   *Health vouchers.* This scheme works thus: health care providers are accredited and contracted to deliver high-impact services to voucher-bearing patients. Health vouchers are provided (at highly subsidized rates) to the poor, allowing them to choose health services free of financial considerations. Such a scheme allows for particularly vulnerable strata of the population to be targeted like pregnant women in urban slums, as is being done in Kenya since 2006.

f   *Health equity funds.* A third-party mechanism for reimbursing health care facilities for the services they provide to poor patients. It has proven to be an innovative mechanism of reducing burden of health care costs in several latecomer countries.

Source: author

2.4.4 State vision and capacity to formulate policy to promote health innovation

The capacity of the state to anticipate the need for local production and formulate policy is perhaps the capstone of those latecomer countries that have managed to build significant capacity in health innovation and are marked out by the success stories of India, Brazil and Cuba, which are often discussed in the literature on health innovation (see articles in *Health Biotechnology*, 2004). In these cases of latecomer success, as Part II of the book shows, the policy vision to produce drugs locally was the trigger to health innovation capabilities. But such policy vision needs to be accompanied by sustained institution building to help achieve health equity as Cuba has achieved. Where latecomer states seem to fail often is in ensuring that the health innovation capacity (in terms of production efficiency of drugs and vaccines) connects directly and proportionately to reducing health inequities within the country. This, it seems, is yet another significant failure of separating health innovation into technological and delivery domains, which this book seeks to bridge.

2.4.5 Significant local demand for particular forms of health innovation

Local demand and acceptance of products locally produced is a significant factor in promoting innovation capacity even in cases where the state only plays a limited role in the growth of the sector. The shift in focus from a more linear model oriented science and technology policy (CIPIH, 2006) to health innovation has helped much in incorporating the issue of local demand into both analytical and policy discourses.[20] Very simply put, the availability of a local consumer base offers security for private sector investment, since often times, firms in an emergent sector tend to grapple with issues of economies of scale, competitive production and technological sophistication that could set them apart in a global market. Compelling local demand for health products is also often the precursor to significant policy changes that encourage local production, such as the cases of HIV/AIDS drugs in South Africa and Brazil in 1999 and 2000 or sickle cell research in Nigeria (see Chapter 6 of this book) illustrate.

As opposed to local demand, the acceptance of health products locally produced has received much less attention although it remains highly important in the case of health innovation, as the chapter on India shows (see Chapter 3).

2.5 Balancing local "push" and global "pull" institutions for health innovation

Global pull institutions are triggered off by a variety of factors whether regulatory changes to the multilateral regime or that are a result of changing science bases in the sector and call for more efficient and systematic organization of innovation activities simply because they tend to interact with local institutions in extremely complex ways. Clearly, several global pull institutions represent the interests of multiple stakeholders from the frontier countries and do not necessarily have much direct value for latecomer countries or their people, as many of the recent global changes in the area of health innovation seem to indicate. Most prominent amongst these is the global IP regime, but other issues such as data protection and data exclusivity, free trade agreements and the so-called TRIPS-Plus[21] provisions are other such developments. Such instruments not only impact on the sources of external knowledge that firms/organizations can tap into, they determine markets for products (either by way of creating export markets or limiting them, and by way of dictating foreign presence in national markets) and impact consumer behaviour.

2.5.1 Global IPRs and the TRIPS agreement

Although the TRIPS Agreement has been around for over a decade now and there is sufficient evidence that it may not embody optimal levels of IP from a social welfare point of view,[22] the question whether it is optimal to have differential IP policies for developing countries from the perspective of efficient policy making has never been addressed. IP regimes can potentially operate in three different contexts. In the first case, only national IP regimes exist and resulting international repercussions and trade distortions are minimal either due to non-existent or low levels of international trade. In this (unimaginable) situation, there would be no need to harmonize national frameworks. A second case is one where national IP regimes clearly operate in an international context and where the gains from harmonization may be lost when considered from the strategic perspective of the competitiveness of individual economies. A weak IPR regime could be beneficial for individual economic interests of some countries, as a result of which it would be individual rationale not to opt for a globalized regime. The third case is a situation of international IPP, but with countries that are not homogeneous and can be differentiated into regional groups because they are at different stages of development. Disparities amongst the countries are widespread and different sets of countries demonstrate traditional and knowledge based sectors that are not well developed and have weak institutional frameworks for innovation. The interesting question that such a global regime raises is whether a uniform IPR regime is the best solution and will it lead to more competition and higher investment in R&D worldwide? Or will it only be better for one set of countries at the expense of another set/sets of countries by helping the innovator countries to exclude a lot of futuristic competition?

We are faced with the third situation presently: as Table 2.3 denotes, latecomer countries are on a continuum of innovation capabilities, ranging from the fast followers (that are dynamic and moving ahead to catch up with other countries at the frontier, such as India, China and Brazil), latecomers (those that remain relatively slow in economic catch-up but have significant institutional basis for technology-led development such as Bangladesh and Nigeria) and very latecomers.

Including this glaring reality into the discourse, a comprehensive analysis of welfare effects and distributional effects of the TRIPS Agreement on countries at different levels of development has to take into account its effects on the precise long-term gains and losses of such a regime (aggregate surplus), how they are likely to be distributed regionally (division of surplus) and whether the gains to the winners are smaller than the losses to the losers (from a dynamic efficiency perspective). Given that such an analysis is extremely complex and that it will be too difficult to predict these impacts conclusively, one is forced to view the problem in narrower terms, with less general assumptions and where useful conclusions on welfare reflects of the regime need to be drawn.

2.5.2 TRIPS, individual policy space and catch-up implications

Given that innovations in latecomers are generated through both formal and informal learning activities at the firm level rather than R&D (see Table 2.1), and are promoted extensively through linkages between various agents in the domestic knowledge system, IPRs impact on the process differentially. The general literature on IP and development acknowledges that certain features of the institutional framework in which learning and knowledge generation is embedded might limit the role of IPRs in inducing innovation. In latecomers, where innovation is not well developed, IPP may have very different implications for innovation, domestic knowledge generation and technology learning among local firms. Intuitively, it may seem that IPRs may not be advantageous for innovation in countries where firms are mainly engaged in incremental innovation, and R&D based innovative activities are not very common. Despite this, if it can be ascertained that IPRs promote firm based innovative capabilities through diffusion of knowledge, technology transfer, foreign direct investments (FDI) and licensing, among others, it may still prove to be beneficial for local firms in latecomer countries in an indirect sense.

Box 2.5 IPRs and technology transfer

Some studies exist on the positive impact of IPRs on technology transfer, but how it translates to strengthening innovation at the firm level behaviour and to what extent this relationship holds true in the case of latecomer countries remains unanswered. Mansfield (1994) notes in a firm level survey within the USA, that the type of IP regime has a definite impact on the decision of US firms on whether or not to invest. More recently, Branstetter *et al.* (2004) performed a 16-country analysis of technology transfer in US multinational firms' changes in response to IPR reforms in countries, to show a positive correlation. Popovici (2006) shows similarly a positive correlation of technology flows and IPR reforms from US multinational firms to domestic firms in countries reforming their IPR laws. These studies consider latecomer countries with some level of capacity and technology transfer is built into quid pro quo relationships. However, in very latecomers where such quid pro quo may not be foreseeable, technology licensing and technology transfer play a very small role in innovation (Gehl Sampath, 2007b; UNCTAD 2007). And finally, there is evidence suggesting that in the case of fast followers who tend to pose competition in global markets, technology licensing and technology transfer are once again difficult options since the larger firms tend to protect technologies that give them the market edge (see Chapter 7). Hence, it seems that there is a small window of space between when countries begin to transition from being very latecomers to being fast followers where technology licensing and technology transfer as a source of innovation becomes an option. However, there are innumerable country/sector specific factors that influence it and no general line can be drawn.

Source: author

Economic history evidences that the ability to design individual technology acquisition, protection and use policies tailor-made to local contexts has been central to catch-up processes. Several scholars have tried to point out the linkages between the level of development of countries and observed levels of R&D investments and patenting activity over the past few years. To summarize it here, the more developed a country gets, the higher the percentage of GDP that gets invested into R&D and higher the patenting activity. The explanation for this correlation, however, seems to rest deeper in the process of technological catch-up itself. Within the spectrum of innovative capabilities, the shift from infant industries to those that are at the frontier is accompanied by a gradual accumulation of capabilities that move from copying and reverse engineering to original innovation (Table 2.1). When countries/sectors are predominantly thriving on copying and incremental innovations, the emphasis is on accumulating knowledge that already exists. The closer they get to developing original innovative capabilities, the more important protecting their innovative edge from competition becomes.

Viewed such, it seems likely that the TRIPS Agreement reduces catch-up competition by limiting the capacity of latecomer countries to access already existing knowledge through reverse engineering and incremental innovation to move along the spectrum of innovative capabilities towards the frontier. This negative impact is efficient only if it is outweighed by long-term efficiency gains on global innovation. If the deadweight losses of extending protection to the entire south in terms of prevention of competition and R&D growth outweigh the gains to global innovation, then the TRIPS Agreement has a negative effect on global welfare (Deardorff, 1992).[23] This however, remains to be proven.

From this, two important issues arise. The trends of proliferation of patents in industrialized countries, especially in high technology sectors, and the strategic use of IPRs leads to a skewed and unfair distribution of future chances amongst firms in sectors between developed and developing countries. Several economic studies on the international impact of IPRs and the underlying decisions of countries to opt for such strong IPP (see Scotchmer, 1991) support this observation. *Individual choices of countries are likely to be prompted more by the motive to cement the advantages of their firms in especially the high-tech sectors at the national or regional levels, and this invariably results in harmonized regimes that reflect high levels of IPP* (Lanjouw and Cockburn, 2000). The logical option of allowing for different levels of IPP that corresponds to levels of development of countries would serve the purposes of development rather than support a strong IPR regime whose concrete impact on innovation and technological change at the global level is yet to be proven. Technological capability has a greater limiting power than any form of IP – countries which do not have the tacit know-how and knowledge base to copy and learn systematically cannot begin to copy simply because the products in question have weak or no IPP.

Second, the detrimental effects of the TRIPS Agreement on catch-up processes in latecomer countries has distributional properties that affects consumers in these countries very adversely, as is the case in access to medicines where IPRs interact with public health concerns.[24] Ideally, given the extreme lack of institutions that underpin knowledge distribution and growth in latecomer countries, burdening them with further limitations in developing their indigenous capabilities (to produce drugs in this instance) does not seem to be the optimal intended outcome of a multilateral regime.

This brings us to a point mentioned time and again, which will also be considered at length in the empirical analysis conducted in the subsequent chapters of this book. The very latecomers or latecomers necessarily need to cope with these negative impacts until they reach a stage of technological development where IPRs could become an asset. Given that the time to argue for weaker IPR regimes seems passé in international political terms, promoting local innovation depends on the ability of countries to manoeuvre their way through the policy flexibilities offered by the TRIPS Agreement. The literature on what flexibilities exist in the TRIPS Agreement and how countries can enact rules based thereupon is vast (Correa, 2002, 2004). In sum, flexibilities in the TRIPS Agreement of relevance to health innovation include (Schmiedchen and Spenneman, 2007):

a   *Exceptions to patent rights.* There are several exceptions to patent rights, such as an experimental use exception. Patent protection in highly convergent technologies limits on access to knowledge in ways and means that were originally unintended, and the limited dissemination effect that is achieved by enforcing publication of information on which protection is sought for has not been enough. In order to deal with these unintended impacts, an experimental use exception can be provided in the national patent framework that allows public research institutes or universities to use patented substances or products as inputs to further research. Taking this a step further, a new proposed law in Switzerland intends to provide the possibility for experimental use for also commercial applications (and not only research) provided such use reveals new knowledge about the patented substance. The new knowledge produced through such an exercise could be covered through patents that do not infringe on the patent protection of the product used for experimentation (Schmidtchen and Spenneman, 2009). India has also enacted exceptions to patent rights that offer interesting evidence of how the TRIPS flexibilities can be used creatively to suit local needs. Under Indian Patent Law, all pre-1995 patents do not qualify for protection in India and all products with patent priority dates between 1995 and 2005 can continue to be manufactured by generic firms despite grant of a patent in India, if the generic manufacturers already had a market approved version of the patented drug in return for payment of "reasonable" royalties to the respective patent holder firms. Although the term "reasonable royalty" is not defined in the Act, this provision creates an exception to products that could otherwise be deemed to be patent protected in order to preserve the interests of public health and the local firms.

b   *Transition arrangements.* Under the TRIPS Agreement itself, different groups of countries have received variable deadlines to conform to the provisions set out thereunder. Countries that qualify as "least developed countries" under the UN classification, have, for example, time until 2016 to comply with the pharmaceutical patents related provisions of the agreement, according to the Doha Declaration on the TRIPS Agreement and Public Health of 2001 (WT/MIN(01)/DEC/2).

c   *Compulsory licensing.* This exception to patent rights has been highly contentious and put to little use. Article 31 of the TRIPS Agreement allows for the issuance of compulsory licences in the interest of public health, but circumscribes it to be predominantly for supply to the domestic market. This brought to the fore the very important question: how can those countries that do not have sufficient local production capabilities ensure cheaper access to medicines in times of public health crises? Both the Doha Declaration and the WTO Decision of 30 August 2003 have tried to spell out operational details on how countries without local production capabilities can issue compulsory licences for manufacture of drugs that are needed by their citizens. In practice, however, there has been little evidence of economic feasibility of this option (see Gehl Sampath, 2005). Most importantly, countries without manufacturing capabilities have hardly used this option over the past six years, and this itself calls for a serious evaluation of the practical issues involved, with the only exceptions being Brazil, South Africa and Thailand. There is a need to establish greater clarity and simplify these procedures substantially in order to make them a feasible option.

d   *Criteria for patentability.* Article 27 of the TRIPS Agreement only states that an invention has to be novel, demonstrate an inventive step and be capable of industrial application in order to qualify for a patent. What constitutes each one of these requirements has not been specified and can be interpreted in more restrictive ways by countries in accordance with public health and their social welfare requirements. The Indian Patent Act for example (see Box 2.6 below) is an example yet again of how countries can use the flexibility inherent in defining the criteria for novelty, inventive step and industrial application to suit local objectives of social justice.

Box 2.6 Definition of patentability in the Indian Patent Act

Section 3(d) of the Indian Patent Act that deals with the definition of patentability specifies that patents will not be granted automatically for different forms of the same molecules, such as salts, esters, polymorphs, and decisions will be taken case by case to establish novelty in an effort to prevent ever-greening[1] of molecules. Novartis challenged this provision in the Chennai High Court in the case of Gleevec.

Gleevec, Novartis's anti-cancer drug, was India's first exclusive marketing right (EMR), on a beta crystalline version of the compound Imatinab Mesylate. Indian generic producers of the drug challenged the EMR on grounds that the compound Imatinab Mesylate was a derivative of a molecule that was known prior to 1995, and therefore does not qualify for patent protection. At the time when the EMR was granted, several Indian companies were producing generic versions of Imatinab Mesylate, including, Cipla, Ranbaxy and Sun Pharmaceuticals. The EMR was withdrawn and Novartis was subsequently also refused a patent on Gleevec. In response, Novartis moved the Indian high court challenging the constitutional validity of section 3(d) in the Indian Patent Act of 2005, claiming that such an interpretation is against the TRIPS Agreement. The High Court in Madras issued a judgement in 2007, deeming Section 3(d) to be constitutional and not against the TRIPS Agreement.

Source: Gehl Sampath, 2008

Note

1   The term ever-greening refers to means by which pharmaceutical firms seek to extend patent protection on expiring products and includes methods where a new patent is sought on an ester, salt or polymorph of the substance on which patent is expiring, or a new combination patent on two or more substances that are going off patent protection, among others.

In addition to these flexibilities, the possibility of denying or devising a data exclusivity framework adept to local conditions (see discussion in next section), and allowing for parallel importation of drugs are also considered to be important flexibilities that countries could utilize in order to protect local health needs. However, a recent study shows that very few developing and least developed countries that are members of the WTO use any of these flexibilities (see Hoen, 2009, Table 6).

2.5.3 *International regulatory measures specific to health innovation*

2.5.3.1 *Regulatory measures for new technologies*

Several regulations in health innovation tend to reflect to a very great extent the pressures on the global industry, and carry forthwith the capacity to shape the industry structure. Owing to the scientific uncertainty attached to newer discoveries in biogenerics, systems biology and other genomics based technologies, a series of new regulatory procedures are being introduced (or have been introduced in) industrialized countries that have the capacity to constitute significant barriers to entry for firms from latecomer countries.

A compelling example is that of biogenerics or follow-on biologics. Biogeneric drugs, most of which are recombinant protein therapeutics (rDNA proteins) and monoclonal antibodies are presently a booming market with several first generation rDNA proteins having gone off (or set to go off) patent protection between 2004 and 2010 (Belsey *et al.*, 2006). However, newer rules continue to be constituted on the circumstances under which a biosimilar may be called therapeutically equivalent to its original product (Johnson, 2007) in the USA, and the EU has an even more stringent framework in place to govern the approval of biosimilars. The problem in biosimilars' regulation is one that can be generalized across all newer technologies in health and the way regulation is being framed. Despite the fact that it remains unclear how and under what circumstances therapeutic bioequivalence can be proven in the case of biosimilars (Woodcock *et al.*, 2007), regulatory regimes have geared up to prescribe ways and means in which this should be established. In other words, the regulatory prescriptions may not be fully equipped and informed of the technological limitations of the process, or they might, in fact, delay the emergence of optimal regulatory systems for the therapeutic classes in question. This, coupled with the fact that marketing of biosimilars requires extensive patient support for the new product constitutes significant market barriers for new entrants into the biologics sector, where the innovation process itself is far more risky and treacherous than other forms of generic products.

Other regulatory rules, even those that can be defended on grounds of safety and efficacy, such as those that lay out good manufacturing practices in various countries (FDA approval for example in the case of the US markets) pose obstacles. They constitute steep learning curves for firms in latecomer countries seeking to export.

Box 2.7 WHO prequalification standards and other technical requirements

In order to ensure that drugs that are produced/sold/exported to latecomer countries, the World Health Organization's List of Prequalified Medical Products contains the products that meet the "unified standards of quality, safety and efficacy for HIV/AIDS, Malaria and Tuberculosis". The WHO prequalification list is the result of a project that was meant for the procurement of the drugs by other UN organizations. As a result, in order for a product to be qualified to compete in procurement bids with organizations such as the Global Fund for AIDS, Malaria and Tuberculosis (GFATM), it needs to at least have a C1 status. A C1 status implies a WHO prequalification letter certifying the compliance of the manufacturing site with WHO good manufacturing practice (GMP) requirements and proof of dossier submission to WHO's Prequalification Program with acceptance letter.

Approval standards and processes for exporting to regulated markets differ from country to country and requires substantial investments on the part of firms seeking to export to learning to meet the technical standards.

Source: www.healthtech.who.int/pq/default.htm (accessed 24 July 2009)

2.5.3.2 Data exclusivity

Article 39(3) of the TRIPS Agreement places a requirement upon member countries to provide protection to regulatory data under specific circumstances. However, it is not clear as to whether a strict reading on Article 39(3) calls for a regime of data exclusivity (Correa, 2002). Data exclusivity, a relatively new form of IPP, refers to the protection of clinical data that contain data submitted by pharmaceutical companies to regulatory agencies,[25] such as the US FDA and the European Agency for the Evaluation of Medicinal Products (EMEA), for the purposes of obtaining market approval of patented drugs (Pugatch, 2004). Grant of data exclusivity (five years in the case of the model proposed by the Reddy Committee Report) prevents the regulatory agency from using the data submitted by the originator company to determine bioequivalence of generic products for the said period.

2.5.4 Global restructuring, knowledge partnerships, international R&D collaborations and value chains

The imperative of innovation is to constantly interpose tacit inputs to learning within a firm/organization at any particular time with newer constructs and ideas, whether through internal R&D or as can be acquired from external sources. Therefore an important point for theory and policy for supporting industrial producers in latecomer development is to understand how the tacit knowledge base in industry and public sector organizations grows and how firms and organizations could best transform codified information into relevant knowledge. Several formal channels of transfer of technology have been identified in the literature including but not limited to: migration of skills, licensing, trade and FDI, turnkey projects, technical consultancy, capital goods imports and joint venture agreements.

While private–private collaborations (between local and foreign firms) could be significant and have been instrumental in enabling knowledge spillovers across various sectors in other countries, they do not just happen. Even in countries where they do occur, the accent of origin is critical – studies of international competitiveness also show that while comparing countries' performances through collaborative networks, the point of origin and initial development of the collaborative projects (the geographical space) play a crucial role in capabilities. For example, a study by the European Commission that compared the performance of US based biotechnology firms versus European biotechnology found that being the originator and the developer of collaborative projects is a significant factor in promoting capabilities formation (Allansdottir *et al.*, 2002). Once again, private–private collaborations depend on what stage of development the firms are in and what they can offer in return for the technology in question, as the previous section on IPRs has discussed.

One of the few empirical investigations on how collaborative arrangements, especially in the form of strategic alliances and know-how exchange, impacts on innovation capabilities of firms in the period between 1993 and 2003 concluded that especially large firms benefited most from such alliances in terms of absorption of strategic inputs to innovation (Ohba and Figueiredo, 2007). This evidence, although limited, reiterates the challenge of being able to foster such linkages for the benefit of local sectors and firms in latecomer countries.

The global restructuring of health innovation activities as a result of the pressure on big pharma and the gradual enmeshing of innovation and health care with a proliferation of user-driven innovation models has indeed encouraged the emergence of newer business models, where the focus is on low cost, high volume innovations, as opposed to high cost, low volume models. This has opened up new channels for firms from latecomer countries with significant health innovation capacity such as India and China to benefit from scale economies, especially given their ability to produce low cost innovations of relevance to the poor in health. A good example of such a case is paediatric anti-retroviral drugs (ARVs) and fixed dose combinations for ARVs, a case study of which is contained in Chapter 3. The case of the Indian sector (discussed at length with empirical evidence in Chapter 3) is an interesting example of how collaborative linkages with international firms can be used not only for knowledge partnerships, but also to learn marketing and management skills (through co-marketing alliances within India) and to tap markets in industrialized countries (through marketing arrangements in Europe and the USA). Another important source of knowledge acquisition in the private sector is acquisition of foreign firms. However, this option assumes the presence of extremely competent and financially endowed local firms.

Contract manufacturing, a process that refers to offering services in niche areas within health innovation is another way to build capabilities. Firms that supply specific services or products form part of global value chains in health innovation, and are thereby compelled to learn and perform at requisite quality levels. Some examples include clinical services, manufacturing intermediates and APIs for drugs, manufacturing non-infringing processes for API production, manufacturing injectables. With the new pressures on the global pharmaceutical sector, newer forms of contract manufacturing have emerged including basic molecular research, gene mapping, drug discovery and discovery chemistry for the global pharmaceutical companies. Indian and Chinese companies are variedly capturing the demand for the provision of these forms of services, often in return for tacit know-how on key emerging areas of health innovation. However, as is the case with most private sector oriented initiatives, these too tend to be restricted to those firms and sectors in latecomer countries that show significant promise.

Newer knowledge partnerships of various forms have been the response to the 10/90 gap in health over the past decade or so which focus on contributing significantly to building local capacity. For example, the International AIDS Vaccine Initiative (IAVI), in an effort to promote ownership of the research (and subsequent products) in the south, chose to locate its R&D in select latecomer countries such as South Africa, Kenya and India (see Chataway *et al.*, 2006). From the success of a few product development partnerships (PDPs) and the emergence of a range of new PDPs that seek to achieve health systems equity in addition to product development partnerships, the relevance of some key issues can be derived:

1   How can international collaborations be best structured to generate and translate knowledge of relevance to local contexts?
2   How can the opportunities that such partnerships provide for capacity development be quantified, and how can they be studied, lessons learnt and implemented in other new partnerships?
3   How to balance the international relevance of these partnerships with local interests that ultimately dictate the extent to which they will be implemented/used in contexts that they are meant for?

Latecomer countries themselves are taking the lead in several public–private partnerships in key areas of health research – the Fiocruz–Genzyme partnership on neglected diseases being one of these.

2.6 State capacity to balance global and local interests in health innovation

State capacity is perhaps the quintessential hurdle in designing and implementing effective policies that promote sustainable economic development in latecomers.[26] Most latecomer countries do not possess formal institutions to support innovation processes (North, 1990; Chang, 2001) and some do not even have the awareness of the imperative of these institutions that result in externalities and coordination failures. These missing institutions include "markets"; latecomer country markets do not function as they should due to costly and imperfect information, and non-market institutions that could mitigate these impacts also do not exist (see Stiglitz, 1998). The failure of markets to provide knowledge inputs such as extension services for standards setting, testing, metrology, quality and information, IP, vocational, technical and skill training, and scientific and technological laboratories that could be private or public research organizations all need to be *corrected through institutional mechanisms* created to bridge these gaps. As Bessen and Meurer (2008, p. 1) note, property systems fail even within rule of law. These institutional mechanisms are therefore critical to resolve the costs of conducting innovation; and this makes viewing issues in innovation policy lens an urgent and immediate imperative for all latecomer countries. The state in these cases needs to be proactive, championing the case of technology-led development, by pre-selecting certain policy choices over others and creating reward structures for actors who follow them. The state, through its policy choices, pioneers technology trajectories, as the East Asian examples lead us to conclude (Amsden, 1989; Amsden and Chu, 2003; Woo-Cummings, 1999).

In the specific context of health innovation, it is the fundamentally weak and limited state capacity in latecomer countries that accounts for the difficulties faced in creating coherent local push institutions; either the state is unaware or not persuaded enough to give the issue the importance it deserves or the state's capacity (as manifested by its institutions) is substantially weak and cannot sustain the policy goals. The latecomer's backwardness manifests in a number of ways: the absence of strong and competent state institutions, weak physical and knowledge infrastructure, low level of skilled engineers, technical personnel and a lack of well-educated and abundant low cost managers. More generally, it finds expression in the inability of the state to effect change in the macro, meso and micro environments for innovation (see Table 2.4) that could enable capabilities formation in a sustainable way.

2.7 Summing up

The analysis conducted here points towards three strong results: health innovation is broader, has different technology and knowledge base and different actor configurations than what has been assumed in the narrower pharmaceutical innovation systems studies up until now. These actors and knowledge bases are dynamic and can differ between countries depending on their stage of capacity, the patterns of collaboration and cooperation as well as the capacity of the system as a whole to respond to internal stimuli and external shocks. For example, the knowledge requirements for a country that is trying to generate production capacity is different from one that is playing at the global frontier. These differences are pertinent and need to be accommodated into the debate on sectoral systems for health innovation and development.

Second, mapping health innovation in the widely accepted sectoral systems format reveals that local institutional capacity is most important because of the science intensive nature of the innovation process and the detailed actor–product lattice that characterizes this sector. Almost all critical elements of capacity are built through state provided public goods, especially in the initial stages of capacity development. Third, local institutions also play a crucial role in structural the local–international knowledge interfaces. Creating positive local–international interfaces is a precondition to building and sustaining health innovation capacity within latecomer countries in the mid or long term. The nature and extent of interactions is such that it calls into question the state's ability to coordinate, negotiate policy space and provide guidance through specific technology choices.

Table 2.4 Institutional limitations affecting health innovation in latecomers

Macro level	Meso level	Micro level
• Lack of coherent policy at the national and sectoral level that sets priorities on the technological side.[1] • Lack of institutional apparatus to promote technological and social innovations for health. • Lack of policy emphasis on collaboration. • Low funding to public sector science. • Weak knowledge indicators. • Low emphasis on local knowledge creation for the sector.	• Overlapping mandates between national, regional/provincial and local institutions. • Disjuncture between demand for health services and products and activities in the sector. • Bureaucratic rigidity and inertia to respond to technological opportunities. • Low organizational competence for policy implementation and coordination between the national and local levels.	• Lack of collaborative culture between scientists, researchers and health practitioners. • Slow uptake of new ideas and incentives by the public sector institutes and universities. • Lack of ability to gauge local demand. • Lack of adequate human skills. • No labour mobility. • Stunted or completely absent private sector enterprise.

Source: author.

Note
1 Most countries, even the very latecomers have some or the other form of clear health policy goals set out, hence the emphasis on the technological aspect in this point.

Part II

Health innovation

Country case studies

An innovation system oriented and policy relevant innovation survey at the firm/ organization level is complex and hardly any such surveys have been conducted in health innovation in latecomer countries. The empirical evidence presented in this Part of the book is one of the few attempts of its kind to apply a common methodology and derive findings of policy relevance. Firm level innovation surveys of the kind commonly prevalent in industrialized countries generally aim at gathering information on innovation inputs (both R&D and non-R&D oriented) and outputs (usually in terms of products or processes of innovation) (Smith, 2005, p. 161). Especially, in the case of health innovation, commonly established indicators include R&D investments, patent filings, products (drugs) introduced in the market on an annual basis as well as the number of staff performing R&D in the firm/organization. While these might be apt to measure innovation trends in the industrialized countries, actors in health innovation are mainly engaged in incremental innovation, and R&D based innovative activities are still not very common. Furthermore, a common weakness of earlier innovation surveys was that they were weakest in precisely the features of greatest utility: few innovation surveys carried out in the 1990s, for example, were consciously designed for policy relevance.

In order to avoid both, the main focus in survey design has been on learning and innovation processes amongst firms and organizations in latecomer countries and how these are affected by internal and external stimuli and not so much on innovation inputs and outputs. Semi-structured questionnaires (which seek to elicit both quantitative and qualitative information on the firm/organization in question through the format of a structured questionnaire that leaves the respondent with significant space and flexibility to add aspects of personal or local importance) were designed to investigate a large range of firm level and organizational level factors and institutional variables and their impact on new product/process innovation in health innovation. This included the contribution of scientific/skilled manpower, the quality of local infrastructure services to new product and/or process development, the financial constraints and availability of venture capital, the collaboration with local universities, local R&D institutes, IPP, the participation in local SME development schemes, participation in government–firm–technology transfer coordination councils, and the transfer of personnel between local firms or R&D institutions. It sought to measure both the direct impact of IPRs on promoting R&D and thus enhancing the innovative performance of firms, as well as its indirect impact on promoting mechanisms of capacity building, such as technology transfer, licensing and technology sourcing through foreign subsidiaries.

Organizations involved in health innovation are typically difficult to quantify since they range from public research institutes to teaching hospitals and hospitals to research and clinical organizations to public foundations. In the sector surveys conducted and presented here, key actors in the health innovation system were construed to include:

a   drug companies, both government-held companies and private companies;
b   biotechnology firms as well as firms specialized in the provision of health technologies, as applicable;
c   governmental agencies especially under the umbrella of the Ministry of Science and Technology, Ministry of Health and the Ministry of Industries, Trade and Commerce;
d   pharmaceutical alliances or sector specific industrial organizations;
e   university departments and university centres of excellence (departments that were surveyed included pharmacy, medicine, biology, biotechnology, microbiology, genetics, pharmacology, pharmacognosy, among others);
f   public research institutes;
g   hospitals and medical service agencies, especially training hospitals;
h   the traditional medicinal sector.

The questionnaires and face-to-face interviews were designed to elicit responses to enhance our understanding of the following issues:

•   the type/nature of collaborations, e.g. research, financing, marketing or distribution, and their impact on capacity;
•   who the key partners and collaborators are (both national and international, private and public);
•   how the linkages were initiated and established, and the factors, which play a role;
•   whether specific trigger points to innovation capacity can be established.
•   the structure and intensity of the agreements with partners/collaborators, e.g. IP clauses, capacity-building elements among others;
•   which legal and institutional factors seem to play a role in the development of health institution within the country.

The sector surveys presented in this part of the book all follow a common format of narration. They begin with mapping the health innovation system in the country, with the key actors, their roles and the existing networks. Empirical evidence is presented to show the current strengths of health innovation in each country and the key local "push" mechanisms that have contributed to sectoral competitiveness. The global "pull" factors and how they interact with sectoral determinants are also discussed. The analysis aims to show how local "push" institutions interact to form capacity, and also how state vision and policy is critical in determining whether and the extent to which global "pull" factors act either as enablers or threats to such a capacity building process in health innovation. The issue of access to medicines and how the formation of local technological capabilities interacts with access is dealt with in the final part of the book.

3 India's advanced capacity in health innovation

3.1 Introduction

India has been projected in policy debates and studies on health innovation capacity as the prime example of capacity building, and at the same time, its stance vis-à-vis IPRs, data exclusivity and how they all relate to public health issues have been controversial. The data presented in this chapter was collected during a sector survey of health innovation in India in 2007 (public sector institutions) and 2008 (firms). The 2008 survey covered 75 of the top firms ranked on the basis of their annual revenues, in addition to surveying a number of biotechnological firms and governmental agencies.

India's compliance with the TRIPS Agreement in 2005 brought the domestic firms into the global landscape in ways unfathomed before. India continues to be a very significant global producer of generic drugs and local Indian firms are actively involved in expanding through foreign acquisitions, setting up global subsidiaries and hiving off separate R&D companies, all of which point to the emergence of new industrial structures. The emergence of this new industrial dynamism is strongly influenced by changes in global regulatory structures for pharmaceutical innovation, influx of newer technologies and strategies of global players that go much beyond outsourcing.

The Indian pharmaceutical sector was estimated to be worth US$12 billion in 2006/2007 according to its local Department of Chemicals and Petrochemicals. Although there are some differences in industry forecasts – the Economist Intelligence Unit predicts it to be worth US$20 billion a year by 2021,[1] a Mckinsey analysis (2007) concludes this to be possible already by 2015[2] and the Indian National Pharmaceutical Policy of 2006 sets this as a feasible target for 2010 – there is no doubt that the sector is thriving despite India's full-scale compliance with the TRIPS Agreement in 2005. In 2005/2006 the Indian pharmaceutical industry's share of the global market stood at 1.5 per cent (ranked thirteenth) in terms of value but at 8 per cent (ranked fourth) in terms of volume.[3] The domestic sector meets 70 per cent of all local demands for drugs despite the increased presence of multinational companies since 2005,[4] and 95 per cent of all products sold in the market continue to be generic drugs.[5]

Box 3.1 Indian pharma: market figures at a glance[1]

- In 2007, the local sector met 70 per cent of the domestic demand for vaccines, APIs, intermediaries and fixed formulations.
- In 2006/2007 around two-thirds of production was for domestic consumption and the rest was exported.
- This represented a 30 per cent increase from 2005/2006 figures and accounted for 2.5 per cent of all exports.
- Generics and active pharmaceutical ingredients are the main exports to over 150 countries worldwide.
- The USA remains the main export market, with the EU becoming increasingly important.
- The pharmaceutical sector is the most R&D intensive sector in the country presently. In 2006, the sector's R&D investments exceeded all other major sectors, such as automobiles and software.
- Nine of the top ten firms continue to be local firms since 2004.

Note
1   Economist Intelligence Unit Forecast, 2007 (hereafter EIU); Guatam Kumra, Palash Mitra and Chandrika Pasricha, "Indian Pharma 2015: Unlocking the Potential of the Indian Pharmaceuticals Market", Mckinsey and Company, 2007 (hereafter, Mckinsey, 2007); Bain and Co., 2008.

3.2 Key actors and strengths in the local innovation system

Private firms, mostly local, are the key set of actors in health innovation in India. Although there are around 10,000 registered local companies (EIU, 2007), the organized sector is relatively small and comprises around 300 large and medium sized firms, which account for 70 per cent of the entire market. Nine out of the top ten companies as of 2007 are local companies and they hold approximately 30 per cent of the entire market (KPMG, 2006). According to the Department of Commerce figures, formulations constitute around 80 per cent of India's total pharmaceutical production and APIs make up for the remaining 20 per cent (also see EIU, 2007 and Mckinsey, 2007). Dr. Reddy's Laboratories is the largest player in the Indian pharmaceutical sector with a market share of 10 per cent, followed closely by Ranbaxy, Cipla, Aurobindo and the rest of the firms in the top ten category (Figure 3.1). The drugs are distributed mainly through retail outlets and physicians maintain a large amount of influence on the introduction of new drugs/substitution of existing drugs through other brand generics. Drug companies employ large marketing forces to penetrate local markets through institutional sales and private sales. Figure 3.1 shows the market structure as well as therapeutic categories for the formulations market. The API market, not represented in the figure, is far more fragmented. In addition to pharmaceutical firms, the sector has numerous biotechnology and other health technology firms, many of which focus extensively on innovative health services delivery.

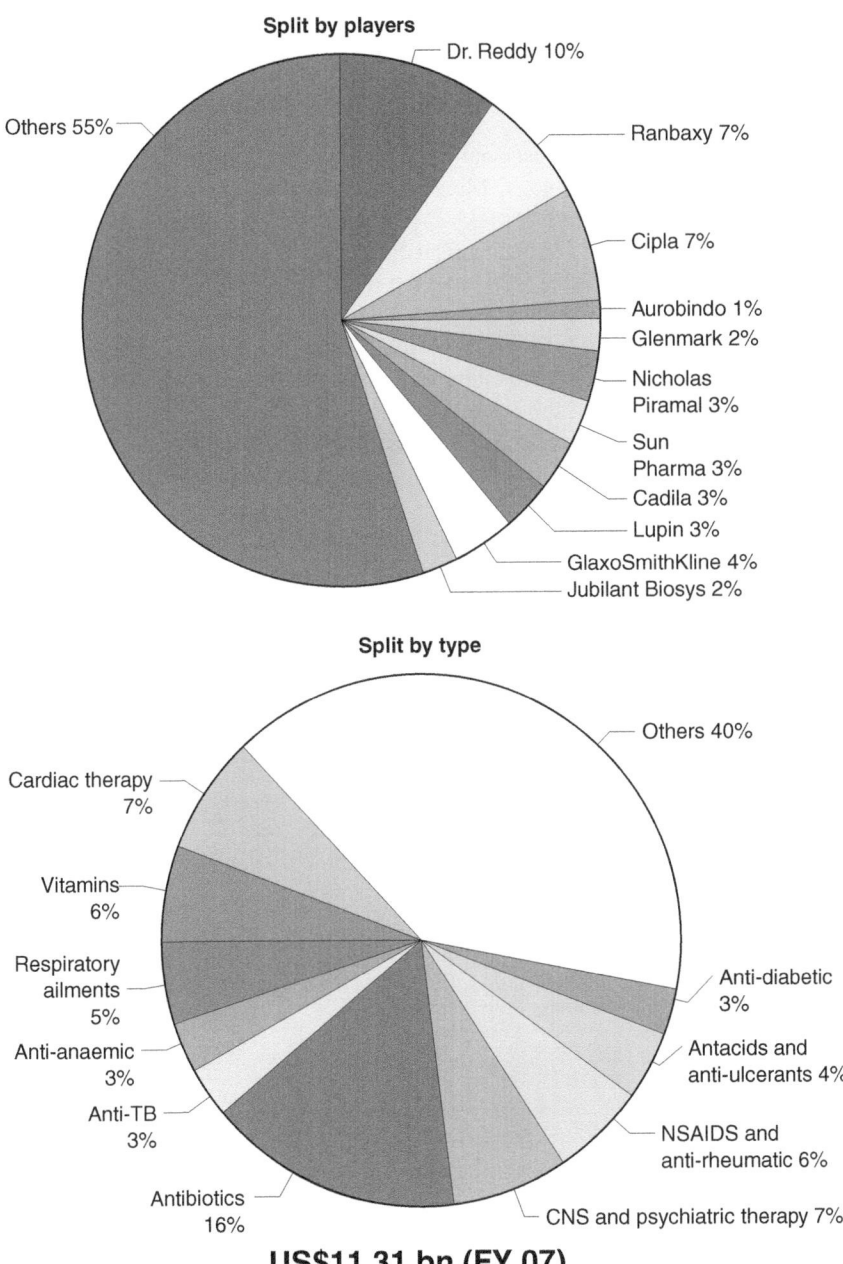

Split by players

Dr. Reddy 10%
Ranbaxy 7%
Cipla 7%
Aurobindo 1%
Glenmark 2%
Nicholas Piramal 3%
Sun Pharma 3%
Cadila 3%
Lupin 3%
GlaxoSmithKline 4%
Jubilant Biosys 2%
Others 55%

Split by type

Others 40%
Cardiac therapy 7%
Vitamins 6%
Respiratory ailments 5%
Anti-anaemic 3%
Anti-TB 3%
Antibiotics 16%
CNS and psychiatric therapy 7%
NSAIDS and anti-rheumatic 6%
Antacids and anti-ulcerants 4%
Anti-diabetic 3%

US$11.31 bn (FY 07)

Figures 3.1 The Indian pharmaceutical sector: market shares and main therapeutic segments[1] (source: author).

Note
1 All figures used for the bottom figure are for fiscal year 2007, except for Ranbaxy, GlaxoSmith-Kline and Wockhardt, whose figures are for current year 2006.

The firms are supported by a wide network of actors in the health innovation system, their activities and the distribution channels are as pictured in Figure 3.2, namely:

- governmental agencies especially those under the umbrella of the Ministry of Science and Technology, Ministry of Health and the Ministry of Industries, Trade and Commerce;
- the Organization of Pharmaceutical Producers of India (OPPI), the Indian Pharmaceutical Alliance (IPA) and the Indian Drug Manufacturers' Association (IDMA);[6]
- public research institutes such as the Centre for Science and Industrial Research (CSIR) and the Institute for Drug and Medical Research (IDMR);
- hospitals and medical service agencies, especially training hospitals;
- the traditional medicinal sector, especially Ayurveda and Unani systems of medicine.[7]

The formulation of policies for the sector is split between the Ministry of Chemicals and Fertilizers, the Ministry of Commerce and Industry (and the Department of Intellectual Property Protection), the Ministry of Health and Family Welfare and the Ministry of Science and Technology (Department of

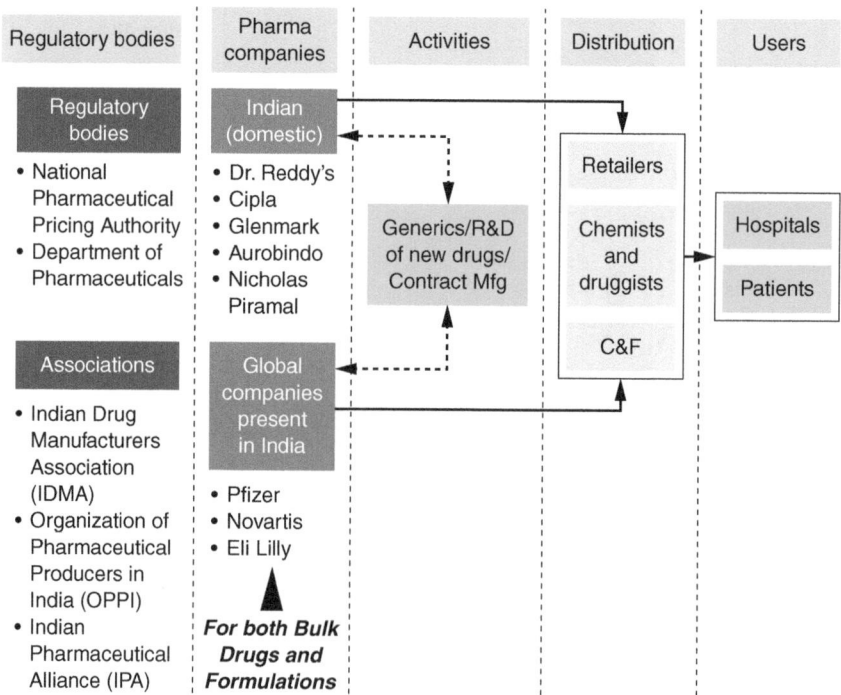

Figure 3.2 Main actors in health innovation (source: author).

Science and Technology and the Department of Biotechnology). Until June 2008, the pharmaceutical sector was under the mandate of the Department of Chemicals and Petrochemicals, located in the Ministry of Chemicals and Ferti- lizers. Recently, a new Department of Pharmaceuticals has been created. The National Pharmaceutical Pricing Authority (NPPA) is an independent agency under the Department of Pharmaceuticals (it was earlier under the Department of Chemicals and Petrochemicals) in charge of fixing/revising prices of selected pharmaceutical products in the country (both APIs and pharmaceuticals), enforc- ing the provisions of the Drugs (Price Control) Order and monitoring the prices of controlled and decontrolled drugs in the country. India has implemented several versions of the Drug Price Control Order since 1964, and the Drug Price Control Order of 1995 brought down the coverage of price control to only 74 drugs. Presently there is a new price control policy (of 2006) under considera- tion, upon enactment of which, over 300 different drugs could be brought under price control. The sector is organized under three main industrial associations: the Organization of Pharmaceutical Producers of India (OPPI), the Indian Phar- maceutical Alliance (IPA), which comprises 15 of the top Indian firms, and the Indian Drug Manufacturers Association (IDMA), which is a much larger organ- ization with medium and small-scale firms in addition to the large firms.

3.3 Current strengths in health innovation

Indian firms were global suppliers of cheaper generic versions of patented drugs to other middle and low income countries worldwide until 2005. In 2005, India enacted its final patent amendment[8] that made it fully TRIPS compliant. Despite this, Indian companies continue to be major suppliers of drugs and medical devices worldwide. According to the Department of Commerce and Industry figures for 2006/2007, India exported pharmaceutical products worth US$3.1 billion thus recording a 30 per cent increase over 2005/2006.[9] Indian drug firms sold finished drugs and pharmaceutical ingredients worth US$800 million in the US in 2006 and accounted for over 20 per cent of all generic drugs approved for marketing by the FDA in 2006, compared with less than 7 per cent in 2002 (EIU, 2007, p. 11). Figure 3.3 plots the revenues from exports for the top ten firms from 2002 to 2007.[10]

Table 3.1 indicates the percentage growth in exports between 2003 and 2007 for the top ten firms.

3.3.1 Generics production

Pharmaceutical production costs are estimated to be 30–50 per cent lower in India than in Western countries (KPMG, 2006), attributable to the expertise Indian firms have accumulated in reverse engineering processes for APIs, scale economies of production and lower personnel and capital construction costs (Bain and Co., 2008. p. 2). The same cost advantages are true in the case of bio- technology firms in India (see for example, Frew *et al.*, 2008).

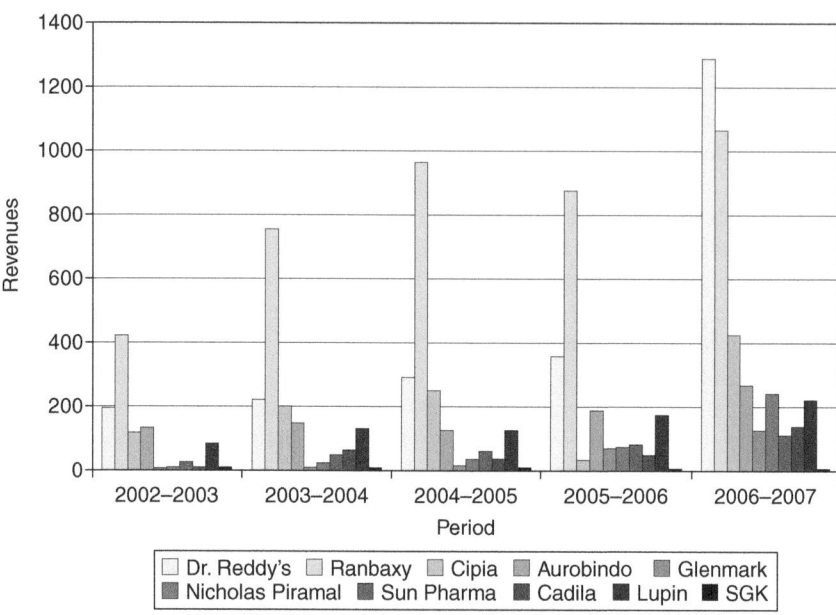

Figure 3.3 Revenues from exports for the top ten firms, 2002–2007.

Box 3.2 Present strengths in generics production in India

- Expertise in reverse engineering processes for APIs.
- Scale economies and production efficiency due to local API production capabilities.
- Lower personnel and capital construction costs.
- Expertise and investments in emerging areas, such as biogenerics.
- Competitive pricing strategies, especially for formulations, where India has a head start of three to five years for finished formulations over China.
- Large pools of English speaking scientific talent.

        Source: Field interviews, Bain and Co., 2008 and KPMG, 2006

Cost competitiveness of Indian generics continues to be the driving force of the expansion of the sector. In a study that compared prices of generic drugs between nine European countries and India in 2005, Indian and Scandinavian generic producers emerged to be the cheapest suppliers of drugs (Simoens, 2008). Amongst the 15 molecules that the study compared, Indian suppliers were 63 per cent cheaper than other suppliers in the generics market in Belgium, and the study found Germany, France and the Netherlands as countries with the highest prices of generic drugs of the ten countries that were compared in the study.

Table 3.1 Percentage growth in exports, 2003–2007[1]

Company	2002–2003	2003–2004	2004–2005	2005–2006	2006–2007
Dr. Reddy's	−1	7	−7	31	138
Ranbaxy	32	−0.5	−5	−16	−3
Cipla	15	44	30	44	18
Aurobindo	16	14	−14	47	34
Glenmark	32	58	–	9	116
Sun Pharma	5	46	35	33	32
GSK	−41	−17	−4	10	37

Note
1 Compiled by author using the annual reports of the top ten firms, except Nicholas Piramal, Cadila and Lupin.

Indian firms have tended to invest historically in R&D activities related to the production of generics. In the years leading up to India complying with the TRIPS Agreement, the dominant business model was one where firms focused on retaining generic product pipelines, albeit extending into more demanding and innovative generic categories, such as novel drug delivery systems (Gehl Sampath, 2005). Now several pharmaceutical firms have established separate R&D companies making the division between generics "R&D" and new drug discovery more explicit. Broadly speaking, R&D investments in the sector can be split up into generics related R&D and proprietary R&D for drug discovery research. The generics R&D is geared towards creating drug master files (DMFs), which are required to get approval in the US market for the sale of active pharmaceutical ingredients and to submit Abbreviated New Drug Applications (ANDAs) that are a prerequisite to receive market approval for generic drugs.

Indian generic firms specialize in developing non-infringing processes for the manufacture of generic products. Production of non-infringing processes helps firms to produce generic versions of a product where the patent on the new chemical entity (NCE) has expired but the product may have process and formulation patents that are still valid (Chaudhuri, 2007). Firms such as Unichem Pharmaceuticals, Matrix Pharmaceuticals and Divi's Laboratories are good examples of firms in this category. Matrix Laboratories' non-infringing process on Citalopram (an anti-depressant) ensured the company a sole exporter status of the API to Western Europe in 2004. Matrix Laboratories has also subsequently developed non-infringing processes for the production of APIs for anti-retroviral drugs. Other categories of generics R&D includes those related to new drug discovery systems and specialty generics as well as biogenerics that are far more complex to manufacture, like injectables, biologics and oncology therapeutics (Bain and Co., 2008).

Since India's product patent protection regime, local firms are no longer able to produce generic versions of drugs patented elsewhere in the world. There have been several estimates of the costs imposed by this restriction on the sector.

However, recent estimates of off-patented products in the Indian market (including drugs whose patents have expired and those which are not patentable in India) are as high as 95 per cent (EIU, 2007). If this is true then there is still a lot of opportunity for the Indian firms to thrive in the generics market both in India and in other latecomer countries (that classify as least developed countries) that are exempt from implementing the TRIPS Agreement until 2016, by offering substitutes to products patented elsewhere.[11] However, in practice, the firms' abilities to cater to the demand for cheaper generics in other developing and least developed countries are determined by their choice of therapeutic product categories. The field survey shows that the most popular product categories are those related to the central nervous system (CNS) and the cardiovascular system (CVS), followed closely by oncology and respiratory ailments. Almost all firms interviewed cited the desire to focus on these products due to the guaranteed long-term markets (since they are chronic ailments) and possibility to sell in regulated markets (which is synonymous with higher pricing abilities and increased profits). The surveyed firms were also asked to quantify the amount of their total research that is focused on local disease conditions. The responses to this question are shown in Figure 3.4. Only 6 per cent of the 49 firms that participated in the survey conducted all of their research on local disease conditions, 18 per cent of the firms admitted to conducting up to half of their R&D on local conditions and a large majority of the firms (75 per cent) conducted only 25 per cent or less of their R&D on local disease conditions.

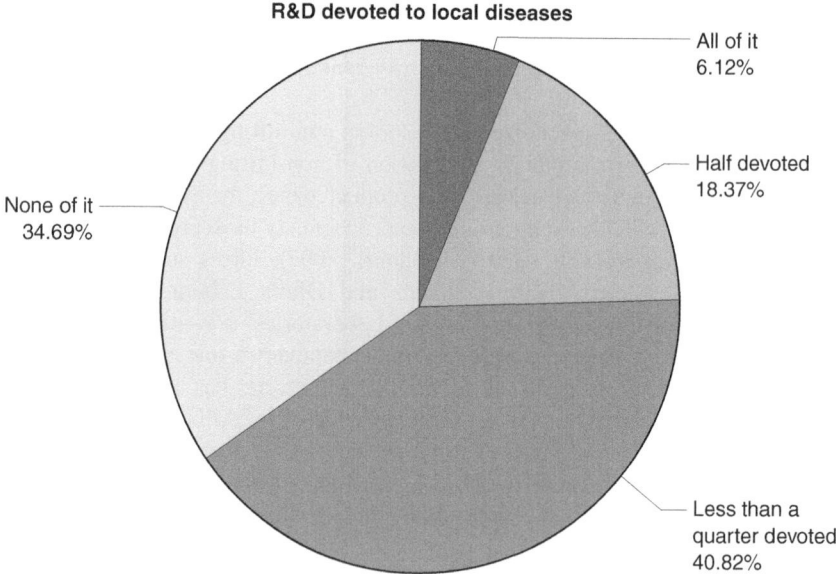

Figure 3.4 R&D on local diseases: results of field survey (source: author's field survey, 2008).

India has approximately 100 FDA-approved plants: the largest number outside the US and approximately twice the amount that China presently has (Bain and Co., 2008, p. 2). Recent estimates expect 250 Indian generics products to be launched in the US market by 2008, as opposed to 93 in 2003 (KPMG, 2006, p. 9).

Up until the end of the 1980s, Indian firms focused extensively on the "rest of the world" markets where there was little or no patent protection coupled with lax registration requirements. Technological sophistication, however, has been accompanied by a gradual shift of focus to the highly lucrative US generics market. In recent years, companies' performances reflect the gains from scale economies and diversification in key markets. The top firms like Ranbaxy and Dr. Reddy's Laboratories that set the trend of focusing on regulated markets initially showed that winning a 180 days exclusivity to sell their generics first in the US markets was a very lucrative option to generate revenues, once the initial barriers to market entry were surpassed.[12] Most field interviews with firms conducted during the survey shows that even when firms do not target the first-to-file 180 days exclusivity afforded to generic drugs in the US market, their gradual expansion in the US market brings in large benefits due to the price competitiveness of Indian generics and the opportunities created by the US$100 billion worth of drugs going off-patent between 2006 and 2008.[13]

Almost all big firms like Dr. Reddy's, Sun Pharma, Cipla and Ranbaxy focus on product portfolios that cater to all the regulated markets and are certified suppliers of generic medicines in the European Union (EU). When compared to the USA, the EU market is viewed as being more problematic by Indian firms due to the costs involved in dealing with the varied regulatory approval processes (which are different for each of the 27 member countries), linguistic difficulties, complex pricing dynamics, greater generic competition and lack of experience of Indian firms to operate in the EU (field interviews). Despite this, the emerging picture is one where firms diversify their exports between the US, EU and other markets in Asia and Africa, albeit to different extents *depending on their product portfolios.*[14]

Hitherto purely generics firms have expanded into more R&D intensive domains by acquiring R&D based firms abroad, thus combining their cost competitiveness with innovative activities to explore upcoming markets such as biogenerics, which are predicted to be worth US$30 billion by 2015 within just the USA (EIU, 2007). In 2003–2004, biopharmaceuticals accounted for 60 per cent of India's total biotechnology market, which was worth an estimated US$709 million (KPMG, 2006). Several firms like Ranbaxy, Dr. Reddy's, Biocon and Wockhardt focus extensively on health biotechnology and biogenerics (field interviews). Wockhardt already had 55 biopharmaceutical registrations pending with 26 approvals in 18 different countries as of 2005 (KPMG, 2006).

Despite the growing emphasis on health R&D, several top firms remain purely generic entities – Aurobindo, for example, the fourth largest firm in the market is a purely generic company. Aurobindo has a large R&D department, which employs 700 people but are all engaged in generics R&D (field interviews). Similarly Cipla is a predominantly generics company. Other firms like Dr. Reddy's, Glenmark and Sun all pursue mixed strategies of generics and drug discovery through varied models (see next section).

3.3.2 R&D capabilities

Industry statistics show that large Indian firms have been investing approximately 10 per cent of their total sales into R&D since the early 2000s. In 2005 when India complied with the TRIPS Agreement, the top five companies increased their R&D spending by 47 per cent on the whole, which amounted to US$192.3 million (as compared to US$131 million for 2004).[15] Table 3.2 shows the R&D spending of the top five firms in the Indian pharmaceutical sector (excluding Cipla). As mentioned previously, a large share of this R&D still goes to developing novel delivery systems, non-infringing processes and similar activities that feed into the generics business thus building upon synergies between the need to be competitive in the present, with the aspiration to build greater innovative capabilities to integrate into the global structure.

The importance that firms place on R&D investments seems to be linked to their strategies on (field interviews):

a   their product portfolios,
b   export orientation and
c   presence (or absence) of a vision to emerge as an R&D based company.

For example, Ranbaxy exports between 65 and 70 per cent of its total production, whereas Nicholas Piramal only exports around 10–15 per cent of its total production.[16] Some firms in the top ten ranking focus extensively on drug discovery, for example, Dr. Reddy's Laboratories, Sun Pharmaceuticals and Glenmark, and this explains their increased emphasis on R&D spending. Leaving the top firms aside, if one would take a sector-wide approach considering all of the 10,000 odd firms, the R&D investments are negligible as one goes down the ranking, if not non-existent. For the 49 firms that participated in the survey, Figure 3.5 shows the rise in mean R&D intensity from 2003 to 2007, from 3.5 per cent of total sales to 5.5 per cent.

Table 3.2 R&D spending as a percentage of total revenues of the top five firms from 2003 to 2006 (excluding Cipla)[1]

Company	2003	2004	2005	2006
Dr. Reddy's	7.6	9.5	12.9	9.6
Ranbaxy	4.5	5.3	6.2	9.4
Aurobindo	1.2	2.0	3.1	3.6
Glenmark	4.4	6.5	5.3	4.4
Sun Pharma	3.4	5.0	5.9	6.3

Note
1 Compiled by author using company annual reports.

Box 3.3 Drug discovery prospects in the Indian pharma sector: Sun and Glenmark[1]

Glenmark presently has eight molecules in clinical trials and its therapeutic areas of focus are inflammation, metabolic disorders (diabetes and obesity) and dermatology. Oglemilast, an asthma drug, is in phase 2-B and the company has partnered with Forest, US, for a deal that guarantees it US$190 million in upfront payment with back-to-back royalties on global sales of the product. Another molecule, GRC 8200 for Diabetes treatment is also in phase 2-B, for which Glenmark has partnered with Merck KGAA. The US$250 million deal for GRC 8200 contains a US$31 million upfront payment and also stipulates back-to-back royalties along with milestone payments. GRC 6211 against Osteoarthritis, also in phase 2, is being jointly developed with Eli Lilly. As part of a US$350 million deal for GRC 6211, Glenmark has received an upfront payment of US$45 million, and the deal also segments the USA, Europe and Japanese markets to Eli Lilly.

Sun Pharmaceutical's lead product is an anti-allergic presently in phase 2 clinical trials. Although its product development is fully funded by Sun, the drug is being developed in collaboration with a clinical research organization since Sun does not have the requisite in-house capabilities. There are three other molecules lined up in preclinical stage; a soft steroid for asthma, a neurological drug and a muscle relaxant. In the last three years, the company has conducted five acquisitions, including three American companies, one in Hungary and one in India. The acquisition of an Israeli company based in the USA was underway in April 2008 when the field interviews with Sun Pharmaceuticals were conducted for this study.

Note
1 Personal communication with Glen Saldanha, CEO, Glenmark, 2 April 2008, and Uday Baldohta, Vice President, Sun Pharmaceuticals, 2 April 2008.

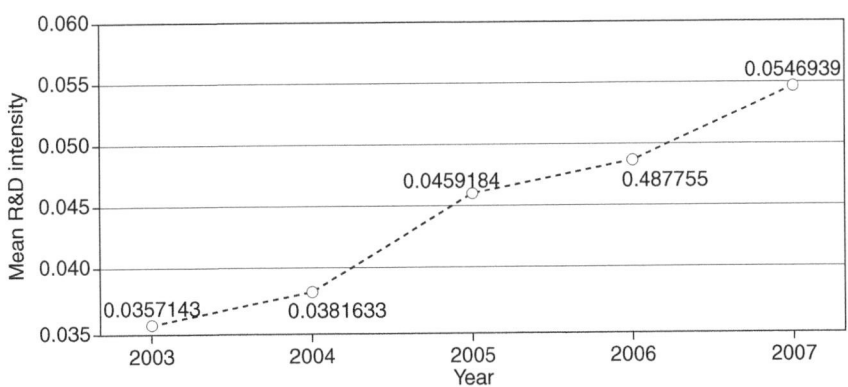

Figure 3.5 Rise in mean R&D intensity from 2003 to 2007[1] (source: author's field survey, 2008).

Note
1 R&D intensity is calculated as R&D as a percentage of total sales.

India's TRIPS compliance has also been accompanied by some increase in R&D investments by the large MNCs. Merck inaugurated its first wholly owned subsidiary, MSD India Private Ltd in July 2005 after being absent in the Indian market for 20 years in 2006.[17] The pro-generics Indian interpretations of the patenting provisions under TRIPS (see upcoming sections) are also encouraging foreign firms to either buy out Indian firms or to set up wholly new production units within the country thus helping the local sector to expand further. The most recent acquisition of a 50 per cent stake in Ranbaxy by Daiichi Sankyo is one such move. The generic firm Actavis (Iceland) bought out the API division of Sanmar Pharmaceuticals Ltd (Chennai) in a bid to get into generic production in India in 2007.[18] Similarly, a Malaysian generics firm, Hovid, plans to establish a manufacturing plant in India in order to be able to produce generic versions of drugs it cannot produce in Malaysia due to Malaysia's more stringent patent regime.[19]

3.3.3 Contract research and manufacturing

Indian firms have developed capabilities in various stages of the drug discovery and development process and conduct contract research and manufacturing for foreign firms. Apart from the low costs of the pharmaceutical production process, the overall R&D costs are about one-eighth and clinical trial expenses around one-tenth of Western levels,[20] which add to the profitability of contracting out activities to Indian firms, in a global pharmaceutical environment that is hard-pressed to cut costs. Local firms conduct contract research and manufacturing (also called CRAM) for foreign firms in areas ranging from clinical trials to drug discovery to non-infringing process development to simply manufacturing APIs and formulations. These factors have accelerated the growth of the local contract research and manufacturing sector, which was estimated at US$895 million for fiscal year 2006.

Some recent, interesting forms of contract research include basic molecular research, gene mapping, drug discovery and managing clinical trials, discovery chemistry for domestic and global pharmaceutical companies.[21] There are over 50 clinical research organizations in the country;[22] the more cited ones being Kendle, Quintiles, Siro Clinpharm and iGate. India rates second on the list of the most attractive low cost global locations to run clinical trials outside the US. According to Mckinsey (2007), India and China will account for almost 40 per cent of global pharmaceutical offshoring in the coming years. Pfizer has approximately 20 ongoing clinical trials in India, GSK has seven and Eli Lilly has 17 trials, in addition to other firms like AstraZeneca and Novartis.[23]

Several large Indian firms have entered into contract research agreements for product development with the big pharma to gain R&D expertise in exchange for cheaper production possibilities. Ranbaxy and GSK reached an agreement in 2007 where Ranbaxy will help develop some of GSK's products in return for tacit R&D skills and experience in handling complex pharmaceutical innovation processes (field interviews). API production for large or international firms and marketing agreements are other popular kinds of cooperation. Matrix laboratories has been very successful as a contract manufacturer of cheaper non-infringing processes of API development for many years now (field interviews). Table 3.3 contains an illustrative list of contract research agreements by major Indian firms as of 2008.

3.4 Local push factors: analysing sectoral determinants of competitiveness

The pharmaceutical sector has been a focal sector in India since the 1960s, and the government has put several incentives in place to enable sectoral competitiveness, with changing emphasis over time. This has included investment in the creation of skilled manpower of relevance to the sector, establishment of public sector institutions such as CSIR and the Central Drug Research Institute (CDRI), investment in biotechnology parks, establishment of export processing zones and easing the emergence of venture capital institutions. Indian firms also receive several other benefits for exports that enables them to price their products

Table 3.3 Some major contract research agreements[1]

Company	Client	Drug
Cadila Healthcare	Altana	Two intermediates for pantaprazole
Dishman	Solvay	Six projects, including supply of starting material and intermediates for eprosartan
Dishman	Astra Zeneca	Intermediate for esomeprazole
Dishman	Merck & Co.	Intermediate for losartan
Dishman	GlaxoSmithKline	Three intermediates
Hikal	Degussa	Manufacturing intermediates and APIs to Degussa on a project basis
Lupin	Cyanamid	Intermediates
Matrix	Wyeth	Supply of acyclovir
Nicholas Piramal	GlaxoSmithKline	MOU for drug intermediates; no fixed tenure
Nicholas Piramal	Astra Zeneca	Intermediates
Nicholas Piramal	Pfizer	Intermediates and APIs
Nicholas Piramal	AMO	Five year contract of ophthalmic products
Nicholas Piramal	Allegran	APIs for levobunolol and brimonidine
IPCA	Astra Zeneca	Contract manufacturing of APIs
Strides Acrolabs	Mayne	Injectables manufacturing

Source: field interviews.

Note
1 Compiled by author.

competitively in export markets. For example, firms located in export processing zones are entitled to customs benefits, tax benefits for export (which could extend up to 15 years) and also Capital Expenditure (Cap Ex) benefits.

3.4.1 Policy choices for developing capacity

The critical policy changes that led to the growth of the sector can be classified into three broad phases, beginning with the key changes that were initiated in the 1960s. In the 1960s, the Indian government, in an effort to boost local production of pharmaceutical products, introduced three major policy incentives: the Drug Price Control Order (to control the prices of drugs), the Indian Patent Act of 1970 that denied product patent protection to pharmaceutical firms and limited process patents for a period of seven years, and government held pharmaceutical production companies (Gehl Sampath, 2005). As a result of the changes introduced by the Patent Act, the number of patents granted per year within India fell by three-quarters between the years 1970–1971 and 1980–1981 (Lanjouw, 1998, p. 4). The Drug Price Control Order, by setting a ceiling on the overall profits of pharmaceutical companies, effectively led to a large-scale exodus of multinational companies (MNCs) operating in India at that point of time. Technology required to enhance reverse engineering skills, specifically those related to imitative process R&D, formulation and production technologies was acquired through public sector efforts, and then passed on to the private sector. The local industries, a large part of which developed through spin-off entrepreneurship of employees of government-held pharmaceutical firms, were quick to take cue from the conducive environment: they developed extensive skills in chemistry based reverse engineering which forms the core of their product and process development skills until today. Indigenous local capacity for production was thus built through a combination of the right policy environment, access to international technology, education and promotion of entrepreneurship, among other factors while the main impetus for learning came from learning-by-doing activities (Mashelkar, 2005).

A second phase of policy changes was triggered off by India's trade liberalization in the end of the 1980s. By this time, the pharmaceutical sector was exporting bulk drugs and formulations, and was recognized to be of strategic importance due to its technological and export potential. Several of the policy changes undertaken in this phase were aimed at enabling the sector take advantage of India's shift from an import-substitution economy to a liberalized one, and helped boost the potential of the sector as an exporter of generic formulations. This, supported by India's continuing minimalist IPR regime created a comfortable and stable economic climate where several of the larger firms, like Ranbaxy and Dr. Reddy's ventured out to acquire facilities in developed countries in the 1990s (for example, the USA).

These two phases of policy transformations were responsible for the radical changes in the foreign versus local firm ratio in the Indian market. From a virtually non-existent domestic sector in 1970 (15 per cent of Indian firms as against

85 per cent foreign firms in the local market), the market structure transformed into one where both Indian and foreign firms held a 50 per cent share in 1982, to a 61 per cent Indian and 39 per cent foreign share in 1999 (OPPI, 2000).

A third phase of policy changes were triggered off by India's entry into the World Trade Organization in 1995, as a result of which it undertook to fully implement the TRIPS Agreement by 2005. Subsequently, India revised its IP regime for pharmaceutical products radically between 1999 and 2005, becoming fully TRIPS compliant in 2005 with the grant of product patent protection. The changes induced by IPP will be profound, because they are accompanied by potential losses to the sector since generic versions of drugs that are patented elsewhere can no longer be produced by Indian firms (see Fink, 2000; Grace 2004, 2005; Gehl Sampath, 2005). However, in order to strengthen the sector's capacity to deal with the threat of foreign competition and potential losses induced by stronger IPP, the government introduced several other policy changes aimed at enhancing the industry's credibility nationally and internationally, one such change being the introduction of good manufacturing practices (GMPs) applicable uniformly across the sector.

Throughout the three phases, knowledge infrastructure policies that targeted India's higher education and health research spending and placed an extraordinary emphasis on science based university education and specialized public research institutes (PRIs) were implemented. The government has invested relatively heavily in setting up excellent university education facilities in key disciplines of relevance to pharmaceutical research (such as those in medicine, pharmacology, chemistry, biochemistry, biology, molecular biology and biotechnology), as well as set up public research institutes such as the Centre for Science and Industrial Research (CSIR), Indian Drugs and Medical Research Institute (IDMR), All India Institute of Medical Sciences (AIIMS), Indian Institute of Chemical Technology (IICT), Indian Institute for Science (IISC). This trend has continued well into the present, with institutes such as the Institute for Human Genetics, the Centre for Biotechnology, Institute of Microbial Technology all being established with the mandate of conducting research on emerging areas of importance to drug research. Throughout the past four decades, governmental spending on health research has been extensive, with up to 90 per cent of all research funds being sourced internally for both the public and private sector (CHRD, 1990, p. 49).[24]

However, the emphatic focus of the sector policy as it was initially laid out, was on encouraging local production of drugs at affordable prices and not on building an innovative industry that could attain global competitiveness. This emphasis remained throughout all policy stages, despite a gradual expansion of industrial and innovation policy incentives. Policy action thus resulted in a strange assemblage of strengths, and significant differences in technological capabilities amongst small, large and medium sized firms in the local sector.

In hindsight, the strengths of domestic enterprise, built over time, are reflected in the way the sector has been able to thrive and advance beyond mere production of generics into innovative territories, expand and tap into modern technologies like health biotechnology. However, the key task of plunging ahead with global aspirations was largely a result of aspirations of local firms. The local firms were quick to foretell how India's compliance with the TRIPS Agreement would fundamentally change the nature of innovative activities they would be able to indulge in, and already began inducing large-scale changes in their activities, several years before India's product patent regime in 2005. In the years leading up to India's compliance with the TRIPS Agreement, the top Indian firms began investing up to 10 per cent of their annual profits into research and development activities (Table 3.2). As the earlier sections show, they diversified their activities to expand beyond generics production to (a) generics based R&D (this includes developing novel delivery systems, non-infringing processes and similar activities that feed into the generics business), (b) drug discovery and development and (c) contract research and manufacturing for global firms, which includes clinical trials work. Such a diversification ensured that they would be able to build upon synergies between the need to be competitive in the present, with the aspiration to build greater innovative capabilities to integrate into the global structure. The sector continues to expand and Figure 3.6 plots the increase in mean full time equivalent employees between 2003 and 2007 for the 49 firms surveyed. Employment rose from 866,419 employees in 2003, to 1,414,286 employees (which is almost the double) in 2007.

Indian firms, however, have been having several difficulties coping with new business models post-2005. Recent years have witnesses a frenzied reorganization in the sector. In addition to the massive buy-outs, several major companies

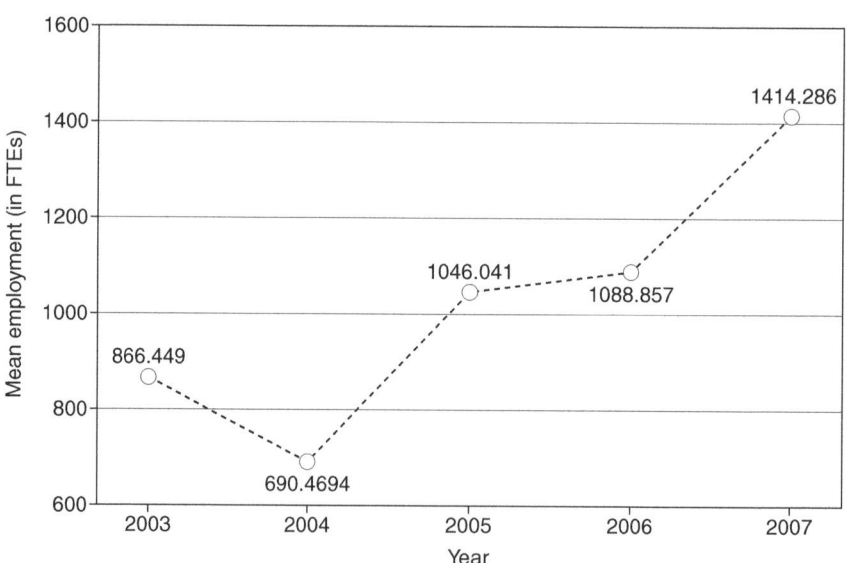

Figure 3.6 Rise in mean employment between 2003 and 2007: results of the survey (source: author's field survey, 2008).

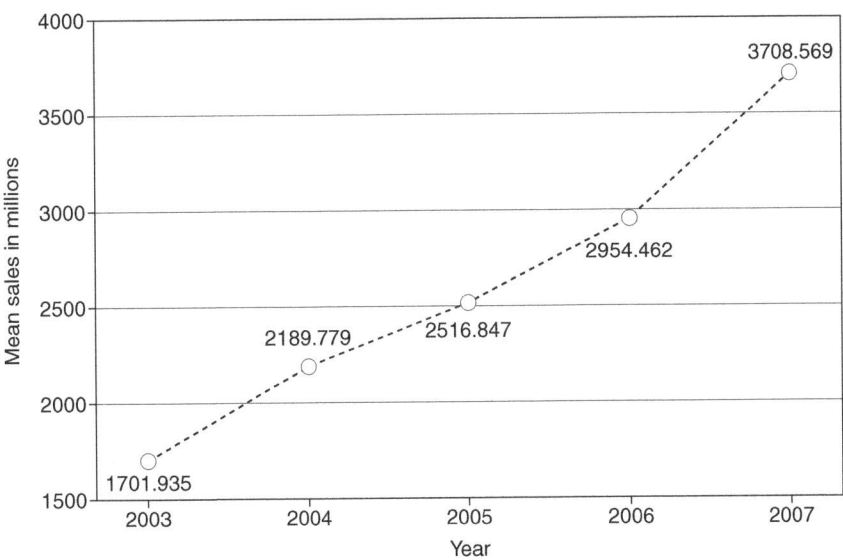

Figure 3.7 Rise in mean sales for the 49 firms between 2003 and 2007: results of the survey (source: author's field survey, 2008).

hived off their R&D operations into newer entities (of which some reversed their decisions). Ranbaxy, Sun Pharmaceuticals and Biocon have launched separate R&D companies of their own. Similarly, Wellquest, a clinical research arm of the Nicholas Piramal Group, launched a research centre in Hyderabad in mid-2007.[25] The centre has an investment of Rs100 million (US$2.5 million) and will focus on clinical trials, generic-drug testing and the development of drug delivery systems. There are several other leading Indian generics companies setting up separate R&D companies, including Cadila Pharma and Lupin. Ranbaxy, the second largest company in the Indian market, was also ranked within the top ten global generics firms and had a good foothold in European markets through a series of acquisitions. In June 2008, Ranbaxy was sold with a 50 per cent stake to the Japanese firm Daiichi Sankyo, making Daiichi the fifteenth largest pharmaceutical firm worldwide (and the second largest in the Japanese market after Tadeka Pharma). The survey and interviews reveal however that as opposed to TRIPS compliance, some of the difficulties faced in implementing the newer business models arose from the overly ambitious internationalization of the firms. This, however, is also a learning process.

Three major factors seem to explain the growing separation of R&D and generics activities in the sector (field interviews). Proprietary R&D involving new technologies in health is a risky option with long incubation times.[26] Second, huge R&D investments reduce the market capitalization of the big firms, which in turn affects their aspirations to acquire more firms abroad. Finally, Indian firms are collaborators and competitors for the global pharma at the same time. While they challenge big pharma patents in India under the local regime and abroad (to win the Para IV 180 days exclusivity in the US market) to protect their generics business, they also collaborate with the multinational companies on several drug discovery fronts, including phase III and IV clinical trials (which very few Indian firms can finance and conduct in-house). And separating their R&D from generics production helps to enhance trust in international collaborations (field interviews).

In order to help the firms cope, the government also plans to introduce several new schemes of relevance to health and innovation.[27] This includes schemes that allow companies participating in R&D to set higher margins for their drugs, soft loans of 3 per cent for companies who collaborate with governmental research facilities, R&D grants for firms who engage in clinical trials for drugs to treat neglected diseases. There are ongoing efforts to revise other rules and regulations related to pharmaceutical research that seem outdated in the present context. For example, in order to encourage domestic R&D capabilities, Indian regulations granted tax incentives to firms to engage in R&D within the country. This was a necessary incentive in earlier times where the government's motive was to encourage local R&D to enable the local sector to grow. However, in today's context, most MNCs are performing R&D in India (and benefiting from this incentive) and most Indian companies are contracting out phase III and IV clinical trials to companies abroad. The government therefore plans to introduce a new scheme that will serve as a fiscal incentive (in terms of tax deduction) for Indian firms that are conducting R&D outside India, recognizing the new realities of the sector.

In biotechnology, the government has recently announced (2007) a National Biotechnology Development Strategy with a budget of 6500 Crores (approximately €1.3 billion). This money will be spend by the Department of Biotechnology to improve biotechnology funding, streamline regulatory processes, enhance technology transfer of relevance for the sector, improve the legal apparatus that supports the sector and generally help in entrepreneurship development and sector growth.

3.4.2 Local and international collaborations

The emphasis on building a local production system in the 1960s and the 1970s was structured around the acquisition of technologies through the public research institutes that was then transferred to the enterprise sector. However, there has been a gradual decline in interactions between the public research institutes and firms over time and, amongst the firms that admitted to having collaborations, most were in the area of research as opposed to product development. Most firms complained that the nature of ongoing research in public sector institutions were not well suited to their needs. Apart form the issue of industry relevant research, lack of quality in the research infrastructure provided in universities – partly due to bureaucratic and financial constraints – is a problem that needs tackling. Research institutes fare much better than universities on the question of finances and human capital for conducting health innovation, notable amongst which are institutes like the CSIR, CDRI and the IDMR. Several of these public research institutes are also very active partners in international public–private partnerships (see Table 3.5).

Private firms, in contrast, had no culture of collaboration until a few years ago (see Gehl Sampath, 2005)[28] since they tended to compete for brand names in the local market where all products sold were generics. The survey captured an emergence of collaborative linkages in both drug research as well as product development. Many contract research collaborations exist between large pharmaceutical companies and smaller biotechnology firms (see Table 3.4 also in this context).

Table 3.4 shows the characteristics both of local collaborators and non-collaborators from the survey data. The two categories of firms mainly differ in their R&D behaviour. In other words, local collaborators on average have higher R&D intensity, and contract local and foreign R&D more frequently than non-collaborators. Furthermore, collaborators and non-collaborators slightly differ in new process development and patents applied for (in India, the US and the EU). As for the remaining characteristics explored in the table, there are no significant differences across the two types of firms. For instance, collaborators and non-collaborators are equally large and have a similar percentage of product innovators and exporters.

Table 3.5 shows the correlation matrix of the intensity of collaboration with key local institutions/partners. The binary variables take on the value of one if the intensity of collaboration is strong or very strong, and zero otherwise. The table suggests that the intensity of collaboration with PRIs is positively and significantly correlated with that of collaboration with the other institutions/partners, except industry association. Similarly, the intensity of collaboration with

Table 3.4 Characteristics of local collaborators and non-collaborators: mean of variables[1]

Variable	Local collaboration		
	No	Yes	p-value
New product development	0.400	0.559	0.305
New process development	0.267	0.559	0.059[†]
Patents	2.933	22.441	0.053[†]
Part of a group	0.267	0.353	0.553
Employment in 2007 (FTEs)	1357.267	1439.441	0.839
Export	0.867	0.794	0.546
R&D intensity in 2007	0.019	0.070	0.014*
R&D contract, local	0.000	0.676	0.000**
R&D contract, foreign	0.067	0.412	0.016*
Number of years established	22.867	21.500	0.806
Gvt-sponsored R&D	0.000	0.353	0.008
Gvt assistance	0.200	0.471	0.073
Number of firms	15	34	–

Source: author survey, 2008.

Notes
1 p-values of t and z-tests of equality of means are reported.
Significance levels: †: 10%; *: 5%; **: 1%.

universities is positively and significantly correlated with that of collaboration with the other previously mentioned institutions/partners, except hospitals. The remaining figures of Table 3.5 can be interpreted similarly.

Despite these encouraging results, there seems to be a need for more policies that foster public–private collaborations for product development and other emerging areas. Many firms interviewed had not collaborated with and were largely unenthusiastic on the question of collaboration with institutes in the public sector due to their lack of product development focus.

3.4.3 Rapid expansion of the local market for health care

Rising personal incomes,[29] changing disease profiles (with a larger share of global diseases within the country) and the increased privatization of health care (with a rise in specialized clinics, hospitals and treatment centres) are creating new market opportunities in second and third tier Indian cities and towns.[30] Although the local market is crowded, has too many small and medium sized firms and has had lower profit margins than what can be gained by entering regulated markets abroad up until now, the increase in local purchasing power along with the changing disease profile of Indians both amount to a lucrative market. The advantage of an expanding domestic market for a wide range of diseases, including global diseases, offers Indian firms a secure base to invest. Several firms are expressly focusing on mass therapies to be delivered through the improving infrastructure and distribution channels into rural India (field interviews).

3.4.4 Rising burden of disease

A vast majority of India's population of 1.1 billion (approximately 300 million) still lives below the poverty line and according to the WHO (2007), lower respiratory infections, TB, HIV/AIDS, diarrhoeal diseases and perinatal conditions are some of the largest causes of deaths in the country. At the same time, there is an increasing incidence of lifestyle and other diseases that are associated with

Table 3.5 Interrelationship between the intensity of collaboration, if local collaboration

	PRIs	Industry assoc.	Universities	Private labs	Doctors	Hospitals
PRIs	1.000	–	–	–	–	–
Industry Assoc.	0.120	1.000	–	–	–	–
Universities	0.471**	0.289†	1.000	–	–	–
Private Labs	0.359*	0.336†	0.310†	1.000	–	–
Doctors	0.412*	0.359*	0.354*	0.120	1.000	–
Hospitals	0.440**	0.195	0.274	0.188	0.566**	1.000

Source; author's survey, 2008.

Notes
Significance levels: †: 10%; *: 5%; **: 1%

industrialized countries in India (WHO, 2007; see table in Grace, 2005, p. 23) and the incidence of chronic diseases is forecasted to rise substantially by 2015 (Mckinsey, 2007). Coronary heart disease is expected to rise from 3.31 per cent in 2005 to 4.91 per cent in 2015, diabetes from 2.80 per cent in 2005 to 3.70 per cent in 2015, asthma from 2.5 per cent in 2005 to 2.70 per cent in 2015, obesity from 1.3 per cent in 2005 to 2.7 per cent in 2015 and cancer from 0.18 per cent in 2005 to 2 per cent in 2015 (ibid., p. 11). Changing disease portfolios of Indians, with an increase in global diseases is a trend in favour of the firms, since the prospect of an assured domestic market attenuates risk of failure in other international markets. India itself has the second highest number of people in the world living with HIV/AIDS, according to the National AIDS Control Organization (NACO) and the Joint UN Programme on HIV/AIDS and only 7 per cent of those people have access to treatment (EIU, 2007, p. 9; WHO, 2007). It is not clear from such statistics as to how much of this lack of access can be attributed directly to the lack of affordable drugs. Inefficiencies in health delivery mechanisms especially those related to drug distribution and procurement impact upon access in the country, and these are dealt with in detail in Chapter 7 of this book.

Focusing on health innovation from the supply side, Indian firms are actively engaged in health products that are cheap and are tailor-made to serve the masses in various disease segments. This *"bottom-of-the-pyramid"* model, which is based on the economies of scale of producing cheaper health alternatives for the masses in India and other latecomer countries elsewhere is a critical step in enhancing global and local access to medicines. It represents a different model of health innovation and access from that being observed in other latecomer countries, such as Brazil (see Box 3.4).

Box 3.4 Introduction of new drugs in Brazil

Recent work that compares the number of new drugs introduced in Brazil between 2000 and 2004 concluded that "the profile of the drugs launched in the Brazilian market does not reflect the country's specificities (geographical, socioeconomic, epidemiological) or the extent of its pharmaceutical market" (p. 38). More specifically, the study concluded that out of the 109 drugs launched in the local market between 2000 and 2004, most of them were used to treat non-infective diseases that generally characterize disease portfolios in developed countries, the rest were general anti-infectives for systemic use (19 drug in total), and antineoplastic and immunomodulating agents (16 in total). Furthermore, the study found that the number of new drugs launched in 2004 was roughly one-third that of 2000. Although the Brazilian government is the largest purchaser of medicines locally produced, there are numerous difficulties in setting public health priorities and enforcing them especially amongst the foreign companies whose sales dominate the local market. The study also found that in comparison to the situation in Brazil, higher numbers of drugs were being introduced in India on a regular basis. Whether this situation persists despite India's compliance with the TRIPS Agreement is still an issue that remains to be ascertained.

Source: Vidotti *et al.*, 2008

A very significant example of such a business model is the production of fixed dose and paediatric anti-retrovirals by Indian firms. Indian firms have been key players in creating fixed dose combinations (FDCs) of recommended first-line regimens, several of which were not available in the market by the originator companies since the early 2000s.[31] These fixed dose combinations are a key example of how Indian firms have been active in evolving new and disruptive forms of innovation in order to create products that are pro-poor by targeting to benefit mainly from the economies of scale involved. The same is true also in the case of paediatric FDCs. Table 3.6 contains a list of adult ARV FDCs that are presently available. Table 3.7 contains a list of paediatric FDCs presently available. Indian firms have created value added by creating paediatric ARVs for children in association with the Clinton Foundation for HIV/AIDS (CHAI),[32] prior to which there were no ready-to-use dosages for HIV-infected children. Both Tables 3.6 and 3.7 contain a list of first line and second line ARVs, with originator/patent holder firms, Indian generic manufacturers who are currently manufacturing the drugs and producers in the rest of the world for the same products. The tables map the global supply of all ARV fixed dose combinations and paediatric combinations, thereby showing the critically important role played by Indian firms in these two therapeutic segments.

Apart from the creation of such new models of innovation that are more bottom-of-the-pyramid oriented, active participation and supply of anti-retroviral and other public health drugs by Indian firms have been an extremely influential factor in the reduction of prices and continued supply of health products to the poor worldwide. These are discussed in Chapter 7 in detail.

3.5 Global pull factors: emerging challenges and policy responses

India's health innovation and pharmaceutical production capabilities were acquired mainly by denying strong IPP to international firms; granting IPRs and ensuring a smooth transition to a product patent regime as required by the TRIPS Agreement was a tumultuous challenge for the policy landscape. There has been and still continues to be intense public scrutiny (both locally and internationally) of the way India perceives and implements its international obligations in this regard. This section summarizes the current IPR landscape, data protection and international collaborations which are the key global pull factors impacting upon the Indian health innovation system in the present context.

3.5.1 India's IPR regime post-2005

Post-2005 policy on implementation of the TRIPS Agreement in India has been an effort to (a) maintain the *availability of drugs* (for local consumption and exports) *at low prices* and (b) to *minimize the impact* of the patent regime on the domestic industry. The Patent (Amendments) Act of 2005 contains some key provisions that lean in favour of public health. All pre-1995 patents do not qualify for protection in India and all products with patent priority dates between 1995 and 2005 can continue to be manufactured by generic firms despite grant of a patent in India, if the generic manufacturers already had a market approved version of the patented drug, in return for payment of "reasonable" royalties to the respective patent holder firms. The term "reasonable royalty" is not defined in the Act and therefore subject to interpretation. Section 3(d) of the Act that deals with the definition of patentability specifies that patents will not be granted automatically for different forms of the same molecules, such as salts, esters, polymorphs, and decisions will be taken case by case to establish novelty in an effort to prevent ever-greening of molecules. This and several other provisions are in place in the regime to ensure a mitigated impact of the TRIPS-compliant patent regime on local pharmaceutical firms.

There have been several patent disputes in local courts on issues of interpretation of section 3(d) and other provisions of the patent regime. The judgements decreed by the Indian courts help gauge the direction in which India's post-TRIPS regime is intended. India's policy vision and trends in implementation, although at times confusing, has been an effort by Indian policy makers to extract and retain flexibilities permitted within the TRIPS framework, in order to promote public health and the local firms.

One of the first cases post-2005 that challenged the stance of the regime on patentability was on the exclusive marketing right (EMR) granted to Novartis's Gleevec, an anti-cancer drug. The EMR on a beta crystalline version of the compound Imatinab Mesylate, was challenged by Indian generic producers of the drug challenged on grounds that the compound Imatinab Mesylate was a derivative of a molecule that was known prior to 1995, and therefore does not qualify for patent protection. At the time when the EMR was granted, several Indian companies were producing generic versions of Imatinab Mesylate, including, Cipla, Ranbaxy and Sun Pharmaceuticals. The EMR was withdrawn and Novartis was subsequently also refused a patent on Gleevec. In response, Novartis moved the Indian High Court challenging the constitutional validity of section 3(d) in the Indian Patent Act of 2005, claiming that such an interpretation is against the TRIPS Agreement.[33] The High Court in Madras issued a judgement in 2007, deeming Section 3(d) to be constitutional and not against the TRIPS Agreement.

The Gleevec case seems to set a precedent of sorts on what is patentable under the Indian patent regime. There are other, newer disputes on similar grounds: *Roche* v. *Cipla* (Tarceva I)[34] and *Roche et al.* v. *Cipla* (Tarceva II)[35] both help show some of the loopholes in the present system and the thin line walked on by the Indian judiciary to promote public health (see Gehl Sampath, 2008).

Table 3.6 Adult fixed dose combinations: patent holders and generic producers[1]

Adult fixed dose combinations

Fixed dose combination (FDC)[2]	Originator/patent holder	Generic producers India	Generic producers in the rest of the world
Abacavir+Lamivudine 600 mg+300 mg (ABC+3TC)	GlaxoSmithKline (UK)	Aurobindo, Cipla Ltd, Hetero Drugs	
Abacavir+Lamivudine+Zidovudine 300 mg+150 mg+300 mg (ABC+3TC+AZT)	GlaxoSmithKline (UK)	Matrix Laboratories, Ranbaxy, Aurobindo, Hetero Drugs	
Didanosine+Efavirenz+Lamivudine (ddI+EFV+3TC) 400 mg+600 mg+300 mg		Cipla Ltd	
Efavirenz+Emtricitabine+Tenofovir 600 mg+200 mg+300 mg (EFV+FTC+TDF)	Merck Sharp & Dohme (Canada; the Netherlands), Bristol Myers Squibb and Gilead Sciences International (Canada)	Matrix Laboratories, Cipla Ltd	
Efavirenz+Lamivudine+Stavudine 600 mg+150 mg+30 mg/40 mg (EFV+3TC+d4T)		Strides Acrolabs, Emcure, Ranbaxy	
Efavirenz+Lamivudine+Zidovudine 600 mg+150 mg+300 mg (EFV+3TC+AZT)		Ranbaxy, Strides Acrolabs, Aurobindo, Cipla Ltd, Emcure	
Emtricitabine+Tenofovir 200 mg+300 mg (FTC+TDF)	Gilead Sciences	Hetero Drugs, Strides Acrolabs	

Compound, strength (abbreviation)	Originator company	Generic manufacturers	
Lamivudine + Zidovudine 150 mg + 300 mg (3TC + AZT)	GlaxoSmithKline (UK), Pharmacare Ltd (South Africa)	Cipla Ltd, Hetero Drugs, Cadila Pharmaceuticals, Ranbaxy, Matrix Laboratories, Aurobindo, Strides Acrolabs, Emcure	Aspen Pharmacare (South Africa)
Lamivudine + Nevirapine + Zidovudine 150 mg + 200 mg + 300 mg (3TC + NVP + AZT)		Strides Acrolabs, Hetero Drugs Ltd	
Lamivudine + Stavudine 150 mg + 30 mg/40 mg (3TC + d4T)		Cipla Ltd, Ranbaxy, Strides Acrolabs, Aurobindo, Matrix Laboratories, Hetero Drugs, Emcure	
Lamivudine + Stavudine + Nevaripine 150 mg + 30 mg/40 mg + 200 mg (3TC + d4T + NVP)		Cipla Ltd, Ranbaxy, Hetero Drugs, Emcure, Aurobindo, Matrix Laboratories, Micro Labs, Strides Acrolabs, Emcure	Duopharma (Malaysia)
Lamivudine + Nevirapine + Zidovudine 150 mg + 200 mg + 300 mg (3TC + NVP + AZT)		Matrix Laboratories, Strides Acrolabs, Hetero Drugs, Cipla Ltd., Ranbaxy, Micro Labs, Aurobindo, Emcure	Aspen Pharmacare (South Africa), Apotex Inc (Canada)
Lopinavir + Ritonavir 133.3 mg + 33.3 mg/200 mg + 50 mg (LPV + r)	Abbot Laboratories (UK and USA, Germany)	Aurobindo, Matrix Laboratories, Ranbaxy, Cipla Ltd. Hetero Drugs, Strides Acrolabs, Emcure	

Notes
1 Data collected from each website of all Manufacturing Companies, The Global Fund, List of ARV Pharmaceutical Products Classified According to the Global Fund Quality Assurance Policy for Single and Limited Source Pharmaceutical Products, Edition 53, June 30, 2008; CHAI, Anti Retroviral Price List, April 2008; WHO Prequalification Programme, Manufacturers And Suppliers Whose HIV-Related Medicines Have Been Found Acceptable, In Principle, For Procurement By UN Agencies, 63rd Edition, February 2008.
2 This column contains the name of the compounds, their strengths, followed by their abbreviations in brackets.

Table 3.7 Paediatric fixed dose combinations: patent holder and generic producers[1]

Paediatric fixed dose combinations

Fixed dose combination[2]	*Patent holder firm*	*Generic producers India*	*Generic producers in the rest of the world*
Lamivudine(20 mg) + Stavudine (5 mg) + Nevirapine (35 mg)		Ranbaxy	
Lamivudine (40 mg) + Stavudine (10 mg) + Nevirapine (70 mg)		Ranbaxy	
Lamivudine (30 mg) + Stavudine (6 mg)		Cipla Ltd	
Lamivudine (60 mg) + Stavudine (12 mg)		Cipla Ltd	
Lamivudine (150 mg) + Stavudine (30 mg)		Cipla Ltd, Ranbaxy, Strides Acrolabs Ltd, Aurobindo, Matrix Laboratories, Hetero Drugs	
Lamivudine (30 mg) + Stavudine (6 mg) + Nevirapine (50 mg)		Cipla Ltd	
Lamivudine (60 mg) + Stavudine (12 mg) + Nevirapine (100 mg)		Cipla Ltd	
Lamivudine (150 mg) + Stavudine (5 mg) + Nevirapine (35 mg) tablet for oral suspension		Ranbaxy	
Lamivudine (150 mg) + Stavudine (10 mg) + Nevirapine (70 mg) tablet for oral suspension		Ranbaxy	
Lamivudine (20 mg) + Stavudine (5 mg)		Ranbaxy	
Lamivudine (40 mg) + Stavudine (10 mg)		Ranbaxy	

Notes
1 Source: same as Note 38.
2 This column contains the name of the compounds, their strengths, followed by their abbreviations in brackets.

Box 3.5 The Tarceva patent dispute

The Indian Patent Office granted a patent on the lung cancer drug, Ertlonib to Roche (brand name Tarceva) in early 2008, around which time Cipla received marketing approval for marketing a generics version of the drug from the Drug Controller's office. Cipla had made no pre-grant or post-grant opposition to Roche's patent, but having received the market approval, it went ahead and launched the drug explicitly violating the product patent on Tarseva that had been granted to Roche. At the same time, another drug company, Natco (which had made a pre-grant opposition to Etrolonib that had been rejected by the Patent Office) applied for a compulsory licence to sell the drug in Nepal (a least developed country).

Roche approached the Delhi High Court requesting the grant of an injunction stopping Cipla from marketing the product. The Delhi High Court, while denying an injunction on 18 March 2008, based the decision on three grounds:

a   the presence of a prima facie case for the plaintiffs (Roche);
b   balance of convenience, which in the court's view shifts to Cipla because it is manufacturing locally;
c   and the degree of hardship (in terms of the price difference between the patented drug and the generics version) that will be shifted to consumers in case Roche is granted an injunction.

Cipla was asked to keep account of its sales of the drug in case it was required to pay royalty to Roche in the event that the latter won the case. The judgement also restrained Cipla from exporting Erlocip (Cipla's brand name) to countries where Roche has a registered patent on the drug during the pendency of the appeal.

Roche appealed against the injunction granted and the Delhi High Court decreed the following on 24 April 2009. Section 3(d) sets a standard of known obviousness as a precondition of patentability. The court also found that the plaintiff ought to have been refused an injunction for their failure to make a prima facie case, which was not the view held in the earlier decision of 18 March 2008. It also held that Cipla had held a credible challenge to the validity of the patent held by Roche.

Source: Copies of the judgements in the two cases; Personal communication with Deepali Talvar, Director Legal Services, Pfizer; the OPPI Representatives and Chan Park of the Lawyers Collective

---

Local firms have also been keen to challenge firms and their patents in international markets. There are newer cases of challenging patents and settlements outside the court (Sun Pharma), which reveal the firms' increasing know-how of in-country procedures in regulated markets like the USA.

3.5.2 *India's proposed data protection regime*

According to Article 39(3) of the TRIPS Agreement, member countries are under an obligation to provide protection to regulatory data submitted for receiving market approval of pharmaceutical products under specific circumstances.

The government of India constituted an expert committee in order to deal with the steps that need to be taken to comply with Article 39(3) of the TRIPS Agreement. The report (also known as the Reddy Committee Report) submitted in May 2007 acknowledges that: (a) data protection is relevant for any product at the stage of market approval, whether or not it is patent protected, (b) it is a protection provided in return of submission of proprietary test data required for market approval and (c) it protects against unfair commercial use and disclosure.

The Committee Report dealt with the issue of data protection for pharmaceuticals and agrochemicals separately suggesting different forms of protection for each of the categories. In the context of pharmaceuticals, the committee concluded that the present legal regime was probably not adequate to address issues on data protection with respect to Article 39.3, and that the Drugs and Cosmetics Act needed to have clearer legal mechanisms to ensure that undisclosed test data was not put to unfair commercial use within India. The Committee concluded that there was a need to improve the system and make necessary legal changes and explicitly provided for the minimum requirements under Article 39.3 of TRIPS.

The Report called for a two-stage approach to data protection for all new chemical entities:[36] a transition stage and a data exclusivity regime to be enacted at the end of the transition stage. In the transition stage, the Report recommended that test data that companies sought to protect could be protected through trade secrets. During this stage, the Drug Regulator of India would continue to be the central body in charge of market approval of drugs, and companies that wished to protect their data could specifically request for protection of the said data as trade secrets. The report provided that in case the data that were supposed to be protected as trade secrets were leaked out, the company in question could receive damages for trade secret violation.

It provides a model of data protection (of five years in duration) to be applied at the end of the transition period. This model of data protection incorporates several features that are meant to make it more public health centred. The main features of the post-transition model of data protection as recommended by the Report are:

a   the test data will not be relied upon by the drug regulator for second or subsequent market approvals;
b   the protection applies with prospective effect only, for all molecules discovered after 1 January 1995;
c   in case of a patented drug, the data protection should not go beyond the term of protection of the patent, failing which it will lead to extension of market exclusivity to the patent holder;
d   the period of protection will be counted from the date of first marketing approval granted anywhere in the world in order to ensure that companies market their new drug in India at the earliest in case they wish to receive data protection for their product;

e   data protection provisions will be over-ridden by all provisions in the Indian Patent Regime on compulsory licensing (sections 84 to 92 A) and Section 107 which provides for the Bolar Exception in order to ensure public health;

f   date protection provisions can be waived by the government of India at any point of time due to any public health emergency;

g   during a public health emergency, the government can rely on data provided by the proprietary firm to grant market approval to any other firm;

h   the government of India reserves the right to control the prices of the drugs under data protection.

The provision of data protection to any firm in India should not restrain manufacture of generic versions (not approved) for export to other countries that do not have data protection for the product in question, or where the data protection for the product in question has expired.

The Reddy committee report is another effort by the Indian government to balance its obligations under the TRIPS Agreement with public health. The Report leaves the length of the proposed transition period in the open (it could extend to anything from five or ten years). Even after the end of the transition period, it recommends that higher standards of data protection should be provided only after careful assessment "of its impact on the sector and public to avoid any adverse repercussions in the long run".

Whereas the post-transition model has incorporated several safeguards in the interest of fastest introduction of generics, and public health (features (b) to (h) above), it still remains unclear why the report concluded that India needs a new system of data exclusivity. India has not had a very reliable system of test data submitted for marketing approval of products, and earlier studies of the sector have shown that domestic firms have relied on access to the data in order to be able to reverse engineer quickly and cost effectively.[37] That said there seem to be sufficient legal mechanisms in place to strengthen protection of test data, without having to provide a data exclusivity term of five years in order to comply with Article 39(3) of the TRIPS Agreement. In common law (on which the Indian legal system is based), unfair commercial use is a remediable ground. Furthermore, trade secret protection, which was earlier on a weaker form of protection under the Law of Torts and Contracts in India (as the report also notes) has been elevated to the status of an IP category under the TRIPS Agreement. Thus, strengthening the existing regulatory mechanism for data protection within the country and relying on trade secrets seems to be sufficient to comply with the requirements of Article 39(3) of the TRIPS Agreement.

Most importantly, the challenge of the Reddy Committee Report remains its holistic enactment as India's data exclusivity regime after the completion of the transition stage. In other words, several provisions remain key to ensure that the data exclusivity regime will not run against the interest of the local pharmaceutical sector and public health. Specifically, the clauses that state that in the case of a patented drug, the data protection should not go beyond the term of protection of the patent and that the period of protection will be counted from the date of first marketing approval granted anywhere in the world are very important safeguards.

As a hypothetical exercise, if India presently had a data exclusivity regime that provided only five years of protection as stipulated by the Reddy Report, but did not contain the provision that it should be from the date of first marketing approval granted anywhere in the world, then the Tarceva case (Box 3.5) would look very different. The producer could have obtained five years' protection of their data under the data exclusivity regime. In such a case, regardless of whether the patents on the products were valid under the Indian patent regime, companies will not be able to obtain marketing approval for generic versions of these products, unless they repeat clinical trials. This would be expensive, ethically dubious and cause undue delays in generic entry.

3.5.3 International acquisitions and knowledge partnerships

Most local firms surveyed reported tacit know-how gains of participating in global value chains, which included manpower exchange and learning on conducting health R&D programmes and marketing skills. In the past few years, especially 2004 onwards, local firms have been engaged in a spate of acquisitions and takeovers that were aimed at entry into newer markets (especially the USA), entry into newer innovation segments (including biologics) and expansion of contract research options. These are listed in Table 3.8.

Examples of acquisitions and expansions to enter new markets. Indian firms made 18 international acquisitions between January 2004 and October 2005, including Matrix Labs' acquisition of Belgium's Docpharma for $263 million in June 2005, Dr. Reddy's acquisition of Roche's API business for $59.6 million, Ranbaxy's acquisition of a 40 per cent stake in Japan's Nihon Pharmaceutical Industry, and Sun Pharma's completion of its purchase of ICN Hungary for an undisclosed sum (see also KPMG, 2006). In 2006, Ranbaxy acquired a South African generics company, Be-Tabs, apart from Ethimed (Belgium), Therapia (Romania) and Mundogen (Spain) (EIU, 2007, p. 11). In 2006, Dr. Reddy's bought out Germany's fourth-largest generics company, Betapharm Arzneimittel, from UK based 3i for $573.6 million, which was the biggest acquisition seen in the sector until then. In March 2007, Ranbaxy and Cipla pulled out of bidding for the generic-drug unit of a Merck (EIU, 2007, p. 12).

Table 3.8 Collaborative and competitive strategies in Indian pharma

Collaborative strategies	Competitive strategies
• Out-licensing research • Out-licensing of discovery services • Co-marketing alliances for the local market • Co-production and co-marketing alliances in international markets • Contract research	• Generics products in regulated markets • New chemical entity research • Patent disputes in national and international courts • Aggressive international acquisitions to enter new markets and to expand into newer areas of research

Source: author.

Examples of acquisitions and expansions to enter newer segments. This includes Nicholas Piramal's acquisition of Avecia Custom Drug Synthesis of the UK for $16.7 million in 2005 and Jubilant Organosys acquired Hollister-Stier Laboratories (US) in May 2007 (ibid.). Wockhardt acquired the Wallis Laboratory (1997) and CP Pharmaceuticals (2003) based in the UK, and Esparma, Germany in 2004 for its biopharmaceutical work.

Example of acquisitions to expand contract research. Jubilant Organosys acquired Target Research Associates plus 64 per cent of Trinity Laboratories and its wholly owned subsidary Trigen Labs, in the USA in 2005. Bilcare Ltd acquired Preclinical Inc., its first manufacturing facility in the United States in 2005.

3.6 Chinese health innovation capacity: a point of comparison?

The Chinese health innovation system is fast evolving with a wide local pharmaceutical base (that runs into thousands of local companies) and biotechnology firms that perform genomics, systems biology and stem cell technologies based research. It is estimated that the Chinese health biotechnology market grew 30 per cent annually between 2000 and 2005 to a total worth of US$3 billion (Frew *et al.*, 2008). China and India have several points of similarity in their health innovation capabilities that are worth noting. First, both countries did not enforce the TRIPS Agreement until recently (China in 2001 and India in 2005). Second, both countries have a very strong local pharmaceutical sector with similar innovation outputs: the Chinese pharmaceutical sector is also actively involved in production of generic drugs, novel drug development and contract manufacturing. India and China jointly account for over 40 per cent of global pharmaceutical outsourcing presently (EIU, 2007) and this figure is set to rise in the coming years. Both countries have each a billion-size pharmaceutical market with a large number of poor people.

The differences however are becoming increasingly relevant. China, more generally and specifically in health innovation spends a much higher amount on R&D than India. There has been a steady increase of R&D expenditure in China by approximately 24 per cent per annum since 1999, and the R&D/GDP ratio has more than doubled in a decade in China, reaching 1.34 per cent in 2005 (UNCTAD, 2006a). Most health innovation R&D in China is conducted by government owned firms, and this ensures collaboration between universities, public sector institutes and firms. Frew *et al.* (2008) for instance, find that most companies they interviewed were intent on commercializing the research results of the local research institutes. These are points of variation when one considers the Indian story. Not only is the government's R&D investment much smaller in India as a whole and in health innovation in particular, R&D of relevance to the private sector enterprise in health innovation has been dwindling over the past decade. The CSIR and its institutions have been criticized for not developing technologies of commercial relevance to be used for health innovation (Abrol, 2007).

A final point of comparison where India seems to be lagging behind is policy coherence. The Chinese government has set in motion a well-structured policy apparatus to deal with the issues confronting its health innovation system, namely, insufficient pools of talent, lack of frontier R&D, low R&D investment from private entrepreneurs and a relatively unequipped legal system (Chen *et al.*, 2007). The policy changes include the creation of a National Biotech Leadership Committee in 2004 which will undertake the building up of sound research funding, recruit Chinese talent from abroad and establish standards of production and research for the biotechnology sector as well as help establish productive international collaborations (ibid.). Although the same shortcomings hinder India's health innovation performance and although several policy initiatives have been put in place to help private enterprise, Indian policy apparatus generally lacks the kind of policy coherence evident in China's economic performance.[38]

3.7 Summing up

This chapter has analysed India's health innovation, which is widely believed to be a forerunner of innovation capacity in this sector using empirical data from 2007–2008. The chapter identifies India's policy vision and institutional investments to be a critical factor that not only helped build capacity in the sector, but one that has also sustained the local firms' competitiveness after India's full-scale compliance with the TRIPS Agreement. Other factors that help the sector to perform well are the availability of skilled human capital, supportive knowledge infrastructure as well as newer opportunities at the global and national fronts. Globally, the restructuring of health innovation and the cost-cutting pressures for the "big pharma" have translated into a wide array of collaborative opportunities for Indian firms to gain a stronger foothold in international global value chains. At the same time, the large domestic markets and the newer health care inroads being made into rural India and associated economic returns promise the firms a sustainable market at home.

4 Health innovation systems in Bangladesh and Vietnam

4.1 Introduction

In this chapter, health innovation capacity in two countries that rank relatively low in terms of both knowledge capacity and institutions are compared. Bangladesh has a "least developed country" status as a result of which it is not obliged to implement the provisions of the TRIPS Agreement on pharmaceutical patenting until 2016. Bangladesh has extensive capacity in health innovation, especially as related to production of generic drugs whereas Vietnam has also been successful in several aspects of health innovation. This chapter presents the results of empirical investigations into health innovation systems conducted in the two countries in 2006 and 2007.

In the sectoral systems survey in Bangladesh, 130 questionnaires were administered to firms, universities and public research institutes active in biomedical research and hospitals in 2007. Face-to-face interviews conducted with a cross-section of firms, as well as a variety of other actors, such as professional associations and agencies and the concerned government departments. A total of 68 persons (including CEOs, top level management and government officials) were interviewed for the study. This information was updated once again in 2010 through interviews with key sector actors. The survey in Vietnam followed a similar format and was conducted in 2007. The information and analysis both draw from the field surveys. While Bangladesh's capacity is discussed in the first few sections, the results of the survey in Vietnam are presented in order to contrast the results.

4.2 Key actors in health innovation in Bangladesh

Similar to India, private firms play a major role in health innovation in Bangladesh, although this has evolved over a period of time since the Drug Control Ordinance of 1982. The other actors – universities and public research institutes, public and private health providers, teaching hospitals and governmental agencies – are all discussed here.

4.2.1 Pharmaceutical firms

The companies include specialized multinational companies, local large companies with international links and smaller local companies. Out of the 237 registered companies, only around 150 are estimated to be in a functional state. The Bangladesh Association of Pharmaceutical Industries (BAPI) is the main professional association for the sector, and has 150 member companies that lobby the government for policy changes, among other activities. Square Pharmaceuticals is the largest firm in the market for many years now, and is followed closely by Beximco, Incepta, ACME and Eskayef (IMS, 2006). Other firms in the top ten bracket include Aristopharma, General, Healthcare Pharma, Novartis and Drug International (ibid.).

4.2.2 Universities and public research institutes

Research of relevance to health innovation is carried out in universities (mainly public) related to pharmaceutical biotechnology, but they are mostly for academic reasons than for direct practical production purposes. The standard of education and quality of research (if any) in the private universities in health innovation is low. But because there is a growing demand for chemists, pharmacists and the like, more and more private universities have introduced courses of relevance to health. In the public sector, there are 13 governmental medical colleges, two institutes for health technology, six post-graduate institutes, three specialized institutes and five medical assistant training colleges in Bangladesh, all meant to impart training of relevance to both the pharmaceutical and health sector (Osman, 2004). Apart from these public universities, Bangladesh has recently seen the mushrooming of several private universities, like BRAC University, North-South University, Stanford University.

There are also public sector specialized research institutions on health innovation in general and biotechnology. Prominent amongst these are the Institute of Diseases of the Chest and Hospital (IDCH), Centre for Industrial and Scientific Research Bangladesh (BCSIR), Infectious Disease Hospital (IDH), Institute of Public Health (IPH) and the Cholera Research Laboratory (all established in Dhaka in the 1970s), and the National Institute for Cardiovascular Diseases (NICVD), the National Institute for Ophthalmology, and the National Institute of Preventive and Social Medicine (NIPSOM) (established in the 1980s). The Cholera Research Laboratory transformed over time into the Cholera Hospital and then into the International Centre for Diarrhoeal Diseases Research, Bangladesh (ICDDRB), which now is one of the most important nodes of health research, training and service delivery in the country. Around this period, the Bangladesh Institute of Research on Diabetic and Metabolic Disorders (BIRDEM) Hospital of the Diabetic Association was also set up.

4.2.3 Governmental agencies

The Ministry of Health and Family Welfare (MHFW) of course is one of the most important actors in the health innovation system. However, the key department through which it oversees its activities in the area of health innovation are grossly under resourced and lacks organizational competence. The Directorate of Drug Administration (DDA) is the key actor, but is equipped with only two laboratory facilities, meant to check quality and efficacy of all drugs introduced in the local market.

4.2.4 Health centres and hospitals

NGOs and special health programmes. Different special health programmes sponsored by the government and donor agencies often use NGOs as key intermediaries and social mobilizers. Some of these agencies have innovated approaches and products in health service delivery in the country. For example, the ICDDRB and BRAC's contribution in finding a popular solution (oral rehydration technology) to the problem of diarrhoeal diseases has set an international standard. NGO-established and run health centres are a major source of health care in rural and urban Bangladesh.

4.2.5 Alternative medicine providers

Although, the Drug Ordinance of 1982 expressed intentions in bringing Ayurvedic, Unanic and Homeopathic medicines under the controlling umbrella of the Drug Administration, nothing seems to have moved so far. These medicines are small competitors to the modern pharmaceutical industry. In other countries (e.g. South East Asian countries, China and India) the linkage between the two broad schools of medicines has now been very close. They complement each other in many different ways. But in Bangladesh there is very little linkage between them. As a result, both are losing the benefit of knowledge and experience gained by each of them. One limitation of the Alternative Medicines is the lack of publications on their work, research findings and products. There is also a serious shortage of research studies and relevant literature in this field of medicine (Ullah and Muhammed, 2002). While the allopathic system of medicine and the pharmaceutical sector in Bangladesh is flourishing very fast under global competition, the Ayurvedic and Unani medicines are struggling to survive due lack of patronage, support and innovations. With a thoughtful and scientific approach, it can actually learn a lot from the allopathic pharmaceutical sector and play a complementary role in the public health care system.

4.3 Current strengths in health innovation in Bangladesh

Bangladesh exports a wide range of pharmaceutical products (therapeutic class and dosage forms) to 67 countries.[1] The Drug Control Ordinance of 1982 placed a ceiling on selling imported drugs in the local market promoted self-reliance in its pharmaceutical sector, prior to which the local manufacturing catered to only 20 per cent of the total needs. Local exports have risen from US$0.04 million in 1985 to US$27.54 million in 2006 (Export Promotion Bureau, 2006). As opposed to relying on foreign companies for 75 per cent of their drug supply prior to the Ordinance, local firms now cater to 82 per cent of the markets, whereas subsidiaries of MNCs supply 13 per cent of the market and 5 per cent of the drugs are imported (ibid.).

Approximately 450 generic drugs, in 5300 registered brands having 8300 different presentations of dosage forms and strengths are manufactured by 237 registered companies (including five multinationals) in the sector. The local companies produce a wide range of products that include anti-ulcerants, flouroquinolones, anti-rheumatic non-steroid drugs, non-narcotic analgesics, anti-histamines and oral anti-diabetic drugs. The survey shows that many of the bigger firms are now venturing into the production of anti-cancer drugs, anti-retroviral drugs for the treatment of HIV/AIDS[2] and anti-Bird Flu drugs. The local market is extremely concentrated with the top ten firms catering to about 70 per cent of the market and only two companies, Beximco and Square, hold 25 per cent of the entire market (Chowdhury *et al.*, 2006). This also points out to the extreme disparities in firm sizes and capabilities, as far as innovation as well as marketing capabilities is concerned.

A major limitation of the innovation process is that the local pharmaceutical firms in Bangladesh are mainly engaged in formulation of APIs requiring manufacturing skills only, and are presently struggling to build capacity in the more knowledge intensive processes of reverse engineering APIs. The few firms in Bangladesh that are presently producing APIs locally are only able to perform the last few steps in the process with help from technologies bought from Indian firms.[3] Square Pharmaceuticals, which is the largest local firm, lists the following 13 APIs as its mainstay: Amoxycillin Trihydrate (both Compacted and Micronized) BP/USP, Amoxycillin Trihydrate (Micronized) BP/USP, Cloxacillin Sodium (Compacted and Micronized), Cloxacillin Sodium (Micronized) BP/USP, Paracetamol BP/USP, Diclofenac Sodium BP/USP, Diclofenac Di Ethyl Amine BP, Diclofenac Potassium BP, Diclofenac INN (Free Acid), Flucloxacillin Sodium (Compacted and Micronized) BP, Cephalexin Monohydrate (Compacted and Micronized) BP/USP.[4] Beximco, another major local pharmaceutical company, has two top-selling brands – Neoceptin R (Ranitidine) and Napa (Paracetamol) in the local market.[5] Formulation activities are carried out in most indigenous firms and a small percentage of subsidiaries of international firms that operate in the market, and both groups were captured by the survey.

The lack of reverse engineering capabilities amongst the pharmaceutical firms was confirmed through observed R&D investments over 2000–2005 as captured by the survey. The survey shows that there was not much difference in the amounts invested in R&D between the pharmaceutical firms, and those in agro-processing and textiles and garments (about 1 per cent). At a first glance, this seems to be a surprising result, since it implies that R&D and innovations are not (statistically and significantly) correlated with one another in the pharmaceutical sector in Bangladesh, although generally speaking the pharmaceutical sector is very technologically intensive and far more innovative in terms of new product/ process innovations when compared to low technology sectors such as textiles and agro-processing (Gehl Sampath, 2007b). But in the context of latecomer countries, it confirms the extensive relationship between firms and the knowledge systems they are entrenched in. The difficult state of the domestic knowledge system in the country (see UNCTAD, 2006b, Chapter 6), forces firms operating in what is normally a high-technology sector to focus on manufacturing and excludes the more knowledge intensive activities from their reach. This lack of capacity to locally produce APIs reduces the competitiveness of the firms enormously, since between 30 and 50 per cent of the production price of the drugs is taken over by the expenses of securing APIs from external sources (Gehl Sampath, 2008; also see Chapter 7).

4.4 Local push factors and their role in shaping health innovation

The top local firms (around six in total) are trying to secure skills and scientific infrastructure in order to venture into API production and reverse engineering. However, they are stifled by lack of adequate scientific and physical infrastructure. Lacking scientific infrastructure includes missing human resources as well as the incapacity of local PRIs and universities in assisting the firms in developing these chemical synthesis skills due to under-funding of research, disillusion of scientists and researchers and lack of a cogent focus amongst core university faculties that do work on medical sciences. While there has been progress and the pharmaceutical sector is recognized as a priority sector in Bangladesh, certain important developments – such as the government's plan to provide a common API park to support the firm level endeavours to locally produce APIs, is yet to materialize. Interviews conducted in 2010 reveal that several firms are discouraged by this delay in the establishment of key industry services.

This disarticulation between various components of the domestic knowledge systems illustrates a prevailing phenomenon that prevents effective learning and absorption by the enterprise sector in most latecomer countries, as the analysis in Chapters 5 and 6 further confirm. Most exporting firms in the survey pointed out cheap labour costs as their main advantage in the international markets, but even the biggest firms like Square Pharmaceuticals were sceptical about whether they could capture markets in other African and Asian countries on the basis of just cheap labour when they did not possess the economies of scale and reverse engineering skills on par with their Indian counterparts (field interviews).

Apart from this, a range of factors, including lack of common industry infrastructure, lack of capabilities to conduct bioequivalence tests in the country and the lack of biotechnological capabilities to branch out into emerging options such as biogenerics, all curb their innovative capacity. The top firms (that also export) are keen on diversifying exports between regulated and unregulated markets, since sales from regulated markets can be huge once the initial hurdles of market entry are countered. Square Pharmaceuticals, for example, has invested huge sums in setting up production facilities that meet exporting requirements to the UK (and planning to expand to the USA too) just outside

Dhaka. The absence of infrastructure support to conduct bioequivalence tests and the lack of biotechnological capabilities pose big barriers to such firms seeking to branch out into emerging options such as bio generics or focus on exporting to regulated markets. All these factors and their impact on innovative capacity are discussed in detail here.

4.4.1 Disarticulation within the local health innovation system

The gradual transition from manufacture to knowledge intensive reverse engineering skills in the local sector assumed the availability of human skills and scientific and physical infrastructure. Specifically in the context of health innovation, the survey reveals that the disarticulation between university and public sector research and the enterprise sector is very strong, and one of the largest impediments to building API skills.

Bangladesh has very weak knowledge infrastructure as measured by R&D investments as percentage of GDP, centres of excellence for basic and applied research in both the public and private sectors of the economy, and scientists and researchers per million of the population. Bangladesh' success in terms of near-universal primary school enrolment (World Bank, 2005b), does not extend to secondary and tertiary education. There is a drastic drop in enrolment rates from primary to secondary and tertiary education, which draws a bleak picture of the human skills available in the country with severe repercussions for innovative capacity, a result that was corroborated by data collected in the survey. There are no data available on researchers involved in R&D and data on R&D expenditure for the country are also not available since 2003. However, UNCTAD (2006b) notes, the gross expenditure on R&D in 2003 was 0.2 per cent of GDP in all least developed countries (about ten times less than in developed countries) and the number of researchers and scientists engaged in R&D activities per million population in 2003 was 2 per cent of the level observed in developed countries.

Available university education of relevance to the pharmaceutical and health sector in Bangladesh can mainly be divided into three fields: medical education, nutrition and biochemistry and pharmacy education. Among the government provided public university faculties, Dhaka University is highly reputed with very established departments that deal with pharmaceutical sciences followed by others such as Jehangir Nagar University. BRAC University's School of Public Health, a private university, is also gradually gaining considerable reputation.

Despite the presence of numerous R&D institutions that are mandated to conduct research on various aspects of health innovation as discussed in the previous section, very low levels of collaboration between firms and public sector institutions involved in R&D, teaching and delivery of health services is observed in Bangladesh. Table 4.1 shows the observable patterns of product and process innovations in Bangladesh's health innovation based on survey data. These patterns of innovation amongst firms and public sector actors are quite different from what one would expect. More specifically, almost no universities and public research institutes and no hospitals are involved in new product development (4.65 per cent

Table 4.1 Observable patterns of product and process innovations in Bangladesh

New product development	New process development												
	Universities/PRIs			Firms			Hospitals			All			
	No	Yes	Total	No	Yes	Total	No	Yes	Total	No	Yes	Total	
No	39	2	41	2	0	2	48	1	49	89	3	92	
%	90.70	4.65	95.35	4.44	0	4.44	96	2	98	64.49	2.17	66.67	
Yes	1	1	2	29	14	43	1	0	1	31	15	46	
%	2.33	2.33	4.65	64.44	31.11	95.56	2	0	2	22.46	10.87	33.33	
Total	40	9	43	31	14	45	49	1	50	120	18	138	
%	93.02	6.98	100	68.89	31.11	100	98	2	100	86.96	13.04	100	

Source: author's survey, 2006–2007.

and 2 per cent respectively) and new process development activities (6.98 per cent and 2 per cent respectively). Furthermore, a very small percentage of universities and public research institutes (2.33 per cent) and none of the hospitals are involved in both product and process development. As for the pharmaceutical firms, a majority of them (95.56 per cent) are involved in new product development. While the percentage of firms involved in new process development is much higher than universities/public research institutes and hospitals, it is much lower (31.11 per cent) than that of firms involved in new product development. When the sector is taken as a whole, only 33.33 per cent of all actors are involved in new product development, 13.04 per cent are involved in new process development and 10.87 per cent are involved in both, when "new" was defined as new to the firm and the organization in keeping with the framework.

Table 4.2 shows collaboration intensities of universities and PRIs, firms and hospitals with all other counterparts in the pharmaceutical innovation system, namely, industrial associations, medical practitioners, NGOs, governmental agencies, among others. The figures in the table present the mean of rankings between 1 (least important) and 5 (most important). Thus, any ranking above 2.5 would represent moderate collaborative efforts between any two sets of actors. The rankings in the table reveal again that there is very little collaboration between different actors in the system as far as innovation is concerned. Firms tend to collaborate strongly with private laboratories and medical practitioners (for sale of their products, see discussion in section 4.4.3), and moderately with industrial associations and governmental agencies (for lobbying). Similarly, universities tend to collaborate strongly with other universities and moderately with medical practitioners and governmental agencies.

Normally, one would expect to see strong collaborations between public sector institutions (who conduct primary and applied research of relevance) and firms (for product development), as well as interactions with other actors such as hospitals (for supply) and governmental agencies (for infrastructure support).

In Bangladesh, there are several reasons for the disarticulation between public sector research and pharmaceutical product development as well as the skewed patterns of collaboration. To begin with, university and research in PRIs is

Table 4.2 Collaboration patterns in the health innovation system in Bangladesh

Collaboration intensity with . . .	*Universities/PRIs*	*Firms*	*Hospitals*
Public research institutes	2.348	1.067	1.440
Industrial associations	–	2.535	1.100
Universities	3.027	1.758	1.700
Private laboratories	2.304	3.796	1.600
Hospitals and medical practitioners	2.790	4.066	2.640
Other firms	1.835	1.935	–
NGOs	1.837	1.510	–
Government agencies	2.736	2.555	–

Source: author's survey, 2006–2007.

grossly under-funded. The government allots only 12 crore takas (equivalent to US$1.75 million) for public sector research for the entire country (as of 2007, which has not seen a big increase as of 2010) which are to be shared amongst universities, PRIs, NGOs and all other public sector institutions. The status of research even under the premier university departments and PRIs is not sufficiently supportive towards developing local API skills. There is a lack of university courses that are tailor-made to produce chemistry based skills of the kind required to reverse engineer and build capacity for health innovation. Additionally, lack of funding and focus are major handicaps for all the universities. The laboratory facilities in disciplines such as pharmaceutical sciences and biotechnology research, which are being taught in several public and private universities, are also not enough to create human skills that can be directly deployed by the industry. Whereas several universities are only now creating courses for both these disciplines (which implies that it will take several years for competent streams of manpower to develop), the curriculum and quality of the courses also need to be assessed. There are no official rankings available of the quality of academic courses in the universities within the country, and the procedures for accreditation of courses for newer universities need monitoring.[6] Most firms surveyed complained that they had to train graduates in aspects of clinical pharmacy for a year after they are employed (field interviews) since university graduates are not geared for clinical work in firms.

4.4.2 Lack of GMP standards and bioequivalence facilities

Presently, there is no law prescribing GMP standards for the pharmaceutical drugs that are sold in the local market. Around six of the big firms are in the process of receiving GMP certification, and Square Pharmaceuticals received regulatory approval from the British authorities earlier this year.[7] The Drug Policy of 2005 states in its objectives that the sector requires the enactment of good manufacturing standards in order to promote safety and efficacy of drugs for the local market. There is a need to enact rules that promote this objective in order to boost the export of pharmaceutical products, as well as to ensure safe and efficacious access to medicines in the local market.[8]

Lack of facilities within the country to conduct bioequivalence tests means that even the biggest firms like Square Pharmaceuticals have to outsource their products to bioequivalence laboratories in countries like Malaysia (field interviews). In addition, the country does not have any good laboratory facilities for biotechnology based work, which is another big hindrance to the bigger firms seeking to diversify their exports to the regulated and semi-regulated markets worldwide.

4.4.3 Nexus between innovations and health delivery and misallocation of human skills

There is a relatively large mismatch amongst the qualifications of personnel as well as facilities available to enable them to perform in the various organizations and several of these accrue from the (dis)incentives to various actors in the local pharmaceutical sector. Aspects of the health sector in the country, especially those related to drug procurement and sales, interact perversely with pharmaceutical production incentives and contribute to low competitiveness of the firms. Since local firms mainly engage in formulation activities, quality control and quality assurance personnel are in large demand. The country produces a large number of qualified pharmacists most of whom are absorbed by the pharmaceutical firms, and employed for quality assurance and quality control activities for the manufacture of drugs. As a result, most pharmacies in the country are run by pharmacy owners, or personnel who have very little professional training (field interviews).

Furthermore, the internal market is characterized by branded competition: each product essentially a generic, competing on the basis of brand names. In the absence of control mechanisms that check for GMP standards and bioequivalence of drugs marketed locally, the drug distribution system is organized solely around pharmacies (run by unqualified or inadequately qualified personnel) and doctors. This offers ample scope for the sale of low quality drugs at high prices, with firms relying solely on extensive distribution systems that promote their brand name products through medical practitioners, often in unethical ways. This is the reason for the skewed patterns of collaboration observed in Table 4.2: firms tend to collaborate very highly with medical practitioners for distribution of their products. Also, drug supplies both through institutional and private pharmacies proceed through suppliers and retailers in a market that is not well regulated, and offers ample scope for price-fixing and other anti-competitive practices (World Bank Indicators, 2007).

Table 4.3 shows, for each group (firms, universities and PRIs and hospitals) and for the whole sector, descriptive statistics of the key actors that are expected to carry out innovation empirically. It lends strength to the analysis on incentives of actors and the performance of the local innovation system. The table shows that employment in 2005 is much larger on average in pharmaceutical firms than in universities/PRIs and hospitals, which confirms again the dismal state of research infrastructure as well as supply-side institutions to provide medical services in the country. Similarly, pharmaceutical firms are much older on average than university departments/PRIs and hospitals, the last two groups being equally old on average. The division of skilled labour amongst these various organizations (universities, PRIs, firms and hospitals) as captured by the survey and presented in Table 4.3 is very important in explaining several of the innovative patterns in the sector presently and call for a closer look. The largest percentage of R&D performers in any year of the period 2001–2005 is found in pharmaceutical firms (82 per cent) and the smallest one is found in hospitals (10 per cent). The pharmaceutical firms, who are the largest R&D performers in the system, have the largest share of personnel with bachelors degrees. This again is an indicator of the kinds of innovation the firms are engaged in. The R&D personnel in 2005 are the largest in universities/PRIs (with the largest share of staff with PhD degrees), which have hardly any funds to support their activities.

Table 4.3 Descriptive statistics: key actors of innovation in Bangladesh

Variable	Universities/PRIs Mean	(Std dev.)	Firms Mean	(Std dev.)	Hospitals Mean	(Std dev.)	All Mean	(Std dev.)
Employment in 2005 (FTEs)	116.837	(324.278)	922.867	(694.716)	181.320	(206.148)	403.036	(578.664)
Age (in years)	10.884	(11.280)	21.444	(15.56)	10.060	(10.296)	14.029	(13.476)
% of staff with PhD	0.146	(0.200)	0.001	(0.001)	0.032	(0.042)	0.057	(0.129)
% of staff with MSc	0.243	(0.240)	0.348	(0.180)	0.107	(0.078)	0.228	(0.201)
% of staff with BSc	0.100	(0.175)	0.298	(0.115)	0.108	(0.090)	0.168	(0.158)
Non-R&D performers 2001–2005	0.535	–	0.178	–	0.900	–	0.551	–
R&D personnel in 2001–2005	0.091	(0.184)	0.008	(0.008)	0.001	(0.006)	0.031	(0.110)
No. of observations	43		45		50		138	

Source: author's survey, 2006–2007.

The survey also found that there is an overlap of competencies between medical practice, teaching and research in the sector, due to the lack of relevant manpower to conduct these activities, as well as regulations that prevent professionals from getting employed in conflicting activities. Practising doctors also teach at university departments (with very little time or effort on improving course curricula) and also are involved with several large/medium scale firms in their formulations activities as research consultants. This is once again confirmed by the collaboration patterns reported in Table 4.2: university researchers, for example, collaborate intensely only with other universities and medical practitioners. This creates inherent conflicts of interest, and is one of the biggest problems in the nexus of the health and pharmaceutical sector in the country.

4.4.4 Policy framework for health innovation

Bangladesh's Drug Control Ordinance of 1982 was, in several ways, very similar to India's policy initiative of a similar kind that triggered self-reliance in its pharmaceutical sector, but this policy has not been supported by complementary industrial policy measures to support the sector. It achieved the reduction of share of imported drugs in the market and also resulted in the creation of production capacity in the local firms in the initial stages of the development of the sector (see Box 4.1).

Box 4.1 Drug control and local production: experiences in India and Bangladesh

The policy changes initiated by the Indian government in the 1960s and the 1970s brought about radical transformations in the foreign versus local firm ratio in the Indian market gradually. As discussed in the previous chapter, in the year 1970, the domestic sector was virtually non-existent, with 15 per cent of Indian firms as against 85 per cent foreign firms in the local market. In terms of retail sales value, in 1970, only two firms in the top ten firms were Indian and the rest were subsidiaries of multinational companies (see Lanjouw 1998, p. 3 and Table 1 on p. 39). This ratio of 15 per cent Indian firms to 85 per cent foreign firms in 1970 grew to 50 per cent each of Indian and foreign firms by 1982, which further increased to 61 per cent Indian firms versus 39 per cent foreign firms by the year 1999 (OPPI, 2000). Of the top ten firms in 2001, eight were Indian firms and only two were subsidiaries of MNCs.

In Bangladesh similarly, although there were 166 licensed pharmaceutical manufacturers in the country in 1981, eight MNCs marketed 75 per cent of the products. The value of locally produced medicines rose from Tk1.1 billion in the 1980s to Tk28.42 billion in 2004. According to local estimates, there were 1495 licensed drug wholesalers and 37,700 drug retailers in the country as of 2000. The history of export of pharmaceutical products from Bangladesh actually saw its beginning within a few years before the close of the decade of 1980.

Source: author

Company interviews revealed that the successful firms all relied on technology transfer arrangements with several MNCs in the 1970s and 1980s to access preliminary technologies as well as tacit knowledge through training. These technology transfer experiences, as company executives confirmed, were perhaps the most important for their abilities to set up local companies in the first place.

Although there have been some policy incentives since the 1980s, such as reduced import tariff on production of exportable and import substitutes that have helped local firms to focus on exports, its present deficiencies can be traced back to the absence of a consistent, strategic policy framework that could steer it into a profitable and competitive trajectory. Table 4.4 contains a comparison of the similarities and differences between India's and Bangladesh's policy support regime for the growth of the pharmaceutical sector. A period of 20 years from the date of the introduction of the drug control regulations in both countries has been taken into account for this comparison. The problems of disarticulation between public sector research and product development, as well as misallocation of skills owing to perverse overlaps between the pharmaceutical and health sectors can all be credited to the lack of a coherent policy regime for the pharmaceutical sector.

Apart from the few similarities, which helped to boost pharmaceutical manufacturing by local firms, the many differences are helpful to unravel the tale of missing competencies amongst Bangladesh's pharmaceutical firms. The missing investments in public sector research, common industry infrastructure services, university education of relevance to building up reverse engineering skills as well as other industrial policy measures for technology transfer and investment all account for the difficulties faced by even the best firms in the country today.

The pharmaceutical sector falls under the MHFW in Bangladesh, rather than the Ministry of Industry and Commerce (or Ministry of Science and Technology), which would be the natural counterpart. The sector has been a leading sector in the most recent economic policies that seek to provide a variety of incentives for exports, and although the government has enacted a New Drug Policy (2005) and a National Biotechnology Policy (2005), some of the key assurances given to the producers, such as the establishment of a common API park, are yet to materialize. Based on the national biotechnology policy framework, the Ministry of Health and Family Welfare produced a "National Guidelines on Medical Biotechnology" in December 2005. The key guidelines set out the key objectives as: (1) judiciously harness the opportunities of medical biotechnological applications for health and livelihood improvement, (2) to prepared a detailed inventory of medically important bio-resources in order to promote conservation of biological diversity and sustainable exploitation of those bio-resources and (3) to conduct genome sequencing of Bangladesh population for determination of variation in human DNA level of our population from that in other nations with a view to understand the overall future health and nutritional implications.[9] Among the other objectives, the guidelines

Table 4.4 Comparing Bangladesh and India's policy regimes for pharmaceutical self-sufficiency

Bangladesh's policy support regime, 1980s to 2000s	India's policy support regime, 1960s to 1980s
Similarities	
• Drug Control Ordinance of 1982.	• Drug Price Control Order, 1970.
• Setting up of public research institutes but lack of funding and vision.	• Setting up of government-held companies to boost the local production of drugs.
• Setting up of government-held companies for production.	• Setting up of extensive public research infrastructure for pharmaceutical research.
Differences	
• No restrictions on pharmaceutical patents under the 1911 Act.	• Restrictions on patenting of foreign pharmaceutical products under the Patents Act of 1971.
• No comparable role of the government or public sector institutions to help firms to acquire reverse engineering skills.	• Proactive role in technology transfer related to reverse engineering to local firms, through public research institutes.
• No funding to public sector institutions; the BCSIR is almost defunct.	• Extensive funding to public sector organizations to boost the capacity for pharmaceutical research, especially CSIR, CDRI and IDMR.
• Lack of vision and funding to reform the university education system.	• Introduction of university education to suit industry requirements (in chemistry and pharmaceutical sciences).
	• Other industrial policy measures, such as investment and ownership restrictions on MNCs.

Source: author's surveys in India (2008) and Bangladesh (2006–2007).

speak about encouraging R&D in medical biotechnology, development of human resources in this area, creation of an enabling environment for biotech industries and creation of public awareness about the safe handling of this technology.

The New Drug Policy (2005) contains provisions for technology transfer and some other incentives to MNCs to set up production facilities in the country both on a joint venture or independent basis. The firm interviews in 2010 reveal that many of them have in fact entered into alliances with companies abroad (European, American, Indian and Chinese) in order to be able to augment their skills. It is however imminent that these are supported through express national and sectoral policies that create further institutional incentives that promote knowledge intensive activities, especially the availability of human skills. The Directorate of Drug Administration is the key department in charge of the sector, and is supported by the IPH, which has the mandate of supporting public health activities, quality control and production of biomedicals, training and research. Both organizations are severely under-equipped and under-funded.[10] One of the few services offered by the Directorate is the Bangladesh National Formulary, produced by the Directorate of Drugs Administration, which contains a list of all drugs available in the country, with manufacturing details and price.

Another peculiar problem with the Ministry of Health is that most government officials (except those that specifically occupy technical positions) that work for the ministry are medical doctors, who are forced to undertake tasks without necessary specialized skills. Doctors are assigned the task of planning and strategy, overseeing functions of the various departments and even handling financial management responsibilities (field interviews). This seriously affects performance of the various organizations under the ministry. The survey found that within specialized institutions like the IPH, production specialist occupations (for production of vaccines) are occupied by medical doctors. The civil service system is also based on regular two-year transfers for many of these positions. Those who invest the time to learn to perform the tasks that they are assigned to are transferred soon thereafter. Hence, most officials interviewed for the study thus expressed their frustration to invest in on-the-job learning (field interviews).

Table 4.5 shows the patterns of the contribution of government policies and institutions to new product and new process development in universities and PRIs (model 1), firms (model 2) and both of them (in the pooled model 3).[11] As the estimation results in the table reveal, the only factor that contributes to present innovation efforts in the pharmaceutical sector is skilled manpower and quality of local infrastructure services. All other governmental policies and institutions, such as innovation incentives by the government and local research in the PRIs and universities, are very weak in promoting innovation activities in the sector.

It also points out to the fact that even if the new Patent Act of 2007 that incorporates the Doha flexibilities for pharmaceutical patents in Bangladesh is

Table 4.5 Bivariate probit ML estimation results: government policies and institutions

Variable	Model 1		Model 2		Model 3	
	Coefficient	(Std error)	Coefficient	(Std error)	Coefficient	(Std error)
New product development						
Government innovation incentives	−1.209	(1.161)	–	–	–	–
Scientific/skilled manpower	0.319	(0.464)	0.836**	(0.307)	0.438	(0.562)
Local university for R&D collaboration	−0.131	(0.811)	–	–	–	–
Local research institute for R&D collaborations	0.615	(1.220)	–	–	–	–
Intellectual property protection	0.673	(0.911)	−0.199	(0.617)	0.458	(1.109)
Quality of local infrastructure services	0.788†	(0.473)	–	–	–	–
Availability of venture capital	0.673	(0.537)	–	–	–	–
Government–firm technology transfer	−2.020	(1.285)	−0.725	(0.847)	−0.239	(2.171)
Staff transfer to local firms	0.610	(0.876)	0.680	(0.702)	1.313	(2.020)
Pharmaceutical firms	–		–		3.687**	(0.585)
Intercept	−0.384*	(0.189)	−0.323†	(0.185)	−2.256**	(0.567)

New process development

Government innovation incentives	−0.374	(1.265)	—		—	
Scientific/skilled manpower	0.303	(0.510)	1.061**	(0.378)	0.870*	(0.40)
Local university for R&D collaboration	0.496	(0.940)	—		—	
Local research institute for R&D collaborations	−0.050	(1.361)	—		—	
Intellectual property protection	0.246	(0.981)	−0.185	(0.710)	−0.084	(0.74)
Quality of local infrastructure services	1.110*	(0.472)	—		—	
Availability of venture capital	0.504	(0.490)	—		—	
Government–firm technology transfer	−1.788	(1.375)	−0.591	(0.899)	−0.279	(0.95)
Staff transfer to local firms	1.125	(0.750)	1.240†	(0.652)	1.207†	(0.67)
Pharmaceutical firms	—		—		0.921*	(0.41)
Intercept	−1.732**	(0.317)	1.570**	(0.288)	−2.089**	(0.43)
Extra parameter						
ρ	0.524*	(0.211)	0.583**	(0.181)	0.618†	(0.33)
No. of observations	88					
Log-likelihood	−80.615		−86.479		−44.606	
LR test	$\chi^2_{(10)} = 11.73$; *p-value* = 0.304				$\chi^2_{(2)} = 83.75$; *p-value* = 0.000	

Source: author's survey, 2007.

Notes

Significance levels: † 10%; * 5%; ** 1%.

enacted, strategic policy support is required to promote API and reverse engineering skills among the local firms, in order for them to effectively supply low cost generic versions of patented drugs to other LDCs.

4.5 Global push factors and their role in Bangladesh

4.5.1 IPRs

As a least developed country, Bangladesh is exempt from implementing the general provisions of the TRIPS agreement until 2013, and has an extension until 2016 to implement its provisions on pharmaceutical patents (in accordance with the Doha Declaration).[12] The EU–Bangladesh Commission is currently negotiating the US–Bangladesh Bilateral Investment Treaty and Article 1(c) of the agreement defines investment to include IPP.[13] Bangladesh's Parliament has been amending the country's trademark, patent and copyright legislations, following a lengthy inter-agency approval and clearance process.

The Law Commission of Bangladesh has formulated a new Trade Marks Law, in consultation with the World Intellectual Property Organization (WIPO) that was recently approved. Similarly, new legislations for Patents and Designs (provisionally called the Patent Law 2007, and the Designs Law 2007) were formulated by the Ministry of Industries. The Draft Patent Law of 2007 granted an exemption to the pharmaceutical sector, and provides:

> It shall come into force at once except the provisions relating to examination, sealing, grant and post-grant matters of the patents relating to pharmaceutical and agricultural chemical products, but excluding the grant of exclusive marketing rights therefore and mailbox filings which shall come into force on and from the first day of January, 2016.
>
> (Section 1)

This Draft Law was replaced by a new Draft Patent Law of 2010 that is expected to come into force soon. The new Draft Law 2010 does not deal with designs. Until the 2010 Draft Law comes into force in Bangladesh, its present policy framework for IPP consists of the Patents and Designs Act of 1911, the Trade Marks Act of 1940, the Copy Right Act of 2000 and the Merchandise Marks Act of 1889.

4.5.1.1 Present patent regime

The present patent protection regime comprises the Patents and Designs Act of 1911 (last amended in 2003) and the Patent and Design Rules of 1933. The Act deems patents to be valid for a total of 16 years (Section 14), calculated from the date of application (Section 7), and allows a further extension of ten years (Section 15(a)(1)).[14] Section 8 contains provisions for opposition to grant of patent (within four months from the date of advertisement of acceptance of application). The law grants process patents on pharmaceuticals. Patent statistics between 2000 and 2005 are contained in Table 4.6. According to the local patent office, of the 182 patents granted in 2005, around 50 per cent are pharmaceutical patents.

4.5.1.2 Export of ARVs and other patented drugs using TRIPS flexibilities

The present patent regime in Bangladesh does not contain a provision that enables firms to export to other LDCs as per the TRIPS flexibilities. Section 22 of the Patents and Designs Act of 1911 deals with the grant of compulsory licences and revocation of patents. According to this section, any person can present a petition to the government of Bangladesh that the demand for a patented article is not being met, but this is presumably for the local market only. Under such circumstances, the government or the high court division may order the patentee to grant licences on terms they see fit. A revocation can also be made within grant of four years of the patent, in case the patentee fails to give adequate reasons for his default (Section 22(4)). Thus, in the absence of a law that contains TRIPS flexibilities for export of generic versions of patented drugs to other LDCs that have TRIPS-compliant regimes, local firms would be constrained to indulge in exports, even if they can/are allowed to produce the drugs locally.

The draft Patent Act of 2007 contains all the exceptions for pharmaceutical products in accordance with the TRIPS Agreement and the Doha Declaration on the TRIPS Agreement and Public Health, but may not be enacted soon due to the political situation in the country. Section 84, clause 10, of the Draft Patent Act of 2007 contains provision for grant of compulsory licences for the "manufacture and export of patented pharmaceutical products to any country having insufficient or no manufacturing capacity in the pharmaceutical sector for the concerned product to address public health problems, provided compulsory license has been granted by such country". This compulsory licence is solely meant to be for the manufacture of that particular pharmaceutical product for which the licence is obtained, and to the country that grants the licence, under

Table 4.6 Patents granted in Bangladesh between 2001 and 2006

Year	Applications filed			Applications accepted		
	Local	Foreign	Total	Local	Foreign	Total
2001	56	239	295	21	185	206
2002	43	246	289	24	233	257
2003	58	260	318	16	206	222
2004	48	268	316	28	202	230
2005	50	294	344	21	161	182
2006	23	287	310	16	146	162

Source: Department of Patents, Design and Trademarks, Bangladesh.

terms and conditions specified by the importing country and the registrar of the Patents Office of Bangladesh (Section 84, clause 11). For purposes of this section, "pharmaceutical products" are defined as "any patented product, or product manufactured through a patented process, of the pharmaceutical sector needed to address public health problems and shall be inclusive of ingredients necessary for their manufacture and diagnostic kits required for their use". Thus, the enactment of the Draft Patent Act is an imperative for the export of patented drugs by Bangladeshi firms.

Closer scrutiny of the patents that have already been granted within the country shows that many of the patents are presently disregarded in the local market. A major explanation for this lies in the technological intensity of the local firms; their inability to reverse engineer offers the best form of protection for the foreign firms who sell their products in the local market. Given this, one is forced to question the motives of foreign firms to patent in the local market. One explanation is that the patent holder firms may wish to prevent competition from companies in other countries, such as India, who may still be keen on

Table 4.7 Exports of patented drugs by Bangladesh's pharmaceutical firms

---

Exports of patented drugs by Bangladesh's firms: key legal prerequisites

---

Local firms in Bangladesh could export to other LDCs generic versions of drugs patented elsewhere, if both Bangladesh and the importing countries do not provide pharmaceutical patents. Bangladesh's own patent regime presently recognizes process patent protection for pharmaceuticals. It is not clear if many of the important drugs that are essential to ensure access to medicines are already patented within Bangladesh as are in the mailbox.

Furthermore, most African and non-African LDCs have granted product patent protection to pharmaceuticals as required by the TRIPS Agreement, despite the 2016 extension (UNCTAD, 2007). Therefore exporting patented drugs to these LDCs could require: (a) a national legislation in the importing country that incorporates the TRIPS flexibilities, including the 30 August 2003 decision and (b) a legislation in Bangladesh that allows the local firms to export to other TRIPS-compliant countries through a compulsory licence (ibid.).

Under the Doha Declaration on TRIPS and Public Health and 30 August 2003 Decision on the implementation of paragraph 6 of the Doha Declaration, LDCs without adequate manufacturing capabilities can obtain supplies from another country with manufacturing capabilities, such as Bangladesh, under a compulsory licence. This compulsory licence would be issued to the local firm in Bangladesh solely for purposes of supplying the patented product to the LDC in need of the product, but lacking the local manufacturing capabilities to produce it.

Under the present patent regime in Bangladesh, if international firms choose to patent their drugs in the country, it would be illegal for the local firms to engage in their production. Section 84(10) of the Draft Patent Act of 2007 incorporated the TRIPS flexibilities in this regard, which is a legal prerequisite for the local firms to produce and sell generic versions of patented drugs to other LDCs that do not have pharmaceutical manufacturing capabilities. How the Draft Patent Law of 2010 deals with this issue needs to be seen.

Source: author.

generic versions of patented drugs that they can no longer sell in the Indian market for exports to Bangladesh. Another explanation is that foreign firms are resorting to patent within Bangladesh if only to avert the potential threat of competition from the local firms.

It is highly unlikely that IPP will provide a direct incentive to innovate for local firms, since they are not into innovative activities at the frontier (see UNCTAD, 2007). An empirical analysis of the impact of IPRs, both as a direct incentive for innovation as well as an indirect contributor to firm level technological upgrading through avenues such as technology licensing, found very little support in the pharmaceutical sector in Bangladesh (Gehl Sampath, 2007c). Technology licensing to local firms is marginal and not a contributor to innovative efforts presently in the local pharmaceutical sector in Bangladesh (ibid.). Although the new Drug Policy has provisions for joint research and technology transfer between foreign firms and local firms, efficient technology transfer for the future, especially in the case of a knowledge intensive sector like pharmaceuticals, will hinge upon transfer of know-how (Arora, 1995, p. 41). Successful transfer of know-how, which is uncodified and costly to transfer, will in turn depend on the technology absorption capacities of the recipient, and not just the willingness of the licensor (see Box 4.2).

Box 4.2 Technology transfer experiences amongst local firms in Bangladesh

Firms in Bangladesh require substantial help in developing local API skills, which could be promoted through south–south cooperation with the pharmaceutical sector in India. Amongst the firms that were surveyed, several large firms are in negotiation for transfer of skills and know-how from successful European, Chinese and Indian firms. Previous experience shows that technology transfer and collaboration helped to develop formulations capacity in the sector. Good examples are Square Pharmaceuticals, which collaborated with Jansen and Vicsenco that received help from Pfizer. In all these cases, the transfer of technology was accompanied by training of skilled manpower. In the case of API skills, this may not be so easy. The firms require new human skills and access to know-how in addition to codified technology in order to build capacity.

Source: author's survey

4.5.2 Too narrow focus on the domestic market

Most of the sales for even the largest firms accrue from the local market,[15] but the size of the local market is quite small.[16] The policy framework protects the local firms from imports of drugs that can be locally manufactured and the present marketing and sales incentives for firms (see next paragraph) are such that there seems to be very little incentive to enhance competitiveness (field interviews). The few firms that are in the process of expanding their range of activities to include API and reverse engineering skills are focusing on the export markets, and will need a lot of institutional support to achieve efficient results.

4.6 Vietnam's health innovation system

In Vietnam, enterprises in the pharmaceutical sector have achieved positive growth with the attempt to produce generic products instead of importation, and, moreover, to export to overseas markets in recent times. In parallel with the increase of the importation of medicine (8.1 per cent in 2005), the exportation also increased recently (7.4 per cent in 2005). Revenue of the sector has continuously increased since 1995, from US$65 million in 1995 to US$248 million in 2003. In 2003, the state owned enterprises production accounted for 40 per cent of all pharmaceutical production, whereas foreign firms produced 44 per cent and the remaining 16 per cent was attributable to other sources (joint stock companies). However, the pharmaceutical firms in Vietnam import 90 per cent of its production material (read APIs) from abroad and are only able to produce generic medicine with relatively simple technologies (90 per cent).

There is a big number of large state owned manufacturing enterprises in Vietnam, including pharmaceutical ones. In recent times, most of these firms have been equitized and turned into shareholding companies, but the state still owns a large number of equities of the firms (usually 51 per cent). SMEs dominate Vietnam's production landscape in general and also in health innovation. However, most of these SMEs are very weak in R&D capacity and lack resources to invest in R&D activities while intermediate organizations are also not available to support them in innovation in general (Nguyen Thanh Tung, 2004). *Government agencies* especially the Ministry of Science and Technology and the Ministry of Health play a key role in promoting innovation.

4.6.1 Current strengths of Vietnamese health innovation system

Although Vietnam only made health innovation a priority recently (in the beginning of the 1990s), it has gained several noticeable achievements. Vietnam has mastered the artificial insemination technology, and genomics and biotechnology techniques are being applied for diagnosis and cure of heredity diseases. Research projects for vaccine production have been the most dominant outcome in the field of medicinal biotechnology. Vietnam has produced several kinds of

Table 4.8 Valuation of the pharmaceutical manufacturing sector

Year	Total valuation of medicine consumption (1000 US$)	Domestic manufacturing		
		Valuation	Percentage of total valuation	Growth rate (%)
2001	472,356	170,390	36.10	100
2002	525,807	200,290	38.10	117.55
2003	608,699	241,870	39.74	120.76
2004	707,535	305,950	43.24	126.48
2005	817,396	395,157	48.34	129.16

Source: Cao Minh Quang, 2006.

vaccines as part of its vaccine programme for eliminating polio since 2002. There are four vaccine-manufacturing enterprises in the country that produce vaccines adhering to WHO standards and export to India, South Korea and Japan. Vietnam has also recently succeeded in research and production of new age B-hepatitis vaccine based on recombinant DNA technologies. In addition, the Vietnamese sector is also presently engaged in genetic engineering, transgenic, GENE-CARD technologies as it applies to identify martyrs' remains (from the Vietnamese war), and to aid criminal investigations (MOST, 2003).

4.6.1.1 A strategic and coherent policy framework

Despite its late prioritization, health innovation has developed remarkably well in Vietnam mainly as a result of the well-configured national innovation framework that is supported by relevant sectoral initiatives. At the national level, the Ministry of Science and Technology, Ministry of Agriculture and Rural Development, Ministry of Health and Ministry of Aquaculture play most important roles. These ministries have departments in every province (more than 60 provinces). Besides, there are other related government agencies involving in the system, such as the Department of Pharmaceuticals Management. These government agencies not only manage the operation of each sector but also set up and fund R&D programmes. However, the finance for biotechnology R&D so far is still not addressed in the requirement for development.

Ministry of Science and Technology (MOST) had built up the state level research programme, entitled "Biotechnology for developing sustainable agriculture, forest and aquaculture, environment and human health protection" (1996–2000) and has been implementing another research programme, entitled "Science and technology for biotechnology development" (2001–2005).

In addition, the Economic–Technical programme in biotechnology was developed with the objective of assisting enterprises in applying R&D results into industrial production. Under the assignment of the government, the Economic–Technical programme in biotechnology was under the responsibility of the Ministry of Agriculture and Rural Development. In the framework of this programme, fund from budget with VND25.4 billion was invested in 11 production units of Cayenne pineapple (segment one), fresh foetus of pig, ox, living stock vaccine, micro organic manure, glucose, unsexed African carp and vaccines for human health. The objective of this programme is to promote the process of technology development and industrial production. However, due to the limitation investment, these projects have been at small scale and lacked industrial application.

Finance for health and biotechnology development is drawn from many channels such as state budget, international organizations, NGOs, foreign governments especially official development assistance and from enterprises. Among these resources, the government funds most of R&D related to health and biotechnology. The product development, however, is funded by enterprises themselves. Products, which are important for public utilization and environment protection, are funded fully or partly by government depending upon concrete cases.

Since the government enacted the Resolution 18/CP, comprehensive biotechnology programmes have been created and invested increasingly. Nevertheless, the total expenditure for R&D activities in biotechnology has only reached VND80 billion (about US$5 million) for a ten year period. Since 1995 the government has invested a further about US$5 million to enhance infrastructure facilities for biotechnological laboratories and R&D institutes. On the average, each of the national key laboratories has had investment from US$200,000–500,000. These numbers are very small, especially compared with other countries (MOST, 2003).

In fact, biotechnology requires high investment, especially, for equipment and other facilities. Although the government had paid attention on developing national biotechnology laboratories, national laboratories on plant, animal cell technology have not been developed effectively.

4.6.1.2 Innovative human skill development initiatives

Vietnam has an extremely sophisticated system of education which has been substantially reformed in the recent years to cater to the manpower requirements of the sector, wherein, in addition to university programmes, the PRIs also conduct practical training programmes to train skilled personnel in relevant aspects of health innovation. In addition to this, Vietnam provides an extensive framework for overseas training and programmes of internships, MSc and PhD degrees for its citizens with state budget funds of VND100 billion per year (or around US$7 million). These funds are disbursed through the Ministry of Education and Training, and just over the past five years more than 30 persons have been trained in biotech areas using these endowments. In the framework of national research programmes on science and technology, hundreds of biotechnology and health research staff are facilitated to establish collaborations in key areas of importance to the Vietnamese economy with colleagues from frontier countries through visits or research projects. In addition, scientists from overseas have been invited to Vietnam to train in research methodology with over 200 groups of Vietnamese biotechnology scientists in recent years.

4.6.1.3 Active private sector enterprise

In pharmaceuticals, approximately 180 enterprises produce modern medicine and about 300 enterprises produce traditional medicine. Among the enterprises that produce modern medicine, 30 per cent of all firms are GMP certified. There is a large number of enterprises that only distribute, retail and package medicines (about 900 enterprises). In addition to these there are approximately ten multinational firms operating in Vietnam.

The share of domestically manufactured medicines in the local Vietnamese market has been steadily on the increase. From 26 per cent of the local market share in 2004, local firms have increased their share to 43 per cent as of 2005. The WHO ranks Vietnam's innovation capacity to be between 2.5 and 3, where being on level 2 signifies a country that is able to produce some generic drugs with a majority of imports, and level 3 applies to countries with a good base to manufacture and export generic drugs and products (Cao Minh Quang, 2006).

4.6.1.4 Well-funded and functional public research institutions

A number of R&D institutes have made and continue to make remarkable contributions towards enhancing the innovation capacity in the system. The National Institute for Hygiene and Epidemiology (NIHE) conduct research on medical microbial-immunology and epidemiology, virology, microbiology, immunology and epidemiology. The institute also carries out research on the development of production/trial of vaccines, biological substances in order to prevent and diagnose some high risk communicable diseases. The Pasteur Institute in Ho Chi Minh City and Nha Trang carries out research on aspects of medical biology including microbiology, immunology and epidemiology of infectious disease. These institutes also provide services such as clinical laboratory analyses, immunization, dispensary services and laboratory analysis for food hygiene safety. Besides, they also produce several kinds of vaccines and bio-products for diagnosis of various bacterial and viral infections. The Institute of Vaccines and Biological Substance in Quy Nhon carries out research on the applicability of advanced biotechnology in production and development of vaccines, serum and other biological substances. The institute also produces vaccines and serum to supply the Expanded Programme on Immunization in Vietnam.

4.6.2 Key challenges for the future

The key challenges faced by the system are as follows:

a   The sector has not been a focal sector in Vietnam, although with the prioritization of biotechnology in 2002, it has received a renewed boost. There is a need to enact sectoral policy for health innovation in Vietnam in order to enable its potential.

b   Although the number of R&D institutes that conduct research relating to biotechnology has increased recently, R&D institutes are still scattered and not integrated. As a result, there is a lot of duplication of research efforts, which are wasteful. Moreover, there is evidence of research programmes that do not necessarily address the need of the market or industrial sector.

c   There is a need to support private enterprise that could emerge as a "spin off" from the governmental enterprises that presently exist. This calls for advanced support structures that mitigate risk and provide financial alternatives on the one hand, and help in acquisition of technologies on the other. The R&D institutes usually do not have an office or unit to carry out technology transfer activities, and this calls for change. This could also help strengthen the linkages between the industry sector and R&D organizations, which is presently weak and needs to be improved (MOST, 2003).

d   Although Vietnam has an extremely sophisticated system of education, which has been substantially reformed in the recent years to cater to the manpower requirements of the sector, the growing demand for professionals especially in the major fields of biotechnology such as genetic technology, cell technology, enzyme-protein technology and microorganism technology needs to be provided for.

4.7 Summing up

In contrasting the cases of Bangladesh and Vietnam, this chapter throws up several important issues. The case of Bangladesh shows impending promise – local firms have, despite little support and coherent policy strategies, achieved production capacity that is unique amongst LDCs. One major challenge that is missing, however, is the need to coordinate the production capacity with the need to provide access to safe and cheap medicines for the local people. This, as the case study reveals, is difficult in the absence of a coherent and accountable policy framework and the enforceable rules on good manufacturing standards. Both of these are not present to the extent required in Bangladesh. When this is contrasted with the case of Vietnam, the first point of note is the relevance of coordinated interventions in building capacity in the sector. Vietnam, despite its late prioritization of the sector, has been able to achieve substantive progress mainly because it has been able to pool together a critical mass of physical and knowledge infrastructure to support health innovation.

5 Kenya's health innovation capacity

5.1 Introduction

The Kenyan economy registered a GDP growth of 6.9 per cent in 2007 and has been in the process of recovering from one of the country's longest recessions (World Bank Indicators, 2007). Despite its relatively good economic performance over the past few years, the country ranks low on knowledge indicators measured in terms of secondary and tertiary schooling, researchers in R&D per million of population and domestic credit institutions. Kenya has one of the lowest scores on the human development index within sub-Saharan Africa and the country's performance on life expectancy, education levels and decent living standards *have remained the same or worsened over the past 15 years.* The Ministry of Health provides public health care services and controls 52 per cent of all medical facilities available in the country (Export Processing Zones Authority, 2005).

Most biotechnology-led research in the country has focused on agricultural biotechnology, where the initial developments can be traced back to the early 1980s with the application of tissue culture in crops such as citrus fruits (at the Kenyan Agriculture Research Institute, KARI) and Pyrethrum (University of Nairobi). Around the same time, the use of biotechnology in livestock and health research also began with a focus on the generation of disease diagnostic technologies employing hybridma and DNA molecular techniques. A major breakthrough was the Rinderpest Vaccine that was jointly developed by KARI, Pirbright (UK) and the University of California (Gichuki, 2006).

Despite these successes, the majority of Kenya's research projects in health biotechnology in Kenya are concentrated in the public sector, involving mainly the public research institutes, often with donor funding (Clark *et al.,* 2005; Kirea *et al.,* 2003). Health innovation in general, and health biotechnology in particular, has been slow to take off, despite the fact that Kenya has a relatively high amount of private pharmaceutical enterprises in the East African region.

This chapter provides an analysis of the current status of health and biotechnology innovation in Kenya and evaluates the relevant policy support that needs to be provided in order to enable innovation activities. The data contained in this chapter is based on a sector survey of health innovation that followed the same methodology as the other chapters in Part II. In some places, the information and analysis is substantiated by additional information that was conducted in 2007 in Kenya on biotechnology research across both agricultural and health biotechnology areas.[1] In total, 41 firms, 32 hospitals and 25 public research institutes were surveyed (98 in total) in addition to 45 governmental agencies. In addition to this, 65 people including top level management in firms (both multinational and local), governmental officials, directors and research staff in PRIs and hospitals were interviewed through face-to-face interviews.

5.2 Key actors in health innovation

Kenya's innovation infrastructure comprises of a strong base of public sector institutions dedicated to research and standard setting, such as the Kenya Industrial Research and Development Institute (KIRDI), Kenya Bureau of Standards, Kenya Intellectual Property Institute (KIPI). Several other research institutes exist in order to conduct research on sectoral priorities, including health biotechnology. It has six main universities, of which the Jomo Kenyatta University and the University of Nairobi are the most important, apart from a range of polytechnic institutions that impart technical education in various science intensive disciplines.

As is the case in most latecomer innovation systems, a large part of Kenya's innovation activities in health are concentrated in the public sector, although there is a relatively vibrant private sector in the country performing manufacturing, distribution and retailing activities in pharmaceuticals.

5.2.1 Governmental agencies

The creation of the Kenya Industrial Property Office in 1990 (and its transformation into KIPI with greater decision-making power and authority) following the enactment of the industrial property Act was a major strengthening act as far as IPP in Kenya is concerned. The National Council on Science and technology in Kenya has a broad mandate of focusing on innovation and new technologies of importance to the country, such as biotechnology and ICTs. There are two other health agencies that are expected to promote entrepreneurship and standard setting: the Pharmacy and Poisons Board and the Kenya Bureau of Standards. The Pharmacy and Poisons Board is responsible for the regulation of trade in health products, including those employing health biotechnology. It prescribes the apparatus and also oversees compliance with good manufacturing practices, labelling and other formal requirements. The Kenya Bureau of Standards (KEBS) operates under the Ministry of Trade and Industry, and is responsible for setting standards for weights and measures, purity and identity. KEBS is the national standards body and is established under the Standards Act (cap 496) laws of Kenya. This Act of 1974 seeks to promote and provide for standardization of commodities and a code of practice.

5.2.2 Research institutes and universities

The Kenya Medical Research Institute (KEMRI) is the premier R&D organization with a national mandate to "conduct health sciences research and generate research findings applicable towards improvement of health status". KEMRI was established in 1979 as one of the five public research institutes under the Science and Technology Act (cap 250) laws of Kenya. The institute has ten research centres located in various parts of the country meant to address various aspects of health research including health biotechnology. These centres have over 800 scientific and technical staff with over 200 biomedical scientists in such fields as microbiologists, clinicians, social scientists, pharmacists, epidemiologists, immunologists, virologists. The technical staff includes laboratory technologists, public health and clinical officers and pharmaceutical technologists (KEMRI website). KEMRI has developed at least two products namely *Hepcell* which is a diagnostic kit for detecting human hepatitis B surface antigen and *particle agglutination*, which is also a diagnostic kit for the same, developed using locally produced reagents, doesn't require electric power and its results can be viewed using the naked eye. The development of both these products has been supported by the Japan International Cooperation Agency, which has also funded the product commercialization facility at KEMRI.

KIRDI is a technology development and management agency of the government, which operates under the Ministry of Trade and Industry. It was established and incorporated under the Science and Technology Act (cap 250) in 1979 with an intention similar to that of KEMRI. The institute has several objectives that are important for all innovation activities including those in health biotechnology, such as enhancing the national industrial technology innovation process as a strategy towards rapid socio-economic development, contributing to the development of sufficient capacity for industrial research and development, contributing to the creation of the national wealth in disembodied technologies that are appropriate and accessible to micro and small enterprises in Kenya, and facilitating access by local enterprises to Business Development Services including cleaner production and industrial information. These two institutes are supported through a range of smaller research institutes and international research institutes operating in Kenya such as African Insect Science for Food and Health (ICIPE) and local universities and firms. KARI has a well-established biotechnology tradition, which also lends strength to health innovation through biotechnology inputs.

5.2.3 Private sector

Kenya's local pharmaceutical sector is made up of firms engaged in production and manufacturing, retailing and distributing of health products in the local market as well as in the COMESA economic region. The range of pharmaceutical products manufactured in Kenya includes antibiotics, anti-malarials, anti-amoebics, analgesics, anti-diarrhoeal, antacids, tranquilizers, anti-spasmodics, vitamins and anti-ulcer treatment, according to the Export Processing Zones Authority (2005). The large Kenyan firms that are involved in production are mostly subsidiaries of large MNCs, such as Bayer, Aventis and Novartis with the exception of some local firms such as Macs Pharmaceuticals and Cosmos Pharmaceuticals.

Box 5.1 Important pharmaceutical firms in Kenya

- Alpha Medical Manufacturers
- Aventis Pasteur SA East
- Bayer East Africa Limited
- Beta Healthcare (Shelys Pharmaceuticals)
- Cosmos Limited
- Dawa Pharmaceuticals
- Didy Pharmaceutical
- Diversey Lever
- Eli-Lilly (Suisse) SA – Nairobi
- Elys Chemical Industries Ltd
- GlaxoSmithKline – Nairobi
- High Chem East Africa Ltd
- Mac's Pharmaceutical Ltd
- Manhar Brothers (Kenya) Ltd
- Novartis Rhone Poulenic Ltd
- Novelty Manufacturers Ltd
- Pfizer Corp (Agency)
- Pharmaceutical Manufacturing Co (K) Ltd
- Pharmaceutical Products Ltd
- Regal Pharmaceutical Ltd
- Universal Pharmaceutical Ltd

Source: author's survey, 2007

5.2.4 NGOs/donors and teaching hospitals

Several international NGOs, like the African Medical and Research Foundation and ICIPE, are actively engaged in conducting research on local health problems like Rift Valley Fever and Sleeping Sickness. Kenya has a large number of such hospitals led by Agakhan University Hospital and the Moi University School of Medicine and Referral Hospital.

5.3 Current strengths in health innovation

Health innovation in the country is relatively successful when compared to other countries in East Africa (see Tanzania in Chapter 6). One of the most important successes of the local system of innovation is the presence of private sector enterprise. While several firms only distribute and are engaged in retailing, some local firms are actively engaged in production and R&D of drugs. Of note in this context is Cosmos Pharmaceuticals, a local firm that is engaged in supplying several ARV drugs (for treatment of HIV/AIDS) to many other countries in the region and elsewhere, and anti-TB drugs to international procurement agencies like the Global Fund (PRM Database, Global Fund, July 2008).

While Cosmos has had some problems in accreditation for ARV drugs (they remain, however, one of the earliest producers of the same in sub-Saharan Africa), they are the fifth largest suppliers of anti-TB drugs and an important supplier of anti-Malarial drugs to countries that receive Global Fund (GFATM) grants worldwide (Grace and Gehl Sampath, 2008). Cosmos is a local success story wherein the company has constantly sought to upgrade its ability to reverse engineer and produce drugs of importance to global and local public health. Apart from drugs mentioned here, Cosmos produces a range of local pharmaceutical products for the Kenyan and COMESA market (field interviews). Another company that deserves mention here is Universal Corporation, again a local firm that has invested enormous efforts in upgrading its pharmaceutical manufacturing capabilities and has commenced the WHO prequalification/accreditation process. It has also established an R&D unit for natural products and has hired an expert from India to assist them in this direction.

5.4 Local push factors in the sectoral system for health

The local push factors are relatively weaker when compared to India and Bangladesh analysis conducted in the previous two chapters. However, Kenya still remains one of the most entrepreneurial sectors in health innovation in the region demonstrating capacity not only for health innovation but also for biotechnology based work (Gehl Sampath and Oyeyinka, 2009a, b). The push factors that are responsible for capacity are not so much a coherent sectoral policy vision, as much as local demand for medicines in the Kenyan market as well as the COMESA region, both of which are discussed here. A third factor, collaborations and linkages (especially international collaborations), play a major role in shaping capacity in the sector, which is discussed in Section 5.5. However, as this section shows, there are significant obstacles to building capacity locally.

5.4.1 Lack of human skills of relevance to health innovation

The university disciplines that deal with various aspects of health innovation, such as pharmacology, medical sciences and newer technologies that could be integrated into health innovation such as biotechnology, are in need of revision. Our surveys also sought to ascertain the kinds of capacity being created to perform biotechnology research. We found that the limited capacity that is being created is focused more on tangible infrastructure (such as laboratories and equipment) and is not matched by the expansion of human skills to utilize these facilities as part of structured research agendas for both health and agricultural biotechnology. This once again confirms earlier results on Kenyan biotechnology capacity (see for example the survey by Odame *et al.*, 2002), which

Table 5.1 Animal health biotechnologies in Kenya (2006)

Technology	Description	Year	Status
Latex agglutination diagnostic test for Contagious Caprine Preural Pneumonia (CCPP)	A quick test for identifying goats that have been exposed to CCPP organism. The test works with either whole blood or serum and is therefore a good field test. The reagent also keeps well in the absence of refrigeration.	1985	Ready for commercialization, but not yet commercialized.
Latex agglutination diagnostic test for Contagious Bovine Preural Pneumonia (CBPP)	A quick test for identifying cattle that have been exposed to CBPP organism. The test works with either whole blood or serum and is therefore a good field test.	1990	The test was undergoing more evaluation.
Latex agglutination diagnostic test for Lumpy Skin Disease	A quick test for identifying cattle that have been exposed to lumpy skin disease virus. The test works with either whole blood or serum and is therefore a good field test.	2003	
ELISA based diagnostic test for Contagious Caprine Preural Pneumonia	The technique uses a unique carbohydrate as an antigen for coating ELISA plates. It is therefore a very specific test.	2005	It is a new test that needs more validation before being availed for wider use.

Technology	Description	Year	Status
RT-PCR diagnostic test for Rift Valley Fever	The technique uses non-structural gene as a template for amplification.	2003	Needs more validation.
Antigen detection test for Nairobi Sheep disease virus	A test for quick detection of Nairobi sheep disease virus without going through tissue culture inoculation.	2004	Under development.
Recombinant capripox/Rift Valley Fever vaccine	A sheep ox virus vaccine which expresses a glycoprotein gene from Rift Valley Fever virus. When inoculated into the sheep, it induces an immune reaction which protects against challenge with Rift Valley Fever virus.	1998	Further evaluation in cattle (calves) and goats in containment.
Inactivated vaccine for Nairobi sheep disease	Nairobi sheep disease virus inactivated with beta-propiolactone or formaldehyde.	2002	Under development.
Vaccinia/Rinderpest Recombinant Vaccine	The vaccines were found effective in confined trials.		The vaccine has undergone confined trials at KARI-Kiboko.

Sources: field interviews; Gichuki (2006).

concluded that over the years capacity building has focused more on hardware components (expanding the physical facilities) and not so much on post-graduate training in MSc and PhD levels. This over-emphasis on hardware components has resulted in an increase on the demand for non-scientific staff to manage the expanded physical facilities, thus explaining the low scientific–non-scientific staff ratios captured in our surveys that covered all five public sector institutes.

Table 5.2 presents the net enrolment from 2000 to 2005, and shows that only half of the amount of students that attend primary school eventually progress to secondary schooling and, alarmingly, only 3 per cent of the total receive tertiary education. The survey also found that the share of staff with PhD degrees in the public research institutes was extremely small, again confirming the findings that most of the "core research" staff required to conduct biotechnology based R&D are missing from the expanding infrastructure endowments (Oyeyinka and Gehl Sampath, 2009b). We found that most of the biotechnology work was concentrated around tissue culture and other basic biotechnologies, rather than seeing pockets of excellence across a broader range of expertise, given the broad range of international collaborations going on in the country.[2]

In recent years, the government has sought to address the issue of adequate human and technical capacity by establishing courses in biotechnology in most of the public universities in Kenya. In fact all the six public universities across the country are offering biotechnology courses at under-graduate and post-graduate levels. For example, Kenyatta University offers both BSc and MSc courses in Biotechnology. The University of Nairobi in 2005 established the Centre for Biotechnology and Bioinformatics as a centre of excellence to facilitate capacity building and generate marketable products by harnessing biotechnology. The centre's mandate is to enhance knowledge and skills in biotechnology and bioinformatics to impact on agricultural and industrial output, health and environmental management.

The centre formation underscores the realization that biotechnology is an interdisciplinary subject with wide ranging applications of scientific and engineering principles in different fields such as agriculture, food and feed, medicine, industry and the environment, which are of profound importance to mankind. The centre aims to strengthen national capabilities in the field of basic sciences and technology and in the development of research in biotechnology and bioinformatics, in addition to promote and conduct basic research in the areas of molecular biology, biotechnology and bioinformatics. It also has the mandate

Table 5.2 School enrolment ratios, Kenya 2000–2005

School enrolments (% net)	2000	2001	2002	2003	2004	2005
Primary enrolment	67	–	63	77	76	–
Secondary enrolment	33	34	35	37	40	–
Tertiary enrolment	3	3	3	–	3	–

Source: World Development Indicators, 2007.

of facilitating the application of biotechnology in research and encourages its use for the development of marketable products and to offer training facilities for manpower development in biotechnology and bioinformatics at the national and regional level. The centre is also expected to institutionalize links between universities, scientific research institutions and the private sector in order to promote the focus on product development, and to network with institutions in developed and developing countries as well as the international centres of biotechnology and bioinformatics.

It is expected that the integration of biotechnology courses within the universities' curricula as well the emergence of training centres such as the Centre for Biotechnology will help boost the country's manpower and skills to conduct biotechnology research and innovation in the years to come. The bigger challenge however is to equip these centres with the necessary training materials and facilities, and relevant manpower, which is very different from merely establishing organizations. Meeting this greater challenge will require that Kenya begins to allocate more of its GDP to science and technology activities (which is currently less than 0.5 per cent of its GDP as noted earlier). It also calls for universities and research institutes to seek alternative, innovative funding mechanisms, the incentives for which are presently not in place.

A National Consortium of National Health Research Kenya (see online, available at: http://cnhrkenya.org/), seeks to address some of these issues particularly of relevance to health and health biotechnology. Its main function is to create collaborative linkages between all health research institutions and universities' centres of excellence, governmental agencies (including the Ministry of Health) and private sector enterprise in the country. The Consortium's primary focus is on enabling health R&D capacity to be built in an innovative manner.

5.4.2 Lack of knowledge infrastructure in public sector institutions

Although the local research institutes have been involved in several projects that involve more demanding technologies for health innovation both animal and human (as shown in Table 5.1), none of these projects have led to the commercial products within the country and most of the products were undergoing evaluations at the time of the survey in 2007. Organizations like KIRDI and KEMRI, which have the mandate to develop technologies for the use of local entrepreneurs in both traditional and new technology sectors, operate with extreme staffing and funding shortages, and hence are not able to fulfil their mandates. It is noteworthy here that although at a first glance, there seems to be a lot of technical expertise in these organizations – for example, the ten research centres under KEMRI are reported to have around 800 technical staff – these figures are often misleading. The personnel reported as "technical staff" cover a host of functions outside the traditional biotechnology R&D domain, and includes public health services and clinical officers. The surveys also found that often the few researchers who are skilled to perform biotech and health R&D in these centres are diverted into other tasks that are not so research and funding intensive mainly due to lacking capacity of the government to endow these centres appropriately to carry out their original mandates. Most researchers at universities and public research institutes complain regularly of a lack of funds and initiative on part of the government to support and strategically direct locally important research in health and biotechnology. The extraordinary reliance on external donor funding for research, which is at best sporadic and not dependable, means that innovative activities in academic institutions in the country continue at a rate that hardly reflects its true potential. The development of health innovation has been stunted by the absence of relevant knowledge infrastructure. The amount of resources that are allocated to public sector organizations for research is negligible.

In particular, the survey shows that the universities fare much worse than public research institutes on a number of fronts. Most researchers and scientists in universities spend over 90 per cent of their time in teaching and administration and suffer from severe intellectual isolation (as a result of lack of opportunities to interact with research institutes and the private sector) as well as lack of mandate. This lack of mandate is a problem common amongst several African latecomer countries and can be traced back to stagnating academic systems that demonstrate inertia to change and revision that could make it more current. The interviews and the survey data show that the universities have much more difficulty gaining access to international funding. Most university staff interviewed complained that the technical assistance to research by donors almost always get channelled through the government into public research institutes and do not find their way to university centres of excellence. This makes the issue of funding even more of a challenge for the universities. The interviewees also expressed the need for the National Council of Science and Technology to review and understand the university needs in this respect (field interviews).

5.4.3 Lack of institutional support to private sector R&D

A majority of the private sector enterprise in the country is engaged in importing, distributing and retailing of pharmaceutical products while some firms manufacture. While there is no reliable data on how much of the private sector is engaged in manufacturing as opposed to retailing and distributing, Kenya fares relatively well in comparison to other countries in the region (and in sub-Saharan Africa as a whole) On the whole, the picture for private sector health R&D as captured by the survey looked rather bleak.

Despite the intent of the National Biotechnology Policy of 2006, little has been done to promote the emergence of a vibrant private sector for health biotechnology. Discounting the few firms that conduct local R&D, engaging in health innovation activities is a tough task due for the sector. There is little governmental infrastructure for technological incubation, acquisition of technology required to pursue innovation and funding, especially small-firm risk sharing and financing initiatives of the kind its local enterprise would need. Some existing incentives to promote local innovation, such as a governmental policy of promoting local production of pharmaceuticals through a procurement process that gives preference to local producers even if the local price is greater than that of exports up to a threshold of 15 per cent, is hardly implemented in practice thus not serving its purpose.

On a closer look, there appear to be inherent weaknesses in several institutions that are fundamental to the creation of new knowledge and the use of already existing knowledge in innovation activities. Financial support institutions to promote local innovation and entrepreneurship in Kenya have not been performing well and have been constantly on the decline since 2000. Reviewing the data available in the World Development Indicators Database (World Bank Indicators, 2007) for the years from 2001 to 2005, we found that domestic credit to private sector has been on the decline (from 28 per cent of total GDP in 2000 to 27 per cent of total GDP in 2005). Similarly, FDI remains close to zero (fluctuating between 1 per cent of GDP and less between 2000 and 2005). Data on other important indicators such as R&D expenditure as percentage of GDP and researchers in R&D (per million people) are not available.

The innovation patterns of the private sector were captured by survey data, which show that the local public research institutes are more often involved in new product development than local firms while both groups of actors are equally involved in new process development. Table 5.3 contains the patterns of product and process innovations both in firms and PRIs, and the impact of governmental support and assistance. While the PRIs are involved more frequently on average in new product development than firms, both firms and PRIs are involved equally frequently in new process development. Governmental subsidies and R&D programmes, however, are mainly directed towards PRIs and not towards firms. As Table 5.3 shows, the percentage of PRIs that benefit from government sponsored R&D programmes is on average statistically and significantly

Table 5.3 Descriptive statistics: innovation and government assistance in Kenya

	Number of firms	%	Number of PRIs	%
New product development				
No	34	82.9	15	60.0
Yes	7	17.1	10	40.0
New process development				
No	29	70.7	21	84.0
Yes	12	29.3	4	16.0
Government sponsored R&D programmes				
No	41	100.0	17	68.0
Yes	0	0.0	8	32.0
Government R&D subsidies				
No	41	100.0	15	60.0
Yes	0	0.0	10	40.0
No. of observations	41		25	

Source: author's survey, 2007.

larger than that of firms that benefit from government sponsored R&D programmes. A similar pattern is shown for government subsidies. Most of the
actors interviewed observed that the level of involvement of the private sector in
health innovation and product development is still very low and urged that the
private sector should be encouraged by enacting appropriate policies and
incentives.

Table 5.4 contains the survey responses of firms and public research institutes
towards various policy incentives and the extent to which they contributed
towards health biotechnology innovation. The respondents were asked to rank
on a scale of 1 (not helpful at all in innovation activities) to 5 (extremely
helpful). Therefore, any ranking above 2.5 indicates a strong impact of the policy
incentive in promoting innovative activity.

Three points stand out from the survey responses in Table 5.4. First, public
research institutes rate (and are relatively better endowed than firms as the
surveys more generally show) on all innovation incentives presently implemented in the system. Second, hardly any of the conventional policy incentives
that are needed to support innovation in health biotechnology in public and
private sectors seem to play a significant role presently, underscoring the low
level of health and biotechnology innovation activity in the system. Third, there
is a very clear consensus on the importance of human skills as an innovation
incentive for the sector. This, although intuitive in general, helps to capture the
most important lacunae in the system as it presently stands.

As in the case of Bangladesh, the subsidiaries of multinationals are mainly
engaged in local manufacturing of drugs across a broad range, but not necessarily those that are technologically demanding due to the difficulties of organizing labour, laboratory facilities and other infrastructure requirements (among
other firm level strategic reasons). It is rather the local firms that have acquired
the capacity to conduct API work and aspire to branch out into more demanding
areas of health innovation that drive the process ahead. The factors that impede
its growth are the unavailability of human capital, regulatory barriers to conduct
biotechnology based research and lack of entrepreneurial support.

Table 5.4 Impact of governmental incentives on firm and organization level innovation

Policy incentive	Firms	PRIs
1 Government innovation incentives	1.63	1.80
2 Skilled manpower	2.05	3.24
3 Local collaboration with universities	1.85	2.84
4 Local collaboration with PRIs	1.90	2.84
5 IPP	1.70	1.72
6 Quality of local innovation infrastructure	1.80	2.24
7 Venture capital	1.92	1.80
8 Government support to SMEs	1.70	–
9 Government–firm technology transfer	1.60	–

Source: Oyeyinka and Gehl Sampath, 2009b.

5.4.4 *Mismatch of skills and resources in new product and process innovation*

Table 5.5 presents descriptive statistics of full time employment in firms, PRIs and training and teaching hospitals, education level of staff and the proportion of staff engaged in R&D. It shows that the mean employment over the period 2001–2005 for firms is not statistically and significantly different (on average) from that observed in the PRIs and hospitals. Second, firms, hospitals and PRIs are statistically and significantly equally old. Furthermore, the staff working in the firms and hospitals is on an average less educated than those employed by PRIs. The percentage of staff working in private firms with a PhD and MSc degree is statistically and significantly smaller than that amongst PRIs with similar degrees, and the percentage of staff in firms that have only a BSc degree is statistically and significantly larger than that in PRIs. More specifically, the mean share of staff with a PhD and MSc degree is statistically and significantly larger in PRIs than in hospitals and firms. Furthermore, the mean share of staff with a BSc degree is statistically and significantly smaller in PRIs than in firms but larger than in hospitals. Finally, mean R&D staff and the percentage of R&D performers are not statistically and significantly different across firms and PRIs. These figures are equal to zero in hospitals.

Table 5.6 presents estimation results of a bivariate probit model that explains jointly the probability of being involved in new product and new process development in Kenya's health innovation sector. The results suggest that employment has a positive and significant, albeit small, effect both on new product and new process development. Firms, hospitals or PRIs with no R&D staff over the period 2001–2005 are less likely to be involved in new product and new process development than those that have some R&D staff in any year of the same period. *Ceteris paribus*, PRIs are more often involved in new product development than firms and hospitals, which confirm the descriptive statistics of Tables 5.4 and 5.5, and firms are more often involved in new process development than pharmaceutical hospitals and PRIs. Finally, the share of staff with a PhD, MSc or BSc degree has a negative and significant effect on both new product and new process development. This is a surprising result, as one would expect the opposite, but it explains the mismatch of skills and activities in the local system. This points to the nature of innovation itself – the firms which have staff mainly engaged in quality assurance and quality control for manufacturing various pharmaceutical products are more engaged in innovation, whereas the R&D going on at the PRIs and the universities (which have the more qualified staff on an average) does not result in much local innovation. The two equations of new product and new process development are shown to be positively and significantly related with a cross equation correlation of 0.879. This confirms the descriptive result of Table 5.6.

Table 5.5 Descriptive statistics: key actors of innovation

Variable	Firms Mean	(Std dev.)	Hospitals Mean	(Std dev.)	PRIs Mean	(Std dev.)	All Mean	(Std dev.)
Employment 2001–2005 (FTEs)	41.814	(66.858)	89.812	(258.01)	34.600	(44.164)	55.647	(155.502)
Age (in years)	12.561	(9.770)	14.813	(12.699)	8.760	(19.023)	12.327	(13.630)
% of staff with PhD	0.000	(0.000)	0.002	(0.009)	0.082	(0.139)	0.021	(0.078)
% of staff with MSc	0.015	(0.038)	0.007	(0.017)	0.103	(0.121)	0.035	(0.077)
% of staff with BSc	0.276	(0.288)	0.020	(0.052)	0.103	(0.159)	0.148	(0.275)
R&D performers 2001–2005	0.098	–	0.000	–	0.160	–	0.082	–
R&D personnel in 2001–2005	0.015	(0.087)	0.000	(0.000)	0.056	(0.161)	0.021	(0.100)
Number of observations	41		32		25		98	

Source: author's field survey, 2007.

Table 5.6 Bivariate probit ML estimation results: main actors of innovation

Variable	Coefficient	(Std error)
New product development		
Mean employment (FTEs) 2001–2005	0.150[†]	(0.089)
Staff having university degree	−0.987*	(0.411)
Non-R&D performers 2001–2005	−1.417**	(0.513)
Pharmaceutical PRIs	1.017*	(0.433)
Pharmaceutical firms	0.561	(0.455)
Intercept	0.063	(0.623)
New process development		
Mean employment (FTEs) 2001–2005	0.167[†]	(0.095)
Staff having university degree	−0.993*	(0.437)
Non-R&D performers 2001–2005	−1.760**	(0.614)
Pharmaceutical PRIs	0.343	(0.497)
Pharmaceutical firms	1.226*	(0.490)
Intercept	0.143	(0.720)
Extra parameter		
ρ 0.879** (0.089)		
No. of observations	98	
Log-likelihood	−68.469	

Source: author's survey, 2007.

Notes
Significance levels: † 10%; * 5%; ** 1%.

5.4.5 Policy vision and guiding framework

The legal framework for scientific and technological research and development are guided by the Science and Technology Act (cap 250) laws of Kenya. The Act establishes the machinery through which the government can avail advice on all matters relating to science and technology activities in the country in order to be able to coordinate research and experimental development. The Act also creates a National Council for Science and Technology under the present Ministry of Science and Technology, comprising all the Permanent Secretaries of the relevant ministries and 12 other members representing eminent scientists derived from various disciplines. The National Council on Science and Technology in Kenya has a broad mandate focusing on innovation and new technologies of importance to the country, such as biotechnology and ICTs. The Kenyan government has also been discussing a new Science, Technology and Innovation bill since 2006. Although the bill has not yet been decided upon, in 2008, a Science, Technology and Innovation Strategy was approved. However, Kenya presently spends less than 0.5 per cent of its GDP on science and technology and several sectors of the economy that have demonstrated significant capacity, such as ready-made garments and the cut-flower sector, are all being held back from progressing to more knowledge intensive domains due to the country's weak knowledge capacity.

Since the Science and Technology Act has no specific provisions on biotechnology, a specific framework to address issues of biotechnology development has been formulated. A National Biotechnology Policy was enacted in 2006 that sets out the safety procedures for biotechnology in the context of research and development, technology transfer and commercialization of products that could result from research undertaken in Kenya. The policy also identifies infrastructure development and the allocation of financial and human resources as key priorities for the growth of local health and agricultural biotechnology industry and research. As part of these developments, agricultural biotechnology and Kenya's biosafety framework have received much more attention than health biotechnology per se.

The Kenyan Health Policy Framework of 1994 sets out the health targets to be achieved by the country by the year 2010, which includes adopting explicit strategies to reduce the burden of disease within the country. Over the past few years, the government has also sought to encourage entrepreneurship in the field of drug development using natural resources, further support research through national institutions like KEMRI and also forge alliances between biomedical researchers and traditional healers. The Pharmacy and Poisons Board and the Kenya Bureau of Standards, discussed earlier in Section 5.2, are expected to play an important role in achieving this. The government has also sought to encourage entrepreneurship in the field of drug development using natural resources in recent years. This is being done by supporting more research in the public sector institutions like KEMRI and by enabling local alliances between biomedical researchers and traditional healers.

However, on a sectoral scale, the policy framework on health biotechnology is fragmented and there is no strategic policy vision in place to promote health biotechnology-led development, especially one that takes into account the technological needs (in terms of both physical and knowledge infrastructure) of the process. While Kenya has a national biotechnology policy, intellectual property law and a framework for establishing knowledge infrastructure of relevance to biotechnology research, there is no broader vision that links these to science, technology and innovation policy for the sector (or national science, technology and innovation policy for that matter), local health needs and competitiveness. The amount of financial resources that are allocated to public sector organizations for research is negligible. The framework is reminiscent of a rather familiar state of innovation in latecomer countries (see Oyeyinka and Gehl Sampath, 2009b), wherein the emphasis has been mainly on replicating a set of agencies rather than to enable the knowledge basis required for the sector to flourish. Even within the agencies that are in place, organizational competence is lacking due to the absence of sustained funding and skilled manpower to steer the organizations in productive directions.

The need for agencies that perform umbrella functions of coordinating innovation policy for the country as well as for the sector cannot be stressed enough. Even if one were to disregard this at the present, the lack of organizational competence as a result of sustained funding and skilled manpower to steer the existing organizations in productive directions is a troublesome reality. A striking difference when compared to the Indian and Bangladesh cases is the lack of a sector specific strategic vision (even partial) to promote local production of medicines. The fact that there is a pharmaceutical sector in the country within which several local firms like Cosmos Pharmaceuticals have excellent API manufacturing skills is a clear success story. This issue of resilience, at least in pockets, within local innovation systems that leads to sporadic success stories is a very interesting phenomenon, which is followed up in the Nigerian example (Chapter 6) and Part III of this book. On the part of the government, there even seem to have been several incentives, which for whatever reasons, have run against the development of pharmaceutical capacity in the country. For example, the survey found that local manufacturers who chose to import ingredients and manufacture drugs locally paid taxes that were much higher than those who chose to simply import the finished forms for distribution and retail. Several smaller firms (and even medium and large firms that were small at their inception) complained that these rules on taxes and tax rebates on importing finished forms were a contributing factor to their firm level strategies to branch out into distributing and retailing and not manufacture and product development. Such rules, over time, tend to get institutionalized in pervasive ways and help explain sectoral growth as we observe it in Kenya today.

Box 5.2 Cosmos Pharmaceuticals

Cosmos Pharmaceuticals manufactures health products in various dosage forms like tablets, capsules, liquid orals, externals and powders both for human and veterinary use. Having been in existence for 32 years now, its main focal therapeutic categories are anti-malarial, anti-retroviral, anti-tuberculosis, anti-diabetic, cardiovascular and gastrointestinal. Cosmos's manufacturing facilities are approved by the Pharmacy and Poisons Board, the National Drug Authority of Kenya and are subjected to regular quality audits by the National Regulatory Agency, Ministry of Health Uganda, Tanzania, Yemen and NGOs like MSF. The drug formulations are manufactured in conformity with the current GMP as laid down by the WHO as well as the drug manufacturing and quality regulations of the Ministry of Health, Republic of Kenya.

Cosmos is the recipient from GlaxoSmithKline and Boeringer Ingelheim for the manufacture of several ARVs and also is amongst the top ten suppliers of Artemesinin based therapy for the cure of Malaria to the Global Fund. For the ACT, it imports the Artemesinin from Tanzanian suppliers and makes the APIs in-house. At the time of the survey, Cosmos had just begun to operate a new facility that conforms to higher drug manufacturing standards of the FDA and some other regulatory agencies.

Source: author's survey, 2007

5.4.6 Local health system specifics and impetus to innovation

As mentioned earlier in this chapter, Kenya has one of the lowest scores on the human development index and life expectancy has remained the same over the past 15 years. General performance of the local health sector can be broken up into two main phases. A first phase ending in the early 1990s has achieved some positive trends in health indicators; for example, life expectancy improved from 44 years in 1962–1960 to 60 years in 1993, infant mortality rate reduced from 120 per 1000 in 1963 to 62.5 per 1000 in 1993. However, a second phase from 1993 up until now has a different story to tell. Life expectancy decreased from 60 years in 1993 to 47 years (largely due to HIV/AIDS), while infant mortality has risen from 64 per 1000 in 1993 to 72 per 1000.

There have been several important policy initiatives in the health sector such as the launching of a Kenyan Health Policy Framework in 1994, which articulates the role of the government in improving the health of the population. This was followed by a first National Health Strategic Plan, which was implemented between 1999 and 2004 and aimed to streamline the provision of health services including redistribution of services to the rural areas, with more emphasis on preventive health services and health awareness.

In the present situation, the Ministry of Health provides public health care services and controls 52 per cent of all medical facilities available in the country (Export Processing Zones Authority, 2005). However, there is immense disparity in the provision of health care services between the urban and rural areas. There is an acute shortage as well as unfavourable distribution of medical personnel, i.e. 1:33,000 in rural and 1:1700 in urban in total as of 2005. The survey also shows that the percentage of hospital staff with Masters or PhD degrees is no more than 2 per cent, which is a really worrying result and calls for health systems strengthening in the most fundamental way (see Table 5.6). A health manpower policy was formulated in 2004 with the aim of addressing the development and retention of human resources in the health sector.

Private health spending is close to 78 per cent (WHO, 2007) and health expenditure is 8 per cent of the country's GDP. Modern medicine still caters to a small percentage of the population, when compared to traditional medicine, which is not well integrated into the modern health care system. To increase access to health care, a national health insurance policy has been proposed but consensus is yet to be reached. Some other policy initiatives seem to be working quite well, which have been initiated locally in collaboration with international funders and donors (see Box 5.3). Although the Ministry of Health is one of the largest purchasers of drugs sold locally,[3] the survey did not find much evidence of a direct linkage between local innovation capacity and better access to drugs and services in the country both in the public and private sectors. The rural areas, especially, are highly neglected and under-privileged in this regard and private sector based distribution systems still have a long way to go in this regard. The Pharmaceutical Society of Kenya is the agency in-charge of issuing licences to pharmacists and ensures that drug dispensaries and stores perform according to pharmacy practitioner standards. Additionally, it is also responsible for ensuring the distribution of pharmaceutical and non-pharmaceutical products amongst local dispensaries and drug stores, monitoring and advising members on new disease control programmes and promoting high quality training of pharmacists. However, the survey found low evidence of well-qualified personnel in pharmacies and drug stores across the country.

Box 5.3 Health voucher scheme for rural and urban health in Kenya

In July 2006, the Kenyan government launched "Vouchers for Health" in a three-year pilot targeting poor women in three rural districts and two urban slums. The programme provides access to safe deliveries, family planning and gender violence recovery services. The initial budget was about €6.5 million.

The project is based on the concept of reimbursing providers for services rendered rather than paying for service inputs beforehand. In this project, providers are accredited and contracted to deliver high-impact services to voucher-bearing patients. Vouchers are sold at highly subsidized prices to poor women, allowing them to choose where to access safe deliveries, family planning services and gender violence recovery services. The subsidized vouchers broaden access for the poor to public, private, NGO and faith based hospitals. Detailed planning was done before the onset of the project through participant observation, community interviews and provider assessments. It provided data for the initial design and benchmarks against which results are measured.

An impact evaluation tool has been developed with the main focus to establish how well the poor have been targeted and to measure impact on maternal and infant mortality and morbidity.

Only 18 months into the project 97,500 vouchers (72,800 for safe motherhood and 24,700 for family planning) were sold to poor women for equivalent of US$2 and 70,600 vouchers were reimbursed. Reimbursed delivery services are worth US$60–200. Due to the project's initial success, the extension to new districts and additional services is planned with additional €10 million. As a national project, it has the potential to inform the creation of a national social health insurance programme. One can view the voucher as an insurance card (with clearly outlined benefits) giving access to services built similarly to insurance. Common elements include accreditation, quality assurance, reimbursement system, claim processing, costing and pricing, integrating private sector, client choice, provider competition, access and equity. The project "Vouchers for Health" and the poverty-grading tool can serve as an international model.

Source: author

5.4.7 The failure to establish local collaborations and linkages

Table 5.7 shows the distribution of collaboration intensity between firms, hospitals and public research institutes in the sector as a whole. As in all the other surveys, all respondents were asked to rate their collaboration with other actors on a scale of 1 to 5, where 1 denoted very weak and 5 denoted very strong.

More specifically, Table 5.7 reveals several important collaboration trends in the country's health innovation system that shed more light on product and process innovation patterns. First, the patterns of collaboration intensity of firms are similar to those of hospitals while both these patterns are different from those of PRIs. More specifically, collaboration intensity is on average rated weak by firms and hospitals (less than 2), but fairly strong, strong and very strong by PRIs (around or above 2.5). Second, universities tend to collaborate and have

Table 5.7 Intensity of collaboration in Kenya's health innovation system

Collaboration intensities	Firms	Hospitals	PRIs
With PRIs	1.43	1.5	3.24
With industrial associations	1.87	1.43	–
With universities	1.41	1.68	3.08
With private laboratories	1.60	2.25	2.64
With hospitals	2.19	2.62	2.60
With traditional medical practitioners	1.41	1.40	1.52
With firms	1.56	–	1.45
With governmental agencies	1.75	–	2.80
With international organizations	–	–	3.32
Total number of observations	41	32	25

Source: author's survey, 2007.

much less interaction with other actors in the innovation system than PRIs, which once again helps to highlight the funding and research difficulties peculiar to university centres of excellence within the Kenyan public sector. Third, firms collaborate mostly with hospitals for the sale of their products. All three key actors – firms, hospitals and PRIs – demonstrate very weak collaboration with traditional medicinal practitioners who treat a large majority of the local population. This is a very important result that shows that traditional medicine, despite its importance in the local health system, is not well integrated into the ongoing innovation activities in any significant way. It also helps to point to the lack of trust between traditional medicinal practitioners and other actors in the local health innovation system. Firms collaborate equally weakly both with universities (1.41) and PRIs (1.43), which points to the lack of sufficient linkages between the public sector and private enterprise for health innovation; usually assumed to be the biggest precondition for successful health innovation. Firms also have extremely low collaboration with other firms (1.56) and no collaboration with international organizations (both in the public and private sectors), which also helps to underscore the low level of product development activities happening within the country. This is a very different result from what was observed, for example, in the collaboration trends in the Indian sector (Chapter 3). Finally, a very important result is that only PRIs have collaboration with international organizations. This issue is discussed further in the next section.

More rigorous econometric analysis to explain new product and new process development by collaboration intensity variables (a bivariate probit model not presented here) confirms these results further. The analysis reveals that collaboration intensity with PRIs and private laboratories affects positively and significantly the probability of being involved in new product development. At the same time, the probability of being involved in new process development is positively and significantly influenced by the intensity of collaboration with hospitals. Finally, *ceteris paribus*, pharmaceutical firms are more often involved in new process development, which once again shows the kind of innovation (when present) in the local pharmaceutical sector.

5.5 Global pull factors and their impact on innovation patterns

Two global pull factors are significant in the context of Kenya's health innovation, one negative and the other positive. Kenya has been considerably successful in attracting several international partners for collaborative research, especially in the area of biotechnology (although agricultural biotechnology is a greater focus of such collaborations than health, see Oyeyinka and Gehl Sampath, 2009b). At the same time, Kenya's intellectual property regime, which is TRIPS compliant, is not necessarily a positive impetus to local innovation given its present status.

5.5.1 International collaborations

Kenya's experience with international collaborations is interesting and calls for a re-look at several levels. At a first glance, it is striking to note, as Table 5.7 shows, that the only set of actors that rate international collaborations as an important factor for new product and process innovations are PRIs (a rating of 3.32). However, there is limited mobility of labour between the public and private sector enterprises (or even within different public sector enterprises) and a large amount of tacit knowledge acquired in the PRIs remains within the organizations. Predominantly, the survey finds that this is because of the lack of linkages between the various actors on the one hand within the local innovation system, and second because of the low product development emphasis on the other.

Kenya has been a partner in several very acclaimed international collaborations in health, especially the Kenyan AIDS Vaccine Initiative. IAVI focused on localizing its R&D efforts in various latecomer countries in order to promote ownership of the initiative (amongst the southern partners) and communication (Chataway *et al.*, 2007). However, most of these projects have not contributed to building local research capacity in ways that spill over substantially to the other actors in the innovation system because of the observed tendency of international private sector companies to bring into the country finished (already modified) products for trials and limited production, thereby circumscribing the active participation of local public sector institutions and their researchers in the research and product development process. This points attention to a criticism that Kenyan international collaborations have met previously (especially in biotechnology), deeming them to be exogenous, driven largely by international private sector interests and supported by the donor community or international private foundations.

The lack of absorption of capacity through international collaborations into the local innovation system can be traced back to the lack of knowledge infrastructure in addition to collaboration incentives, as the survey data reveal. The survey finds a strong relationship between national strategy for biotechnology development, availability of relevant human skills in the local research institutes and international collaborative efforts. In other words, if there were more relevant human skills that could be deployed and if national and organizational strategies for biotechnology were more clearly set out and implemented to make capacity building a priority in international research collaborations (both of which rely on policy capacity, see next section), strategic involvement of local researchers in international collaborations could have been effected, which is now not the case. The survey also found that most researchers who take part in such capacity building and training are disgruntled by the low state of innovation capacity in the local system which constantly acts as a hindrance to applying their acquired skills to research and innovation activities to the local context.

5.5.2 *IPRs*

The country's intellectual property regime is compliant with standards set out by the Agreement on Trade Related Aspects of Intellectual Property Rights of the WTO. The IPRs in Kenya are covered under four Acts of Parliament, namely: the Intellectual Property Act (cap 509), the Trademarks Act (Act 506), the Seeds and Plant Varieties Act (cap 326) and the Copyrights Act (cap 150). Kenya has a very low score of local patent applications when compared to foreign ones, which once again acts as a measure of the low level of local entrepreneurial activity. Patent registrations amounted to 61 in the year 2001, with two of these being registered by residents and the rest by non-residents. The number of international patents operational in Kenya as of 2002 amounted to a total of 89,180 according to 2002 data available with the WIPO (WIPO Patent Information 2007). The extremely stringent intellectual property regime certainly poses limitations on reverse engineering activities in health innovation and Kenya is yet to enact several flexibilities that are allowed and important under the TRIPS Agreement,[4] such as a research exemption to universities and public research institutions. There is also very little awareness of patenting possibilities in the public sector. The survey also reveals that all actors advocating and negotiating for royalty-free access to biotechnologies in Kenya (such as the International Service for the Acquisition of Agri-Biotech Applications and the African Agricultural Technology Foundation) are non-governmental in nature, underscoring the lack of awareness amongst policy makers and KIPI on the impact of the present intellectual property regime on local entrepreneurial ventures.

Although Cosmos Pharmaceuticals has acquired voluntary licences for the production of some ARVs, the Kenyan government has not compulsorily licensed the production of any drugs in the interest of public health.

5.6 Conclusion

The key actors and their constraints identified in this chapter point towards a very low capacity to carry out health biotechnology innovation in Kenya. The policy framework is highly fragmented and unable to coordinate the technological requirements of health biotechnology with the local health needs of the population. The universities, local research institutes and governmental agencies suffer similarly from lack of funding, organizational competence and knowledge infrastructure of the kind required to embark on health biotechnology. The private sector remains stunted due to difficulties of accessing relevant technologies, venture capital and risk-sharing mechanisms. These limitations in the innovation environment also limit knowledge spillovers from international collaborations into Kenya's health biotechnology innovation system. In particular, the following challenges will need to be overcome in order to promote the growth of innovation capacity in the sector.

5.6.1 Challenge 1: promoting a vibrant private sector for innovation

Kenya's local private sector enterprise in health and biotechnology is a critical asset in promoting innovation capacity. It is presently highly challenged by foreign competition and lack of technological support from the public sector and the government. Despite the intent of the National Biotechnology Policy of 2006, little has been done to promote the emergence of a vibrant private sector for health biotechnology. Emergence of a vibrant private sector is a reflex to the presence of risk attenuating mechanisms that offer business support and promote enterprise. Innovation experiences in health biotechnology both in the frontier countries and relatively successful latecomers find evidence of several innovative financing activities for both technological and health care services. There is little governmental infrastructure for technological incubation, acquisition of technology required to pursue innovation and funding, especially small-firm risk sharing and financing initiatives of the kind a country like Kenya would need.

5.6.2 Challenge 2: a highly fragmented policy framework for health and biotechnology

The policy framework is highly fragmented and unable to coordinate the technological requirements of health biotechnology with the local health needs of the population. The universities, local research institutes and governmental agencies suffer similarly from lack of funding, organizational competence and knowledge infrastructure of the kind required to embark on health biotechnology. The private sector remains stunted due to difficulties of accessing relevant technologies, venture capital and risk-sharing mechanisms. These limitations in the innovation environment also limit knowledge spillovers from international collaborations into Kenya's health biotechnology innovation system.

5.6.3 Challenge 3: lack of skilled human capacity

A review of previous studies all agree on this point: Kenya still has a shortfall of adequate laboratory capacity and facilities needed to effectively exploit biotechnology (Wafula and Falconi, 1998, and Odame *et al.*, 2002 to mention a few). Human skill, the other component of knowledge infrastructure, is highly limited, a point that has been discussed at length in the previous section.

6 Nigeria and Tanzania's incipient health innovation capacity[1]

6.1 Introduction

Nigeria's economy depends very significantly on the oil and gas sector, which contributes 99 per cent of export revenues, 85 per cent of government revenues and about 52 per cent of GDP. GDP grew from US$28.5 billion in 1990 to US$115.338 billion in 2006. With its large reserves of human and natural resources, Nigeria has the potential to build a prosperous economy, reduce poverty significantly and provide the health, education and infrastructure services its population needs. Despite the country's relative oil wealth, GDP per capita is about US$752 (2005), and poverty remains a big challenge – about 54 per cent of the population lives on less than US$1 per day. However, Nigeria's macro-economic performance over the last two years has been relatively strong.[2]

This chapter provides a broad analysis of the current health and biotechnology innovation dynamics in Nigeria with a view to understanding the policies and institutions necessary to advance the growth of the sector. The data derives from two separate surveys carried out by the authors in 2004 and 2006 as part of two separate projects. The 2004 study was jointly conducted with the National Biotechnology Development Agency (NABDA) and a local research team, and focused on surveying health and biotechnology systems of innovation in Nigeria. The 2004 study was initiated with an inception seminar that included over 100 policy makers and followed with pilot testing of the questionnaire and an empirical survey that administered and retrieved 170 questionnaires in total and conducted over 100 interviews with individual actors from the health innovation system. The study tried to identify the triggers to innovation amongst the major actors, follows through some of the processes and identified the obstacles to creating a dynamic system. The main emphasis was identifying inter-organizational interactions and their impact on performance and innovation in the sector in Nigeria. A second survey[3] was conducted in 2006 and focused specifically on the biotechnology systems of innovation in Nigeria. A total of 240 questionnaires were administered this time around and again over 100 field interviews conducted with actors in health and agricultural biotechnology. In both studies, the questionnaires and field interviews were aimed at all critical actors in the system including university centres of excellence, public sector research organizations, biodiversity related organizations, pharmaceutical and biotechnology enterprises, drug certification bodies, health practitioners, NGOs and donors, governmental agencies and policy makers. The analysis presented in this chapter draws equally on the empirical data collected in both studies.[4]

6.2 Key actors in the innovation system

The critical actors in the sector remain within the public sector and as such the government of Nigeria still conducts a large part of agricultural and health research and there is little research capacity in the private sector. In addition to government established and controlled PRIs, the country has always placed great emphasis on health based universities, all of which emerged as the country expanded university education in the 1960s.

6.2.1 Government

In part resulting from its colonial legacy, policy for S&T emphasized largely agricultural research until the early 1960s until government began to pay attention to the industrial sector. An international conference on the organization of Research and Training in Africa held in the mid-1960s led to the establishment of a National Council for Scientific and Industrial Research (NCSIR). Subsequently in December 1966, the Federal Military Government promulgated Decree No. 83 establishing the Nigeria Council for Scientific and Industrial Research. The NCSIR was replaced within three years with the repeal of the NCSIR Decree, and the establishment of the Nigeria Council of Science and Technology (NCST) Decree of 1970. The promotion of research in other sectors of the Nigerian economy started with NCST powers and mandate now covering agricultural sciences, experimental sciences, engineering and technology, medical sciences, environmental and social sciences. Specifically NCST had to oversee and manage research and development activities across ministerial lines, with four sectoral councils.

6.2.2 Public research institutes

Five PRIs play a major role in the development of health and biotechnology innovation to varied extents deriving from their institutional focus and specialization. The Sheda Science and Technology Complex (SHESTCO), Abuja, is a science village that was established by the federal government of Nigeria as a multidisciplinary R&D centre in 1993. The main aims are to (a) initiate and promote rational and innovative uses of Nigeria's natural endowments, (b) provide a centre of excellence for research and training addressed to the socio-economic progress of Nigeria, (c) train and develop manpower in research methodology and programme formulation and (d) develop results of research for application in the areas of agriculture, health, industry and environment. The Biotechnology Advanced Laboratory, which is part of the complex is meant to provide advanced technological facilities for research in the main sub-disciplines of biotechnology – agricultural, medical, industrial and environmental.

The National Institute for Pharmaceutical Research and Development (NIPRID) was established in 1987 based on the recommendation of the Pharmaceutical Society of Nigeria by the federal government of Nigeria as an agency under the Ministry of Science and Technology. The primary mandate of the institute is to exploit local raw materials through the application of modern scientific research and development methods into high quality pharmaceutical-grade raw materials, drugs and biological products for the management of tropical diseases and other global ailments. The National Veterinary Research Institute (NVRI), Vom, can be traced back to 1913, when West Africa suffered its first major Rinderpest infestation. What started as a veterinary department to deal with the problem, was shifted later on to Vom.

The Nigerian National Institute for Medical Research (NIMR), Yaba, was established in the 1940s as a West African initiative, but is now a federal institute that conducts research and carries out studies that influence health policy making in Nigeria. In its latter role, it serves as an adviser to the government. The institute has five major departments – biochemistry, microbiology, molecular biology and genetics, public health and clinical sciences division. The National Centre for Genetic Resources and Biotechnology (NACGRAB) was established in 1987 by Nigeria's Federal Ministry of Science and Technology to act as the centre of focus in the country for research, data gathering and dissemination of technological information on matters relating to genetic resources utilization, conservation and biotechnology. It is also involved in the development and servicing of the activities of the National Committee on Naming, Registration, Release of Crop Varieties and Livestock Breeding. To date, NACGRAB has evaluated and characterized some exotic and indigenous plant germplasms. It has also undertaken exploration and collation of some endangered plant species. It has collected about 25 lost lines of *Vigna unguiculata* from the International Institute for Tropical Agriculture. It has currently a total collection of about 12,000 plant species maintained as seeds in storage rooms or on the field as a field gene bank.

6.2.3 Universities

There are more than 70 universities in Nigeria with ownership spread between federal, state and the private sector especially religious organizations. Relevant faculties where health and health related R&D are ongoing include pharmacy, pharmacology, pharmacognosy, biochemistry, chemistry, botany, biotechnology/ bio-engineering and wildlife and forestry.

6.2.4 NGOS and donors

There is a wide array of collaborations with donors, NGOs and international organizations. While the section on universities and public research institutes has discussed to some extent the reliance on donor and external funding in health and biotechnology innovation, we focus here on important collaborative ventures. Nigeria is active in the Human Genome Mapping project and has been an active partner in the International Cooperative Biodiversity Group's Programme of the USA which sought to devise newer partnership models that combined drug discovery, protection of local traditional knowledge and biodiversity conservation.

6.3 Current strengths in the health innovation system

The local innovation system is highly constrained and actors are faced with a series of institutional shortcomings that are discussed in Section 6.4. Despite this, there have been several cases of product development success, all of which have been presented here. A key commonality among all these cases is that they were all enabled through the informal linkages of the key actors in the health innovation system, rather than any formal collaboration incentives. Furthermore, they have all been developed through the local PRIs.

6.3.1 Anti-sickle cell drug, NIPRISAN

At the time of the surveys, NIPRID has succeeded in producing an anti-sickle cell drug called Niprisan. The drug illustrates an interesting case of local collaboration since it was based on traditional medicinal knowledge of a local healer to solve a very important local health issue, sickle cell sickness. Although NIPRID was successful in isolating the main molecules and conducting clinical trials in the initial stages, it licensed out the final stages of clinical trials to a US based company. The case was also important since it creates a precedent for collaboration between a traditional medicinal healer and a public research institute (NIPRID in this instance). The institute received information on the potency of the natural product that formed the basis of the drug from a healer with whom it formed an agreement to share benefits arising from the sale of the drug (field interviews, 2006).

6.3.2 Bacterial vaccine for livestock and poultry

The Bacterial Vaccine Production Department of NVRI has been responsible for the production of various bacterial vaccines for use in the control of livestock and poultry diseases. These vaccines include anthrax spore vaccine, black quarter vaccine, contagions bovine pleuropneumonia vaccine (live) wet and dried, contagions bovine pleuropneumonia vaccine (live) freeze dried, contagion bovine pleuropneumonia vaccine-inactivate, haemorrhagic septicaemia vaccine, fowl typhoid vaccine (wet and dry forms), fowl cholera vaccine, BBG vaccine, hantavac vaccine and the vomac-3 vaccine. Although most of these vaccines are only for local use, these are important examples of product innovation in local PRIs.

6.3.3 Typhoid vaccine

A typhoid epidemic in 1993/1994 in the city of Minna provided the innovation trigger that moved a professor at the local university to put together a team of researchers from within the local university and a medical doctor from a public sector research institute (MVIR). The team collected samples of the local strain from the local people, successfully isolated the organisms within the samples and purified the isolates. However, there were no facilities in the university where these organisms could be characterized and so the isolates were sent to the UK to be characterized there. In addition, the laboratory provided samples from their own stock of Typhoid isolates so that the team in Minna could prepare vaccines both for the Minna and other strains in the future. Candidate vaccines were prepared and tested on 4000 mice after which 30 types were retained. These were tested in rabbits and in monkeys at another collaborating public sector research institute. All three were effective, with the most effective being retained for clinical testing at the General Hospital. The typhoid vaccine has since been patented in Nigeria and 18,000 dosages were produced for a local immunization campaign.

Two broad factors were responsible for the success, namely, the focus on local problems and local physical and knowledge resources, fostered by both researchers and the state, and, second, was the collaborative approach to share between universities and public sector research institutes. Trust amongst stakeholders led to the support of local industry and knowledge sharing between the local Association of Traditional Medical Practitioners and local researchers and distant partners. Greater success will evidently result if government policies and priorities are directed at fostering partnership through incentives and infrastructure.

6.4 Local push factors in the innovation system

6.4.1 Lack of funding and mandate in the public sector

R&D efforts both in universities and PRIs have been constrained over time due to the absence of good libraries, poor internet connectivity, brain drain, poor laboratories, declining per capita funding of tertiary education, declining funding for R&D, decaying facilities for R&D, poor research training of academic staff (partly due to the declining priority on research), inability of many academic staff to access research grants from international agencies and inadequate contribution of the private sector and industry to local R&D. Table 6.1 presents the results of our survey in four of the most prominent universities in the area of health and biotechnology. The table shows the extreme reliance on overseas research funding when compared to local collaborations for research.

Table 6.2 shows that except for NVRI, all the PRIs rate foreign collaboration much higher than local collaboration, although they consider it only of average importance.

Table 6.1 Local versus overseas collaboration at universities in Nigeria

Institutions	Overseas (%)	Local (%)
ABU	14	12
Federal University of Technology, Minna	3	12
Obafemi Awolowo University, Ife	25	32
University of Ibadan	58	44
Total no. of respondents	68	68

Source: authors' field surveys, 2004, 2006.

Some PRIs, of which NIPRID is a notable example, have established extensive collaborations with international organizations for R&D, tacit knowledge transfer through skills training. Prominent partners for collaboration are the National Institute of Health, Washington, DC, USA, in the area of training, laboratory infrastructure development, ICT; Howard University, Washington, DC, USA, in the area of capacity building and training of pharmacists on monitoring of anti-retroviral drugs; Xechem Pharmaceuticals Company on Pilot Scale extraction of herbal products in order to make NIPRID's research and development activities industry demand driven and private sector funded.

Field interviews show that the reason why foreign collaborations are rated higher than local collaborations is because foreign collaborations are often the only stable source of funding seeking to establish a reasonable working environment in Nigerian public research institutes and universities. Even the international collaborations are stifled to a large extent by the lack of internal funding and mandate within the country and interviews reveal that most national actors do not know much of the kind of research ongoing within the other universities and PRIs in the country due to the very low importance placed on collaborative linkages in Nigeria's present policy framework. The extreme lack of funding also creates an environment where there is a large amount of artificial competition (which is unproductive for the system's performance as a whole) between organizations to attract funding from national and international sources alike, in order to survive.

Table 6.2 Intensity and partner in collaboration in Nigeria's health innovation (scale 1–5)

Institutions → Collaborators	NACGRAB	NVRI	NIPRID	SHESTCO
PRIs	5.0	2.0	1.8	2.57
Industry associations	4.0	1.4	1.6	0.72
Universities	None	2.7	3.0	1.86
External/private institutions	4.0	1.1	2.1	1.72
Hospital and health centres	None	0.9	2.3	1.14
Traditional medicinal practitioners	1.0	0.6	2.7	0.72
Others	3.0	0.7	0.5	0.14

Source: authors' field surveys, 2004, 2006.

Universities also have similar experiences in establishing collaborations, and although some of them have been very successful in generating results that are far reaching for the local system of innovation, sustained support from the government is required to help further these achievements.

Box 6.1 The Malaria Research Group: an example of long distance partnership care

The Malaria Research Group at the College of Medicine, University of Ibadan is a multidisciplinary research group comprising physicians and scientists from four faculties of the College and Hospital with physical facilities at the Institute of Advances Medicinal Research and Training. The group focuses on basic and applied research for the control of malaria and reduction of associated morbidity and mortality. The group's principal areas of research concentration include chemotherapy, development and novel treatment modalities, development of novel diagnostics techniques, epidemiology, community and public health education. The group also devotes effort to training young physicians and scientists from the region in tropical disease research. Clinical and laboratory based scientists trained by the group are currently participating in various aspects of health care, research, medical education and decision making in Nigeria.

The Malaria Research Group has benefited from productive relationships with established research teams in the USA (Walter Reed Army Institute of Research; Harvard School of Public Health, Harvard; Oregon School of Health Science, Oregon) and Europe (Karolinska Institute; London School of Tropical Medicines and Hygiene). These relationships culminated in the establishment of the group's interdisciplinary laboratories and facilities at the Institute of Advanced Medical Research and Training. The group has also established linkage and collaboration with national and state health control programmes including the Federal Ministry of Health and the Oyo State Ministry of Health.

The current focus and strength of the Malaria Research Group at Ibadan now comprises studies on pharmacological and clinical efficacy of anti-malaria drugs, basic laboratory research on chemotherapy, parasitology and biology of malaria parasites and application of social sciences in tropical diseases control. Over the past ten years, ten doctorate and 12 masters degrees were awarded to graduate students receiving training through the group's facilities. The group has received support from WHO, IAEA, Rockefeller foundation, British Council and the Wellcome Trust.

Source: Oyeyinka *et al.*, 2004

6.4.2 Low level of skilled manpower of relevance to the sector

Nigeria lags behind its Asian counterparts in school enrolments, especially for secondary and tertiary education. As expected, the schooling ratio falls from primary to secondary to tertiary in the country drastically and the same is true for other conventional knowledge indicators, such as researchers in R&D per million of population and R&D investments as a percentage of GDP, which although not presented here, have been analysed by us in a broader context.[5] The proportion of the population enrolled in science, engineering, mathematics and computing in Nigeria in 1997 lag far behind the level in Taiwan in 1985 and has now fallen behind that of Vietnam at the most basic levels, primary and secondary enrolment. If Nigeria were to "catch up" to that of Taiwan's 1985 level by 2005 (i.e. to reach a stage that would follow 25 years behind contemporary Taiwan), the scale of enrolment would need to quadruple over several years.

6.4.3 The marginal presence of a local private sector

Within Nigeria, the universities and PRIs currently drive the process of change. Firms' capacity to exploit biotechnology innovation is at a very elementary phase in Nigeria mainly due to a weak private sector, low level of entrepreneurship and poor institutional capacity support for translating inventive effort into innovation. In recent years, there has been a tremendous upsurge in the market for phytomedicines in Nigeria, but there is a lack of regulatory infrastructure to test and control efficacy and safety of such medicines. The Nigerian Agency for Food and Drug Control (NAFDAC) focuses on this to a limited extent, but there is a need for an entirely different regulatory mechanism for the control of traditional medicines that are introduced in the market. This is accentuated by low private sector capacity in drug development: presently, most of their research (90 per cent) focuses on screening and secondary screening, with only a last 10 per cent focus on product development activities. When compared to the 2004 survey where most local firms were focused on developing natural products based remedies for which there were no strict certification procedures, we saw a clear shift towards more sophisticated enterprise in the sector in the 2006 survey with a focus on biotechnology. However, the local firms had developed no products when the surveys were concluded. PRIs, in this context, have been instrumental in exploring the potential of applying biotechnology related techniques to existing research bases. Recent studies cited in the literature on the point show that between 1990 and 2004, about 98.8 per cent of all R&D funding came from government sources, further supporting our results. They also claim that industrial firms operating in Nigeria prefer to use foreign consultants rather than local consultants and rely more on international results of innovations and inventions rather than local sources of knowledge.

6.4.4 The need for a coherent framework for health innovation

In 1977, the NCST and its sectoral councils were dissolved and in its place, the National Science and Technology Development Agency (NSTDA) established in order to promote a more coordinated approach to science and technology development in Nigeria. The NSTDA was then later transformed into the Federal Ministry of Science and Technology, which has since formulated a national S&T Policy for the country. Currently a major reform started in 2007 is ongoing to further strengthen the S&T function and to incorporate issues of innovation into the ministerial activities (to expand the mandate from S&T to science, technology and innovation) and to take on board emerging areas such as ICT and biotechnology.

The federal government of Nigeria has also developed a National Biotechnology Policy in April 2001. For effective implementation of the policy the government took a further step to establish NABDA under the Federal Ministry of Science and Technology in 2002. NABDA's mandate includes developing an indigenous critical mass of human resources and infrastructure for biotechnology in Nigeria; ensuring that biotechnology is profitably applied to government's stewardship such as assurance of high quality health services, food security, environmental protection and safety; ensuring a sustainable mechanism for adequate funding of biotechnology activities through national and international funding agencies and ensuring that Nigeria becomes self-reliant in the development and application of biotechnology based products and services, among other objectives. As part of these functions, NABDA undertook a detailed survey of biotechnology innovation in the country with the United Nations University in 2004 (Oyeyinka *et al.*, 2004) in order to inform sectoral policy on biotechnology. The Nigerian Natural Medicine Development Agency is another important policy initiative of the federal government and the main aim of the agency is to foster and facilitate the development and accreditation processes of natural medicines in the country. NAFDAC has the mandate to set standards of drug quality and efficacy procedures and drug approval.

In the area of health innovation, NABDA is expected to interact with the Ministry of Science and Technology and the Ministry of Health, and agencies such as the Nigerian Natural Medicine Development Agency. A new National Health Policy was formulated in 2004 to provide a new institutional framework for health care activities, the goal of which is to develop a comprehensive health care system that is based on primary health care. The policy describes the goals, structure and strategy and policy direction of the new health care delivery system in the country. It articulates the roles and responsibilities of the three tiers of government in addition to non-governmental actors. Its long-term goal is to provide the entire population with adequate access not only to primary health care but also to secondary and tertiary services through a well-functioning referral system. However, one of the biggest obstacles to the development of health and biotechnology innovation of importance to health is that this progressive policy was not conceptualized in systems terms and did not give explicit priority to either science, technology and innovation generally or health biotechnology specifically. Previous research (Oyeyinka, 2006; Gehl Sampath and Oyeyinka, 2007) provide useful insights into the functioning of government institutions at both the national and sectoral levels in Nigeria and highlight several such deficiencies that arise from the lack of well-coordinated policies that oversee sectoral growth trajectories.

Nigeria, as a developing country, which is part of the WTO, has also implemented the TRIPS Agreement locally and has had a draft bill on traditional knowledge and biodiversity protection that has been pending for several years now.

6.5 The case of Tanzania's health innovation system[6]

The case of Tanzania is an interesting departure from the Nigerian experience because its health innovation sector has a relatively successful entrepreneurship model that is largely private sector based, which is precisely where the Nigerian health innovation system shows a major setback. The main actors in the health innovation system remain similar, with the prominence of two key research institutes, namely, the Nigerian National Institute for Medical Research (NIMR) and the Institute for Traditional Medicine.

The NIMR is a parastatal institution, which is mandated to: (i) carry out, and promote the carrying out of, medical research designed to alleviate disease among the people of Tanzania among others. Since its inception in 1979 NIMR has evolved from a disease specific approach to the current wider mandate that includes all health research at the local, zonal, national and regional levels. NIMR endeavours at the local level to establish close collaboration with the district Council Health Management Teams and health facilities to address local priority problems. At the national level, NIMR's major responsibilities include supporting the Ministry of Health in disease control activities and building zonal and district capacities for health research and service delivery.

The Institute of Traditional Medicine started as a Traditional Medicine Research Unit in July 1974, and was later elevated to an Institute of Traditional Medicine in 1991. The mission of the institute is to act as a centre of excellence in the evaluation, documentation, creation and dissemination of knowledge on traditional medicine and drug discovery and, hence, contribute to the intellectual life of Tanzania, educate the public and ensure that research in traditional medicine responds to the health needs of the people and acts as a catalyst to improve health care services in the country.

Apart from the public sector research institutes, the local health innovation system comprises pharmaceutical firms, but local producers of pharmaceutical products in Tanzania depend on collaboration with pharmaceutical companies from frontier countries or the fast following countries. Many pharmaceutical substances, such as APIs, are imported from outside the country. The survey showed four important local firms. One of these is Shelys Pharmaceuticals, which is also the largest company in East Africa and has been in existence since 1988. It manufactures a diverse range of 80 products in different therapeutic segment including anti-malarials, pain management, haemaatinics, anti-infectives, nutraceuticals etc. In 2003, the company acquired Kenya based Beta Healthcare to make Shelys the largest firm in the regional market. The company now owns household brands, like Koflyn, Coldril, Sheladol, Action and Mara Moja, and now aims to be one of the largest pharmaceuticals companies in Africa. The Tanzanian Pharmaceutical Industry is partly government owned and also produces some first line anti-retroviral drugs and sells through government procurements. This firm has technical assistance from Indian and Thai firms. Tanzansino is yet another local firm that is presently being resurrected using Chinese collaborative expertise. The local firms supply to around 70 per cent of the local market and also export drugs to Malawi, Congo, Zambia and Mozambique. The fourth prominent local firm is Keko, which is a local private owned enterprise. All the firms import APIs from India and China in order to manufacture medicines locally.

Tanzania has also been successful in creating a cluster of firms that are actively engaged in the production of long-lasting insecticidal nets (LLINs), as discussed in the case study below.

6.5.1 Case study: mosquito net manufacturers in Tanzania

Tanzania has a large number of domestic mosquito net manufacturing firms with a total annual net production of over five million nets, of which about two million entered the domestic market in 2004 (Magesa *et al.*, 1991). These local net manufacturing firms have made substantial progress in expanding the distribution of network for mosquito nets. The net manufacturing firm in Tanzania include the A to Z Textiles Mills Ltd, Sun Flag Ltd and TMTL.

For instance, A to Z Textile Mills Ltd is a fully integrated plant with spinning, knitting, weaving, dyeing, finishing, cutting and making departments. The private firm is based in Arusha, Tanzania, and was established in 1966 as a small garment making enterprise. A to Z Textile Mills started manufacturing polyester mosquito net fabrics in the mid-1970s, which were sold locally. Presently, mosquito nets account for 80 per cent of the total production of the factory, which employs over 1500 people of which over 85 per cent are women. Its capacity is close to eight million nets per annum and it exports to over 25 countries in Africa.

A to Z Textile Mill Ltd employs a technology from Sumitomo, Japan, in the manufacture of Olyset Nets. The Olyset net is a long-lasting insecticidal net (LLIN) made of polyethylene whereby the insecticide is already in the resin, which is the main raw material. The estimated lifetime of an Olyset net is four years minimum, and is a very sophisticated product.

Since mid-1980s, much work has taken place on insecticide-treated nets ITNs in Tanzania (Table 6.3). A number of research institutions, donor agencies, NGO, the private and public agencies have been closely involved in the improvement of this tool and preparing ground for national scale expansion.

Initially, a number of studies on ITNs focused on its entomological actions. This was followed by work on a number of small scale trials to demonstrate epidemiological impact under controlled conditions (efficacy trials) (Lines *et al.*, 1987; Magesa *et al.*, 1991; Curtis *et al.*, 1996; Maxwell *et al.*, 1999). Subsequently, the emphasis was put on larger trials and exploring community-wide benefits of ITNs on both morbidity and mortality (Schellenberg *et al.*, 2001; Abdulla *et al.*, 2001; Marchant *et al.*, 2002). Accessibility and distribution of nets occupied much of the research during the late 1990s (Njunwa *et al.*, 1991; Makemba *et al.*, 1996; Fraser-Hurt *et al.*, 1999). Studies on community based net distribution and socio-marketing formed the largest part of the studies during this period. Other studies included the design and testing of insecticide home treatment kits (Miller *et al.*, 1999a, b) and factors influencing net retreatment among

Table 6.3 Critical path of insecticide treated mosquito net research and implementation in Tanzania

Efficacy studies	Effectiveness studies	Policy developments	Scale developments
1983–1995	1992–2000	1997–2000	2000–2008
Reducing malaria vector exposure (including net and insecticide developments)	Impact (morbidity and mortality) and cost assessment in pilot programmes	National strategies and partnerships for an enabling environment	National ITN strategy and policy NATNETS
1985–1995			Rethinking of ITN national policy on possible free net coverage of all sleeping beds
Reducing malaria morbidity and mortality			

Source: modified from Magesa *et al.*, 2005.

Tanzanian communities. In recent years, most work concentrated on the efficacy and introduction of long-lasting insecticide treated nets (Tami *et al.*, 2004).

The scaling up of net distribution in Tanzania has been enhanced by public–private partnership policies. A close collaboration among the public and private organizations and NGOs was advocated around the issue of demand creation and increased supply and use of ITNs. In this scenario, the public sector role is focusing on consumer protection, policy and regulatory issues, as well as generic demand creation, in order to create an ITN-enabling environment. The NGO role focuses on more local, grass-root demand creation and support for specific niche supply. The commercial sector role focuses on supply and distribution, product development, and brand specific demand creation (Magesa *et al.*, 2005). All these activities are supported by the research community (public and private) in product development, operations research, market research and monitoring and evaluation. The involvement of regulatory bodies in the scaling up of ITN also needs to be recognized. Regulatory issues included insecticide registration, definition of authorized retail outlets, consumer rights and product quality. More remarkably, was the opening of windows for more agents in the sales of ITN kits. Until recently, only registered pharmaceuticals were allowed to sell home insecticide retreatment kits. However, with the collaboration between the Tropical Pesticide Research Institute and Ministry of Health, such kits are now distributed more widely by social marketing agents.

6.6 Summing up

An outstanding feature of Nigeria's health and biotechnology innovation system is the product development successes that have been achieved by some of its PRIs. A closer scrutiny of the products developed shows that the key factors that played a role in the success were the focus on local health and veterinary needs and informal contacts between actors in the innovation system, rather than formal linkages. Another strength of the health innovation system is the ability of the local PRIs to conduct research until advanced stages of the innovation process. While NIPRID and NIMR have very good facilities for preclinical and clinical development, SHESTCO has advanced biotechnological techniques for recombinant DNA and genomics and NACGRAB has an extremely diverse gene bank to source novel compounds for screening purposes. These investments by the federal government in recent years show a serious, sustained interest in promoting the sector. Nigeria also demonstrates a significant level of very qualified researchers working in the various public research institutes and parastatal agencies. It is the capabilities of these researchers that have made it possible for them to initiate product development successes in an otherwise hostile innovation environment. However, these need to be strengthened by sector-wide reform, failing which the potential for health innovation in Nigeria cannot be realized. The case of Tanzania, which has also demonstrated significant success in product development initiatives in some key areas, also poses the same question: How can the isolated cases of product development be made a sector-wide success?

Part III

Comparative insights

A comparative institutional perspective such as the one that guides this book helps to further our understanding of the ways in which national trajectories for development are shaped by historical circumstances. The context specific nature of the process (level of technology and the quality of scientific and technological infrastructure) as well as the nature of institutions (the scientific culture and support systems) means that the factors that foster or hinder the translation of research into innovation differ not only in frontier and latecomer economies, but also can have further variations within latecomer contexts. For instance, in a study that investigated the decisions to commercialize new technologies within a large number of research establishments in India, patentability of technology was ranked seventh in importance (Kumar *et al.*, 2004), but the same assumes extremely little importance in the context of research establishments of a similar nature in several sub-Saharan African countries.

In other words, in what ways have institutions shaped the emergence of scientific research and its observed path to the market in health innovation? Why have there been so few successes in taking inventions to the market in Africa, whereas in Asia even countries with significant lags in policy initiation of capacity programmes such as Vietnam, show greater results? In this book, the sectoral systems framework has been applied to test the hypothesis that the institutionally predetermined policy processes have impacted significantly on the ways inventive activities travel/or do not travel from the laboratory to the market and thus account for varying levels of innovation capacity.

On the surface, all latecomer countries have public sector research institutions with some level of endowments dedicated to health innovation, but, as the sectoral investigations in Part II show, it is the differences that matter. Several key results accrue from the individual country experiences and the comparative insights on the issue of institutional capacity. This Part of the book has two chapters that mainly focus on collating the key insights from a comparative perspective (Chapter 7) and present the policy relevant results (Chapter 8).

7 Health innovation and latecomer development

7.1 Introduction

The six-country analysis of health innovation systems in latecomer countries at different stages of development presents a complex range of challenges and triumphs in building local capacity. The six countries presented in Part II are very varied and some of them have been discussed in the literature on economics of innovation and health for the first time here. They add new dimensions to our understanding of health innovation trends in latecomer contexts. The uniformity and rigour of the field methodology that blends field interviews and case studies with quantitative and qualitative data collected through questionnaires provides a unique basis for comparison. The country case studies have sought to examine the following issues:

a   What are the specific characteristics of health innovation systems in latecomer countries at different stages?
b   What are the dynamics of inter-firm/inter-organizational collaborations in generating new knowledge (defined as knowledge new to the firm or the local context) in this sector, in ways that lead to sustained technological learning? What systemic imperfections affect inter-firm/inter-organizational collaborations and how can they be classified?
c   Are there specific factors that lead to learning and capabilities formation in health innovation in latecomer countries as opposed to what we already know from similar comparisons of their more well to do counterparts in the West? Are these specifically related to development?
d   What is the impact of international policies, especially those related to intellectual property and global trade on technological capabilities building in this sector for the latecomers and the very latecomers?
e   Are there newer models of south–south cooperation and technological learning that are emerging, or are there specific trends observable that could inform policy?

This chapter re-examines the key findings of each one of the chapters in a comparative light in order to derive results of relevance to the discourse on health innovation. The chapter focuses on four main issues. First is the question of institutional capacity that is so central to the framework for health innovation created and elaborated upon in Chapter 2. Institutional capacity was defined as not just the capacity of the sector to borrow rules and regulations, but the capacity of the sector to respond both to external (global rules, IPRs, new markets) and internal stimuli (local diseases and availability of local knowledge infrastructure). Institutional capacity therefore is determined by: (a) the ability of the country to deal with a sector's potential by providing physical and knowledge infrastructure at the basic level, but also by providing rules that diminish information asymmetry and promote mutually beneficial exchange (local "push" institutions), (b) the ability of the country to balance the local "push" with the global "pull" institutions in a way that the local interests prevail and, finally, (c) regulatory capacity to enact new rules and regulations that achieve this balance and change inefficient rules at the margin. The six countries that have been analysed at length in Part II of the book demonstrate different levels of institutional capacity and these are comparatively analysed in the first part of this chapter.

Second, can latecomer countries hope to develop capacity in health innovation? Gerschenkron's suggestion (1962) that relatively greater backwardness requires much more support to overcome and the technological and managerial sophistication applies well to health innovation and seems to point towards the fact that latecomers might not be able to invest and build sustainable health innovation systems that can compete globally in today's context. However, the data presented in Part II seems to suggest that as opposed to the latecomers that rank higher on the knowledge and institutional capacity indexes (such as Kenya and Nigeria), it is the very latecomers (Bangladesh and Vietnam) that perform better in health innovation. How can this be explained and understood, and what implications does it hold for policy?

Third, is the issue of promoting global access to medicines a separate one from that of promoting industrial capacity in latecomer countries? In other words, are these completely different goals in global health innovation, and, if so, what motivations separate the two policy goals? And finally, what is the evidence from the six-country comparison on the impact of IPRs on access to knowledge as is needed for health innovation? Are IPRs a significant barrier to building health (and biomedical innovation) in latecomer countries as literature seems to suggest or does one need to take a more cautious view?

Although evidence from all countries have been discussed, due to difficulties in presenting and comparing econometric data across all countries, econometric analysis presented in this chapter is only for India (as a fast follower), Kenya (as a latecomer) and Bangladesh (as a very latecomer), whenever comparative evidence is presented as graphs or tables. These three country comparisons are used to throw light on the differences in stages of development and how that impacts health innovation capacity. This, however, is substantiated with evidence from the other three countries of Part II to enrich the analysis.

7.2 Local institutional prerequisites for health innovation

The survey results from all six countries unequivocally support the importance of three factors: quality of local infrastructure (physical and scientific), the presence of skilled manpower and the importance of financial instruments for supporting private sector enterprise (as proxied here by venture capital) as the primary factors that structure collaboration. This corroborates the theoretical framework set out in Chapter 2 on the importance of these elements as building blocks for this sector.

Table 7.1 contains a probit model that compares the contribution of various firm and organization level factors to foster local collaborative learning and innovation in the sectoral systems of health. A range of potential factors, including governmental incentives for innovation, skilled scientific manpower, R&D collaborations with local universities and PRIs, IPRs, quality of local infrastructure (which includes physical and scientific infrastructure), venture capital and firm size (probability of being a small firm) have all been considered. Only quality of local infrastructure, skilled manpower and financial support (venture capital as proxy) emerge as factors that are statistically and significantly associated with collaborative learning and innovation. In the case of Nigeria, once again, the table reflects the current state of innovation. Skilled manpower, infrastructure and venture capital availability all, once again, statistically and significantly impact innovation. The table also shows important results that explain the relative role of IPRs for health innovation. In the case of India, due to its relatively advanced capacity in health innovation, IPRs also are significant for health innovation, which is not the case for the other two countries, Kenya and Bangladesh. In these other countries, survey data show that IPRs negatively impact innovation because of the lost possibilities of reverse engineering. The same results, although not presented here, apply to Vietnam, although during field interviews, firm executives tended to view the issue of IPRs as a limitation that could not be avoided due to the WTO set of agreements. In the case of Tanzania, since local production was at such infancy, IPRs did not have any impact at all.

Two key results that accrue here are as follows. In a knowledge based and innovation driven global environment in which countries have to compete, explicit effort to building knowledge-centred capabilities are required to promote health innovation. There are three dimensions to the innovation investments that latecomer countries need to make.

The first relates to the scale and scope of public sector funding directed at building capabilities to exploit technology and generate innovation both in terms of domestic R&D as well as support pilot and design related activities in health. All countries analysed in Part II of the book have invested into public sector research institutions to support health innovation. What has made the difference has been their sustained performance over time, as differentiated by:

a   National funding for health research. India has sustained the vigour of its
    public science research largely despite some critical interludes in the past

Table 7.1 Factors for local collaboration in India, Kenya and Bangladesh

Variable	India		Kenya		Bangladesh		Nigeria	
	Coeff.	Std error	Coeff.	Std error	Coeff.	Std error	Coeff.	Std error
Government innovation incentive	-0.237	-0.365	-0.254	(0.680)	–	–	–	–
Skilled manpower	1.311*	0.632	1.644*	(0.922)	0.836**	(0.307)	0.742**	(0.283)
R&D collaboration with universities	0.093	0.385	-0.102	(0.802)	–	–	0.489*	(0.234)
R&D collaboration with institutes	0.073	0.376	0.147	(0.770)	–	–	–	–
IP protection	1.192***	0.422	0.568	(0.693)	-0.199	(0.617)	0.607†	(0.263)
Quality of infrastructure	-0.973*	0.448	1.264*	(0.623)	–	–	-0.349	(0.266)
Venture capital availability	-0.798*	0.359	-1.977*	(1.019)	–	–	0.649*	(0.332)
Local SMI participation	-0.819*	0.398	–	–	–	–	0.517*	(0.245)
Government–firm technological transfer	0.897*	0.381	-0.664	(0.636)	-0.725	(0.847)	0.613*	(0.272)
Transfers of personnel	0.447	0.378	0.718	(0.668)	0.680	(0.702)	–	–
Small firms in 2004	-0.943*	0.399	2.699*	(1.098)	–	–	–	–
No. of observations	102	–	66	–	88	–	165	–
Intercept	1.624*	0.731	-3.615**	(1.136)	-0.323***	(0.185)	-1.671**	(0.304)
Log-likelihood							-208.184	

Source: author's field surveys in India, Kenya, Nigeria and Bangladesh, 2006–2008.

Note
Significance levels: *** 10%; ** 5%; * 1%.

few years (see, for example, Abrol, 2007), whereas in contrast, Nigeria, Bangladesh and Kenya have all established institutions that over time have tended to become trapped in various forms of inefficient organizational rigidities that get internalized from shortage of funding, lack of interesting research initiatives for scientists to get involved in, general bureaucratic rigidities and inter-organizational competition for survival. Field interviews in all countries revealed that scientists' attitudes are shaped perversely by the lack of policy support in extreme ways, and contributes to brain-drain.

b   Reward system for researchers. In Bangladesh, Nigeria, Tanzania and Kenya, surveys reveal that scientists have extremely low salaries and often have to resort to running parallel enterprises to support their needs. Since there are no specific incentives for researchers to involve themselves in locally relevant research (aimed at local disease), rewards such as promotion, travel abroad and collaborations with laboratories overseas come less from focusing on local problems than from publishing in foreign journals and working on problems of global importance where the "global" is most often defined in terms of drug issues that have a "world market". Strikingly, the country case studies found that in many research institutes in the African countries that were surveyed for the book, even HIV research focuses largely on those strains of the virus that are to be found in the USA and Europe.

This is what sets Vietnam apart from Nigeria, Bangladesh, Kenya and Tanzania. Despite the fact that Vietnam has begun to invest in promoting health and biotechnology innovation at a relatively late stage, the policy framework within which it has sought to do so is coherent and well coordinated. It seeks to provide fresh impetus for health innovation by creating incentives for researchers as well as by providing support to its public sector research institutions that strengthens their mandates and outcomes.

The second dimension relates to the scale of capabilities in the private sector, which equally lags far behind the sort of investment that supports competitiveness in similar firms and industries (see analysis in Section 7.2). Most infrastructure elements span equally across all sectors of the economy and this makes the basic institutional framework as within the national system of innovation highly relevant in latecomer countries. Regardless of the specific needs of health innovation, the missing institutional dynamism that underlies all economic activity is poignantly evident across the most productive sectors of the economy. The three countries that perform very well – namely, India, Bangladesh and Vietnam – all have an enterprise sector that is well functioning (although in the case of Vietnam it is largely state owned). This is an important issue to tackle in the case of health innovation systems in latecomer countries: namely, the uptake of public funded research to create marketable innovations through the enterprise sector. This finding can be applied more generally to latecomer countries trying to build capacity for local disease issues.

Table 7.2 Sources of technology for product development in the health innovation system

Source of technology	India	Vietnam	Bangladesh
Licensing	0.27	0.75	0.01
Foreign subsidiaries	0.23	0.015	0.00
Own development	0.89	0.87	0.82
Total no. of firms	103	66	45

Source: author's surveys in the three countries.

In India, Bangladesh and Vietnam, most firms relied on developing products through their own efforts (which included reverse engineering and copying) and this led to the development of the sector in completely different ways. Vietnam's excellent performance in health innovation in the past decade is attributable mainly to its investments in physical and knowledge infrastructure and skilled manpower. It is the relatively low financial support to the private sector that is presently slowing down the process of innovation (see Chapter 5).

The third relates to the importance of focusing on local needs. All country case studies show that there have been sporadic cases of success that resulted from the health innovation systems. Some of the PRIs have made commendable progress within a very hostile scientific environment and, in the process, developed notable drugs and vaccines. The hallmark of these centres that have been relatively successful is their focus on local needs and problems, which seem to be a major trigger for innovation, and their sustained focus to bring their research to a successful conclusion. The notable examples include:

1 the Malaria group at the University of Ibadan, Nigeria;
2 Typhiod vaccine development at the Federal University of Technology, Minna, Nigeria;
3 the work on the sickle cell drug at NIPRID, Nigeria;
4 biological vaccines to combat livestock disease, at NVRI, Nigeria;
5 the development of LLIN in Tanzania;
6 Cholera research and the development of Baby Zinc tablets by ICDDRB, Bangladesh.

These are clearly cases where the impetus for the most significant changes came from the desire to solve local disease problems.

The failure of the institutional framework to provide the three core institutions of physical infrastructure, knowledge infrastructure and financial instruments for both the public and private sector result in serious challenges to health innovation systems: the lack of interactive linkages for learning and collaboration, institutional rigidity and the challenge of duplicating isolated cases of success at the sectoral level.

7.2.1 Enabling interactive linkages

One of the most severe constraints to the health innovation system as observed in all countries in Part II is the low propensity of critical actors to interact. Interaction is however fostered by common concerns and shared values. However, these actors – be it universities, PRIs, firms or governmental agencies – have operated independently of one another over time, although there seems to be closer interaction between some actors than others. In this milieu, actors foreclose the potential sources of exploring new ideas for innovation inherent in other organizations and the knowledge sources that could provide a basis for action.

Industry involvement in most countries under investigation is low because private sector involvement in health innovation is itself in need of basic support such as sources of finance (e.g. venture capital), better infrastructure and technology diffusion activities that could enhance their internal capacity. The exploitation of biotechnology innovation by firms is once again at a very elementary phase due in part to a weak private sector, low level of entrepreneurship and poor institutional capacity support for translating inventive effort into innovation. The country chapters in Part II show that while the stock of knowledge and other assets are important, more crucial is the relational dynamics among the key actors. In other words, how do the actors interact and what learning takes place in the course of research and production? There is a historical lack of collaborative interactions between industry and public research and these manifest poignantly in health innovation. Interactions between university departments are weak due to poor information flow and lack of incentives amongst researchers to engage in joint research. Universities also do not collaborate sufficiently with traditional medicine practitioners and hospitals.

The country case studies reveal *the context specific dimension of reward systems and collaboration incentives.* This is important and shapes the ways and means through which inventions are translated to the market across all countries and sectors. While researchers interviewed in the sector surveys tended to rank lack of facilities and research funding as the most critical factors that affect university performance, incentive systems tend to develop from more fundamental institutional roots such as labour laws, commercial laws and even a country's constitution. Terms of employment and work environments, both tangible (research and teaching facilities) and intangible (possibilities for institutional collaboration, quality of networks and colleagues) play a pivotal role in retaining skilled professionals and promoting commitment to work for local solutions to health issues.

Furthermore, the firms and organizations *tended to interact with product development and local market demand as a parameter* in the main and these need to be enabled through appropriate policy changes. This has been substituted through the mediation of donor funding or international grants in the case of Kenya, Nigeria and Tanzania, as the country chapters show, but its sustainability is unclear. The case of Kenya for instance, Chapter 5, shows that although there are several research initiatives going on in the country in the area of health innovation and health biotechnology, most of them are in partnership with international agencies and product development focus has been very low.

7.2.2 Lack of funding and institutional rigidity

There has been a *persistent lack of governmental funding* in conducting research. Within Nigeria, for example, presently 90 per cent of the research funds are from international sources, with only 10 per cent from the Nigerian government. The story is much the same in Kenya, Tanzania and even Bangladesh. In all countries, the grant funds to university departments and other specialized public sector institutions are hardly adequate to purchase sophisticated laboratory equipment as required for health innovation and are mostly used to sustain whatever little work that has been ongoing in the laboratories for decades. Progressive decline in science, technology and innovation investment activities due in part to economic problems in the countries, consistent poor funding of health innovation, have all adversely affected the system in profound ways in past decades. These factors add to the rigidity of the system and its inability to adapt to dynamic prospects brought about by new technologies that could otherwise help in reducing the prevalence of diseases. This calls for a more holistic perspective wherein health innovation is viewed much more broadly as elaborated in Chapter 2 of this book.

A major reason for institutional rigidity lies with state involvement itself, which tends to create its own idiosyncratic "lock-in" conditions for two main reasons. First, instead of governments playing a supportive role to rectify market imperfections, governments in latecomer contexts have over time lent their strength to the creation of institutions that override market forces, thereby creating alternative institutions to which actors have to respond albeit to promote self-interest based, inefficient outcomes. This *capture of the entire institution building process* is a commonplace occurrence. As a result, while there is a general agreement that latecomer countries need to create organizations and institutions where they do not exist and reform those that are functioning poorly, institutions for policy making themselves lack both broad and specific competencies in their coordination functions. This is a serious drawback for latecomer countries and leads to a situation in which policy coordination is largely political, sporadic and unpredictable in the absence of strong market coordination.

Second, institutional rigidities that hinder actors from responding to technological change manifest at several levels that attenuate the consequences. At a very basic level, the processes that give rise to organizations and the mandate that drives their programmes may offer resistance. For instance, the Ministry of Science and Technology oversees most of the institutes that carry out research in health, whereas the Ministry of Health in responsible to ensure that these products and services reach the poor and needy. However, the dynamics of innovation require that they interact with agencies that are under each other's purview or even outside the two ministries. Typical bureaucratic rigidities often make this difficult, if not impossible, and, in the process, a lack of systemic articulation is perpetuated. Maintaining these organizations to achieve effective service delivery depends to a considerable extent on available public resources. But poor financial commitments stunt organizational growth further and result in disillusion of scientists and researchers over time, a lack of private sector trust in collaborations with public sector institutions and often even prevent the rise of a private sector itself since organizations to promote the growth of private sector firms do not function effectively. At another level, we find that the norms of behaviour of academics do not predispose them to activities that are of commercial description; and the innovation process certainly entails strong economic considerations.

This calls for a rethink on newer forms of incentives such as (a) involvement in collaborative research that can foster mobility of labour between research and industry, (b) consultancy possibilities to augment income, (c) provision of state owned common services to public and private sector institutions alike, to enable partnering, competition and product development, (d) patenting possibilities and (e) promoting full-scale commercialization of research results. Furthermore, the country case studies reveal certain trends that run common to a large extent in the latecomer context such as the duplication of research efforts across public sector organizations, lack of coordination functions amongst governmental agencies that are overseers of key sectoral activities, lack of academic vigour and accountability of research.

The implications of these for reforming health innovation systems in latecomer countries are threefold. First, significant institutional reform will be required to overcome the current organizational ineffectiveness of the sectoral systems. Second, new institutions would be required due to the new technical-scientific demand imposed by emerging technologies both on the technological side and on the service delivery side for health. The most urgent institutional innovations would seem to revolve among three institutional factors: (a) the framework governing the exploitation of academic research output, that for now does little to promote academic entrepreneurship, (b) the system of financing university research and knowledge creation and dissemination in general and (c) the structure of health systems research and science and technology investments into health innovation which for the time being are separated by superficial terminological and ideological perspectives that delay the integration of the most important issue of access in the discourses. Last, and most important, the surveys show that a large majority of ongoing collaborative efforts in health innovation in the countries tend to be based on informal contacts of researchers and scientists and not formalized links of the institutions per se with other institutions in-country or abroad. As a result, the risk that these contacts will be lost when the people move out of the organizations or leave the country is extremely high.

7.2.3 Duplicating isolated cases of success at the sectoral level

How does one use the lessons from individual success stories observed in some of the latecomer countries, and seek to duplicate them on a broader sectoral scale?

Duplicating the individual cases of successes in product development poses issues of systemic coherence that needs to be addressed. The surveys and field interviews show that collaboration has been limited by three main factors, namely:

- the inability of scientists to move their work beyond the individual organizations,
- the absence of formal institutions supporting collaboration,
- poor incentive structures to motivate scientists.

The third factor was evident in all the PRIs, universities and even firms that were visited across all countries. The institutions in which scientists work hardly reward entrepreneurship and there is no motivation to make additional effort beyond publication of academic papers. Most academics do not understand the institution of patents for instance and have had little guide as to what to do to move inventions to the market. Moreover, the sheer weight of infrastructural constraints leaves them with very little energy to think beyond their immediate concerns. The concerns with short-term goals was evident and long-term commercialization efforts were down the priority list of scientists. It was evident to the research groups that major institutional shifts would be required to change the present habits and practices of the PRIs. While individual researchers are able to carry on working up to a point, the odds rise dramatically as projects demand better facilities, skills and knowledge than the lone scientist could offer. Formal institutional arrangements which were found missing in almost all cases would then be required.

These results point strongly towards the need for secondary institutional "signals" in the form of dedicated sectoral policies that help internalize policy changes in the local systems of innovation and revitalize the efforts of the actors to configure new solutions. These institutional signals are key to effecting change in the systems locally and point to the fact that it is not identifying the policy that is important, but how the policy is set into motion (its implementation) that embodies its success. For example, as opposed to simply identifying and promoting IPRs for research institutions in latecomers, it is the countries that set up Offices for Technology Transfer that manage to internalize the norms of IPRs amongst academics. Secondary, dedicated policy instruments, however, play a role only when the sectoral system already has a critical basis for innovation, as specified by the quality of physical and scientific infrastructure, skilled manpower and financial support for enterprise activity.

7.3 Institutional capacity and competitiveness: main results

In health innovation systems, decisions to building local capability ultimately translate to an enquiry into whether local firms or organizations can supply reliable, good quality medicines for local use or export. A range of issues is critical for building competitive supply, and Table 7.3 presents results on the indicators of competitiveness in the countries under consideration. Total employment (in FTEs), the percentage of gross inputs sourced domestically, R&D intensity expressed as the ratio of R&D expenditures over total sales and R&D personnel expressed as the ratio of R&D employment (in FTEs) over total employment of three countries (India, Kenya and Bangladesh) are contrasted over a period of five years (2000–2005). The results are contained in Table 7.3 and Figures 7.1 to 7.3.

These results imply the following. Employment is increasing on average both in India and Bangladesh's health innovation system over time and is much larger in India than in Bangladesh (see Figure 7.1). The percentage of gross inputs that is sourced domestically slightly increases on average over time in Bangladesh, from 20 per cent in 2001 to 28 per cent in 2005. That figure slightly increases on average in India from 2000 to 2001 then jumps from 38 per cent to almost attain 80 per cent in 2004. This, as Chapter 3 shows, was a result of the greater investments made by local firms in order to move to new innovation domains (new drug R&D among others) as a result of India's impending compliance with the TRIPS Agreement in 2005. Domestic gross inputs are much larger in Indian firms than in their Bangladesh counterparts, and the pattern is persistent over time (see Figure 7.2). This is due to the fact that Bangladesh's firms are unable to largely produce APIs locally whereas Indian firms are one of the main suppliers of APIs locally and globally for the production of drugs. R&D intensity and R&D personnel are much larger on average in Indian pharmaceutical firms than in Bangladeshi and Kenyan counterparts, and the pattern is persistent over time. In India, R&D intensity first exhibits a steep increase from 2000 to 2002 then shows a less steep increase until 2004, and R&D personnel shows a rather steep increase from 2000 to 2003 then decreases from 2003 to 2004. In Bangladesh, both R&D intensity and R&D personnel show a flat increase from 2001 to 2005 and do not go beyond 2 per cent (Figure 7.2). When this is compared with

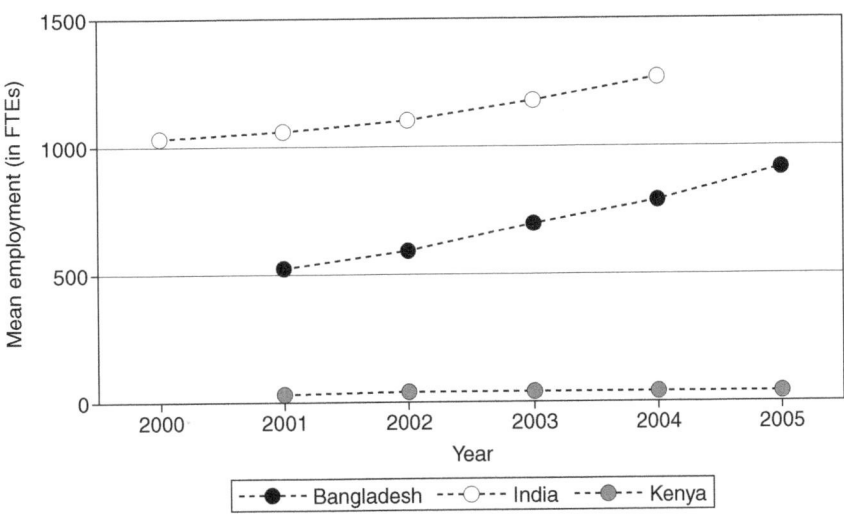

Figure 7.1 Comparison of employment over the period 2000–2005.

Table 7.3 Comparison of employment, domestic inputs and R&D over the period 2000–2005

Country	Bangladesh		India		Kenya	
Variable	Mean	(Std Dev.)	Mean	(Std Dev.)	Mean	(Std Dev.)
2000						
Total employment (FTEs)	—	—	1032.767	(908.404)	—	—
% of gross inputs sourced domestically	—	—	34.592	(42.584)	—	—
R&D expenditures (% of total sales)	—	—	3.704	(5.911)	—	—
R&D staff (% of total workforce in FTEs)	—	—	3.029	(6.087)	—	—
2001						
Total employment (FTEs)	519.178	(501.230)	1061.408	(923.140)	39.061	(63.349)
% of gross inputs sourced domestically	19.800	(13.788)	38.214	(42.582)	10.000	(26.926)
R&D expenditures (% of total sales)	1.023	(2.238)	4.956	(8.083)	1.583	(7.918)
R&D staff (% of total workforce in FTEs)	0.570	(0.648)	3.961	(7.170)	1.320	(7.808)
2002						
Total employment (FTEs)	597.778	(583.952)	1110.699	(955.507)	39.549	(65.002)
% of gross inputs sourced domestically	21.844	(13.575)	66.097	(36.685)	10.366	(27.212)
R&D expenditures (% of total sales)	1.160	(2.968)	6.374	(8.535)	1.583	(7.918)
R&D staff (% of total workforce in FTEs)	0.607	(0.829)	4.602	(8.205)	1.320	(7.808)

2003					
Total employment (FTEs)	703.622	(608.062)	1186.350	(1012.656)	40.841	(66.201)
% of gross inputs sourced domestically	23.844	(12.428)	75.146	(29.849)	12.439	(29.392)
R&D expenditures (% of total sales)	1.393	(3.684)	6.856	(8.785)	1.632	(7.915)
R&D staff (% of total workforce in FTEs)	0.742	(0.844)	4.951	(8.442)	1.347	(7.809)
2004					
Total employment (FTEs)	793.133	(637.774)	1270.515	(1095.903)	43.598	(70.639)
% of gross inputs sourced domestically	26.289	(10.092)	77.466	(27.050)	11.951	(28.392)
R&D expenditures (% of total sales)	1.632	(3.282)	7.194	(8.407)	1.924	(9.454)
R&D staff (% of total of workforce in FTEs)	0.970	(1.274)	4.767	(8.144)	1.605	(9.369)
2005					
Total employment (FTEs)	922.867	(694.716)	–	–	46.061	(71.16)
% of gross inputs sourced domestically	28.400	(11.610)	–	–	18.390	(31.831)
R&D expenditures (% of total sales)	1.917	(3.606)	–	–	2.534	(12.546)
R&D staff (% of total workforce in FTEs)	1.041	(1.217)	–	–	1.849	(10.928)
Number of firms	45		103		41	

Source: author's surveys.

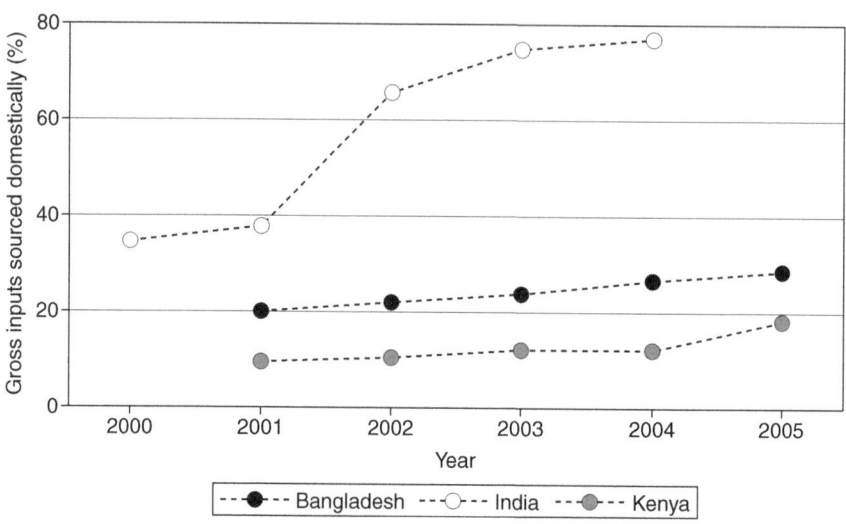

Figure 7.2 Comparison of domestic inputs over the period 2000–2005.

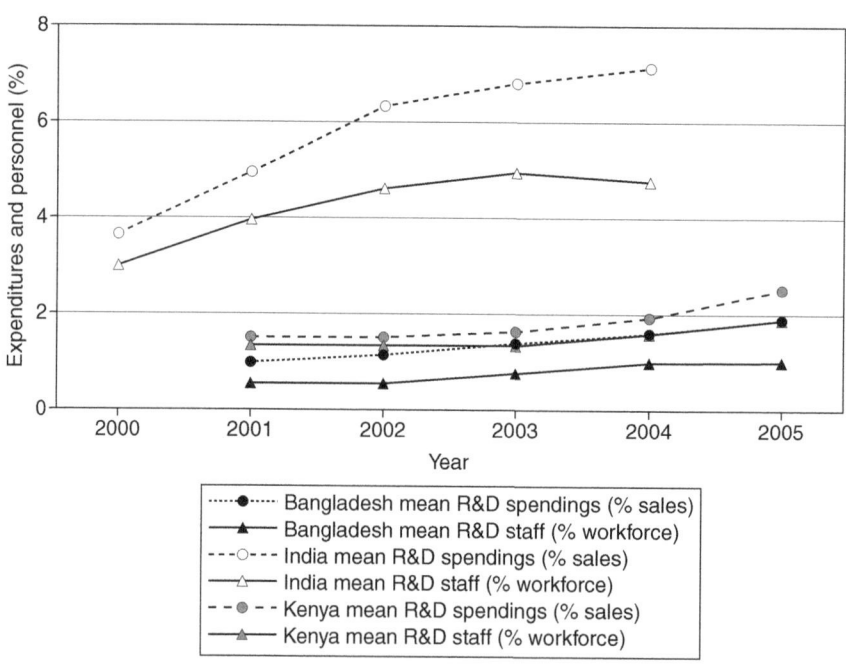

Figure 7.3 Comparison of R&D expenditures and R&D personnel over the period 2000–2005.

Kenya, it shows the very little investment in R&D personnel and R&D intensity in Kenya's health system in comparison with its Asian counterparts. Unlike Bangladesh's and Indian firms, total employment of Kenyan firms hardly increases over time. It starts at a very low level in 2001 to remain almost at the same level in 2005. The percentage of gross inputs that is sourced domestically in Kenyan firms follows a rather similar trajectory to that of Bangladeshi firms. Domestic gross inputs are persistently larger in Indian firms than in Bangladeshi and Kenyan firms. Finally, R&D intensity and R&D personnel of Kenyan firms show a flat increase from 2001 to 2005 similar to that of Bangladeshi firms. The figures hardly go beyond 2 per cent over the time period.

An issue that emerged to be very significant for local competitiveness of production is the cost of APIs as a percentage of total cost of finished dosage form varies significantly from molecule to molecule. For instance, high value/low volume drugs like cardiovascular medicines where it is common to have tablets of 1 mg or 5 mg may have higher component of the APIs when compared to low value/high volume drugs (with tablets of 250 mg or 500 mg). The latter kind of drugs will have relatively lower component of APIs in the cost of the finished dosage form. On average though, one could consider APIs as 50 per cent of the total cost of finished dosage form. In the case of ARVs, most firms in India and Bangladesh were of the view that API costs comprise around 40 per cent the total cost of the finished formulation. In the case of very high API component drugs, such as those for cardiovascular system disorders, the API component of the drug could be as much as 90 per cent.

Countries that do not manage to upgrade their innovation capacity from purely manufacturing drugs to reverse engineering fail to attain the required threshold of competitiveness in health innovation (see also Figure 7.7 and the analysis in section 7.3.3 in this context). This is a key result in understanding why firms fail to produce good quality medicines at reasonable costs on a sustainable basis in other latecomer countries, as is observed in the case of Indian or Chinese firms. In the case of ARVs, most firms in India and Bangladesh were of the view that API costs comprise around 40 per cent of the total cost of the finished formulation.

Some of the key constraints in competitive production of drugs and innovation capacity as observed in countries at the three levels of capacity – namely, fast follower (India), latecomer (Kenya) and very latecomer (Bangladesh) – are analysed here.

7.3.1 Export intensity as a measure of competitiveness

Figure 7.4 shows that the percentage of firms exporting in India is at least twice as much as that of firms exporting their products in Bangladesh (80 per cent versus 40 per cent) and almost three times as much as that of exporting firms in Kenya (80 per cent versus 30 per cent). Furthermore, export intensity, as measured by the ratio of foreign sales over output, is statistically and significantly larger in India than in Bangladesh and in Kenya and is not statistically different between Bangladesh and Kenya.

The percentage of exports is usually a very useful indication in latecomer countries also of the ability of the firms to produce good quality drugs. Many countries, such as Bangladesh, exhibit a lack of regulatory capacity to prescribe local standards for good manufacturing practices and monitor the enforcement of these standards. The regulatory authority is also expected to regulate the code of conduct of manufacturers, distributors, prescribers and dispensers on issues of drug quality, prescribing clinical guidelines and facilitating appropriate training of health personnel and enhancing the availability of information, awareness and education of patients (see Box 7.1). Therefore, when firms begin to export, they are required to upgrade and demonstrate their ability to comply with the standards of safe and efficacious medicines as established in other semi-regulated and regulated markets.

Box 7.1　Regulatory competencies to promote safe access

Drug registration is a process through which the drug regulatory authority of each country approves the use of any particular drug based on the evidence of their quality, efficacy and safety. Effective drug registration entails several pre- and post-registration activities that are required to be performed by the national drug regulatory authorities. The national drug authority is also expected to prescribe regulations for and enforce preclinical, clinical, pharmaceutical and analytical processes as well as have the technical competence to check the data submitted to ensure compliance with regulatory standards. These standards, which are also expected to be set up by the drug regulatory authority, include those for good manufacturing practice of drugs, good clinical practices and good laboratory practice. In addition to this, the authority is expected to continuously monitor the quality of drugs through pharmaco-vigilence activities, market surveillance and random testing.

Source: Matsoso *et al.*, 2004

In several cases, the regional portfolio of firm level exports is a very good indication of the ability of the firms to produce good quality drugs and health products. For example, the survey results show that the top five firms in Bangladesh are just beginning to export to the UK and US markets and the rest are more focused on exporting to the semi-regulated and the unregulated markets.

7.3.2　Nature of innovation and product differentiation

Figure 7.5 shows differences in the percentage of product and process innovators among the three countries. The percentage of product innovators in Kenya is statistically and significantly smaller than that of product innovators in Bangladesh and in India and this is because a large majority of the firms in Kenya that were surveyed were distributors or retailers of medicinal products (in keeping with the structure of the industrial activity in the country). That percentage is not statistically and significantly different between the last two countries. However,

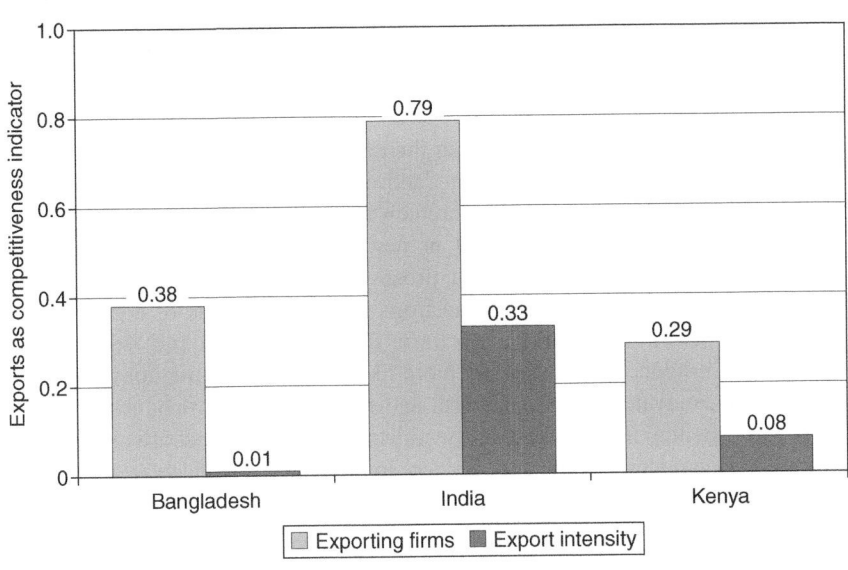

Figure 7.4 Comparison of exports as a competitiveness indicator (source: author).

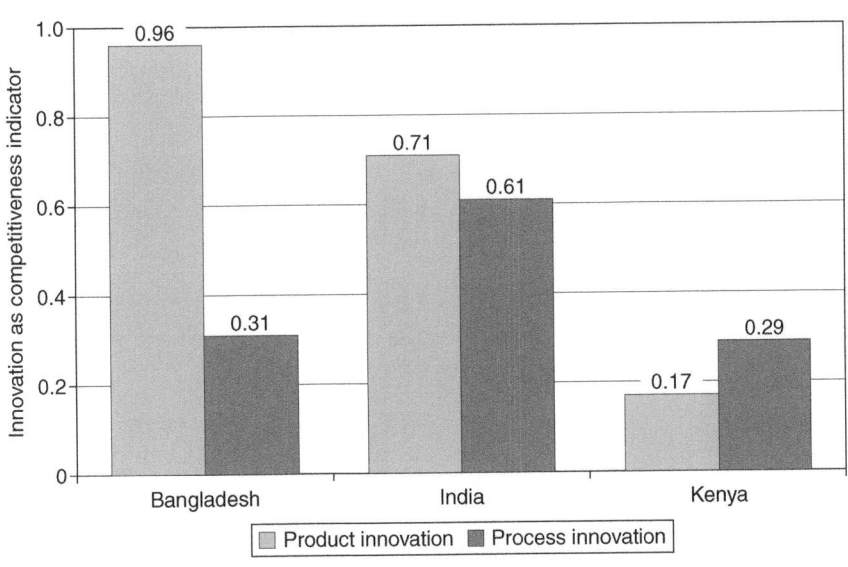

Figure 7.5 Comparison of innovation as a competitiveness indicator (source: author).

this large percentage of product innovators in Bangladesh is due to the fact that a great majority of local firms in Bangladesh simply copy product innovations and then claim to be innovators. Figure 7.5 also shows that percentage of process innovators in India is statistically and significantly larger than that of Bangladesh and India. That percentage is not statistically and significantly different between those two countries.

Figure 7.6 shows the distribution of the degree of novelty of product innovations in the three countries. The firms and organizations were asked to rate in each country whether their products are new to the firm only, or new to the local market, new to the regional market or new to the global market in order to understand the nature of innovation processes that dominate the sector. The responses as plotted show that Indian firms are more capable of competing on the regional and global market than those from Bangladesh and Kenya. More specifically, product innovations are more likely to be only imitations and small incremental innovations in Bangladesh and in Kenya, while they can be imitations, incremental innovations, fairly radical or radical innovations in India. Firms in Bangladesh copy and imitate innovations significantly more than Kenyan and Indian firms.

7.3.3 *Economic viability and sustainability of production: sources of production inputs and machinery*

When latecomers are at the initial stages of productive capacity, it is likely that the drugs/medicinal products produced locally are more expensive than those

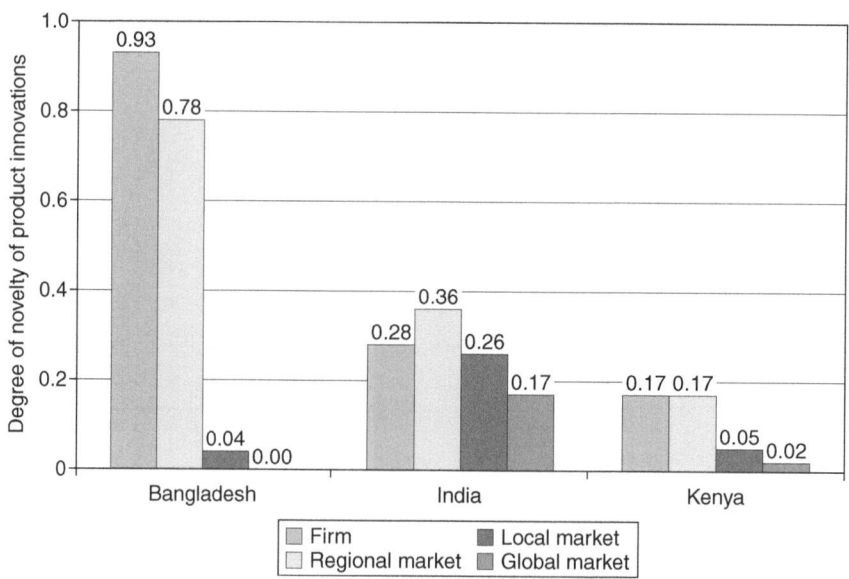

Figure 7.6 Comparison of degree of novelty of innovations (source: author).

that can be procured from internationally established firms. This static cost of developing productive capacity can be offset by the dynamic gains of local production of medicines or related health products if countries ensure that investment into the sector are secured in ways that promote technological learning and competitiveness of local enterprises thus leading to a increasing returns over time. A disproportionate amount of the total cost of producing drugs is associated with the raw materials that form the core of the process (see Box 7.2). Reduction of drug prices is possible only when productive capacity is built with significant parallel emphasis on skills and learning required to boost innovation capacity of the local firms to enable them to gradually progress to reverse engineer drugs. Until firms and countries reach this stage of technological mastery, drugs produced locally in latecomers using imported raw materials will remain somewhat more expensive (about 20 per cent) than those that are produced by established firms elsewhere.

Box 7.2 Cost considerations of producing generic drugs in LDCs

Generic manufacturing of pharmaceutical drugs consists of three main components: (a) the production of APIs, which requires chemical synthesis skills commonly referred to as "reverse engineering" capabilities, (b) production of exipients and other non-active ingredients and (c) formulation skills that are required to manufacture, which involve the mixing of APIs with other non-active ingredients into pill, tablet or other dosage forms.

The cost of APIs as a percentage of total cost of the finished dosage form varies significantly from molecule to molecule. For instance, high value/low volume drugs like cardiovascular medicines where it is common to have tablets of 1 mg or 5 mg may have higher component of the APIs when compared to low value/high volume drugs such as Aspirin (with tablets of 250 mg or 500 mg). The latter kind of drugs will have relatively lower component of APIs in the cost of the finished dosage form. On average though, one could consider APIs as 50 per cent of total cost of finished dosage form. In the case of ARVs for example, the API costs comprise around 40 per cent of the total cost of the finished formulation. However, the API component of drugs rises significantly in the case of specialized drugs, such as those used to treat cardiovascular system disorders, where it could be as much as 90 per cent.

Producing APIs and exipients locally therefore are essential to lower costs of production in the mid or long term. This calls for a larger set of skills that goes beyond simply formulation capabilities. It calls for developing reverse engineering skills that are primarily chemistry based, with some expertise in biotechnology and genomics.[1]

Source: author

Note
1 While several drugs presently being used require chemistry based skills to reverse engineer, there are a range of newer drugs that employ biotechnology, such as second-line ARVs.

It is important to bear in mind that this static cost of building productive capacity has been borne by all countries that succeeded in the sector worldwide. In view of this, the challenge is one of building capacity while making sure that this additional cost of doing so in the short term – in the form of higher drug prices of drugs produced locally – is not passed on to the poor consumer in these countries. This is, however, not an easy task. Latecomer experiences in countries that have managed to set up some production capabilities for pharmaceuticals such as Bangladesh, Kenya and Vietnam all point to the greater complexity of balancing these concerns.

A fundamental issue in ensuring that the production capacity of firms gradually evolves substantially towards cutting costs is one of ensuring that they are able to access local and regional markets well (to sell their products) and also have access to financial means at low interest rates (see next section). Firms in latecomer countries also function in an environment where generic markets are not well established and there is an excessive reliance on branded medicines (produced by multinational companies abroad) by consumers as well as by governmental agencies that play a key role in the procurement processes. A prevailing general perception seems to be that locally produced products are not of a good quality and this stems from low confidence in the industry. As a result, even those local firms producing good quality medicines are confronted by major difficulties in penetrating the market. The extensive marketing and distribution networks of multinational firms that have an incumbent advantage in the market do little to help the local firms battling for some ground in their own countries to win the confidence of their consumers. The same marketing and distribution disadvantages apply when local firms seek to capture regional markets.

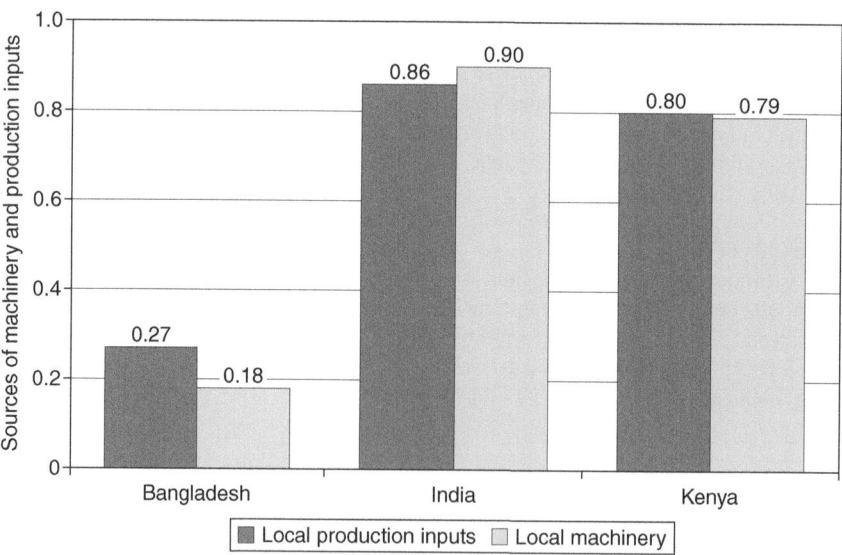

Figure 7.7 Comparison of sources of machinery and production inputs (source: author).

For the six countries analysed in Part II, in order to understand to what extent the sector has forward and backward linkages in the economies (which help indicate the scale economies of production), the surveys sought to ascertain the extent to which the firms sourced local production inputs and local machinery. Figure 7.7, which contains the responses to this question, shows that firms in Bangladesh, despite their production, use local production inputs and machinery statistically and significantly less than Indian and Kenyan firms. The Kenyan result here (which shows a parity with India) needs to be understood in context: since most firms are engaged in Kenya in distribution and retailing, the survey responses only capture the sourcing of machinery and inputs for retails and distribution (of which they are clearly able to provide a large part within Kenya).

Figure 7.8 captures another important factor that promotes health innovation: the quality of production machinery. Bangladeshi and Indian firms use on average world-class production machinery significantly more than Kenyan firms. Firms in the first two countries use "world-class" production machinery significantly alike.[1] Bangladeshi and Kenyan firms use advanced production machinery significantly less than Indian firms that themselves use highly advanced production machinery significantly less than Bangladeshi firms. Kenya's low score is also explained by the fact that most of its firms are only involved in drug distribution, packaging and retailing as opposed to the other two countries, where the firms are in fact extensively engaged in production. The other countries surveyed had very little or none of these indicators, since private sector participation in Nigeria, Tanzania and Vietnam is presently extremely minimal.

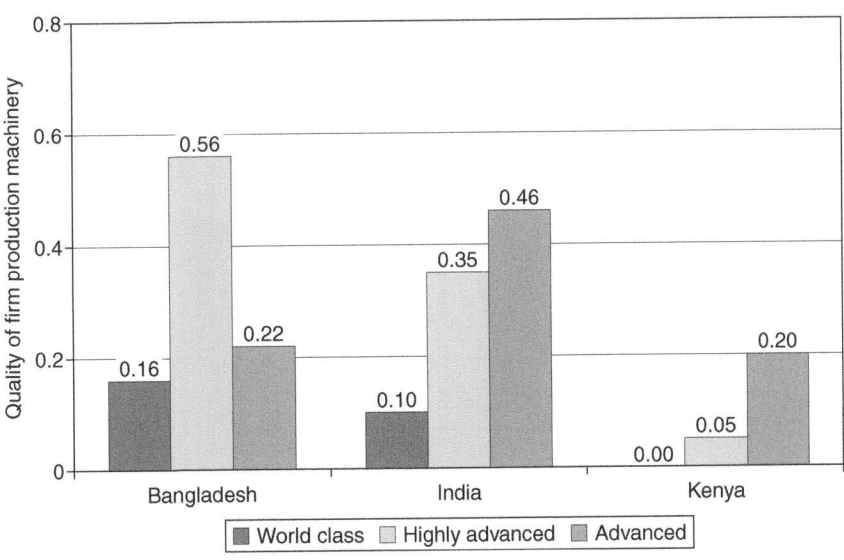

Figure 7.8 Comparison of quality of production machinery (source: author).

7.3.4 *Financial constraints as a barrier to upgrading innovation capacity*

Another extremely important result relates to the presence of financing options available to the firms. Firms involved in production and struggling to cope with pressures of international and national competition (in India and Bangladesh) tend to face constraints in financial support institutions (thus rank them from fairly severe to extremely severe). This is true across all the countries surveyed, where firms seek to engage in local production. Access to credit, if available, is only at very high interest rates and the threat of not having regular and reliable access to credit as well as access to local and regional markets really impacts on firm strategies to venture into local production. The rankings for Kenya (where a large majority of the firms rank them as not severe at all) in Figure 7.9 is once again because most firms surveyed were distributors and retailers and did not face any issues of accessing credit.

7.3.5 *Informal institutions and their impact on firm behaviour*

The survey questionnaires sought to measure the impact of informal institutions and the attitudes of system actors towards innovation in several different ways. One important issue that the questionnaire considered was the impact of official corruption. The question was phrased so as to elicit a qualitative response, that is, to what extent do the firms consider corruption as a major hindrance to the innovation process? Figure 7.10 shows official corruption constraints in the three countries. The pattern is that Indian firms face on average statistically and

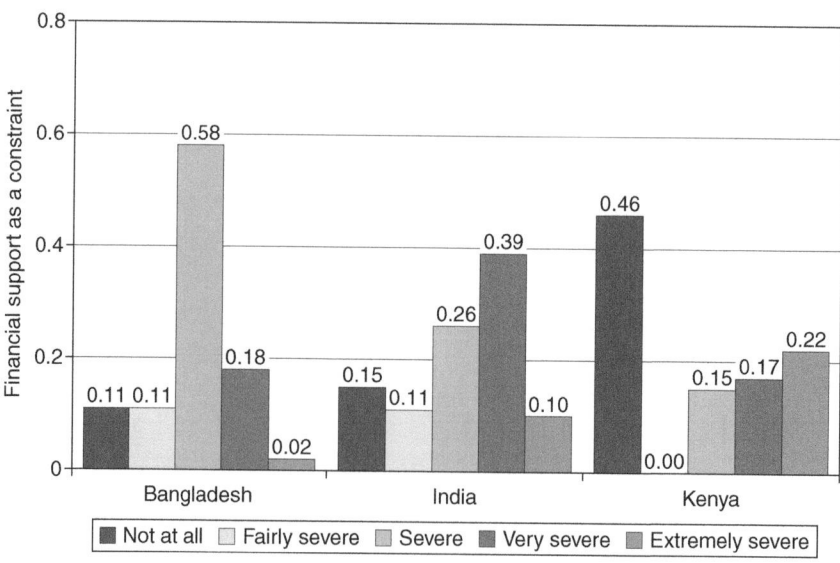

Figure 7.9 Comparison of financial support constraints (source: author).

significantly more severe corruption than Kenyan firms that themselves face more severe corruption firms than in Bangladesh, although all three countries perform almost equally badly on the corruption index. This is an important result, and highlights the informal behaviour of firms and organizations in the innovation process. Bangladesh's firms view corruption as not such an important issue not because there is no corruption in the system, but rather because they have been able to subvert the system to cater to their gains. Indian firms, although also functioning in a corrupt institutional framework have not been able to subvert the gains by joining hands and being able to share the market, simply due to the nature of excessive competition prevailing in the market. Although India and Bangladesh both have had similar policy frameworks, the limited number of firms producing drugs in Bangladesh (147 in total, of which the top ten have a large share of the market) is different from the way the Indian market was structured even before India's compliance with the TRIPS Agreement. Intense inter-firm competition in India was able to incidentally prevent cartelization of drugs and health services of the kind observed in Bangladesh: the local pharmaceutical firms in Bangladesh have been able to organize themselves in ways that are not in the interest of health systems equity. The results presented in Figure 7.10 confirm this further.

7.3.6 The importance of secondary innovation incentives

Finally, Figure 7.11 shows the distribution of patent office delays and animal testing restrictions (for clinical trials) in the three countries. Once again, Indian firms on average statistically and significantly are more affected by patent office

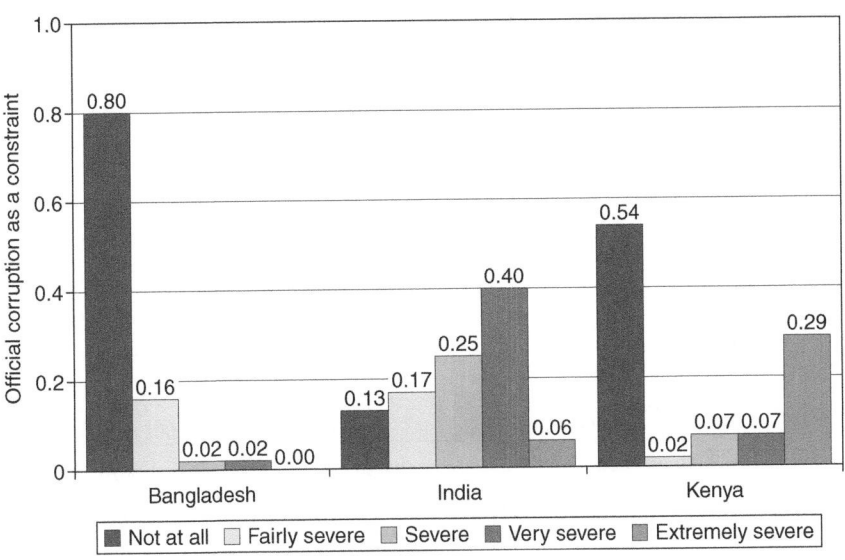

Figure 7.10 Comparison of official corruption constraints (source: author).

delays and animal testing restrictions than their counterparts in the other two countries. This follows from the result in Section 7.1: rules and the impact of rules correspond to the level of innovation capacity in the country. Where there is no capacity, the rules on clinical trials or patent office delays do not matter.

The tables and figures shown above indicate the extent to which firms differ on average across different categories of latecomer countries with regards to the characteristics of health innovation. Each table or figure considers partial competitiveness indicators that need to be analysed in a unified framework. Furthermore, while the above shows differences across indicators of firm level competitiveness in the three countries, it does not indicate why these differences occur. In other words, so far we fail to explain, for instance, why export intensity is so much larger in Indian pharmaceutical firms than in Bangladesh's pharmaceutical firms and so low in Kenyan firms. In order to do so, we derive a composite competitiveness index that is computed as a residual of the estimated model.

In order to compute the model, we chose only Indian and Bangladesh health innovation systems, simply because including Kenya, with its majority of firms focused on retailing and packaging, will skew the results. Table 7.4 shows summary statistics of the dependent and explanatory variables included in the model. The output indicator of ability to compete is export intensity measured as the ratio of foreign sales over output. Explanatory variables include R&D intensity measured as the ratio of R&D expenditures over total sales, total employment expressed in FTEs, indicators for product innovation, radical innovation (products new to regional or global market), institution and infrastructure constraints,

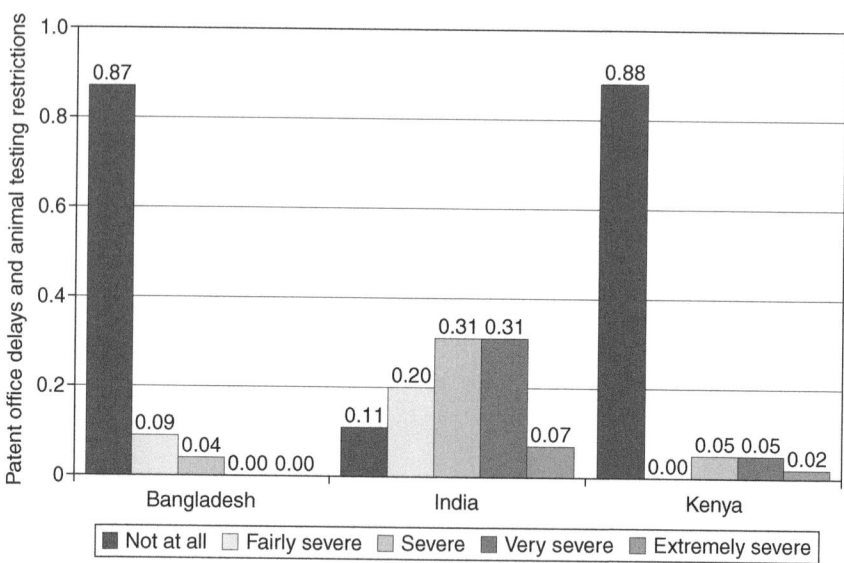

Figure 7.11 Comparison of patent office delays and animal testing restrictions as constraints (source: author).

Table 7.4 Summary statistics across country: dependent and explanatory variables

Country	Bangladesh				India			
Variable	Mean	(Std dev.)	Min.	Max	Mean	(Std dev.)	Min.	Max.
Export intensity if exporting (% output)	3.535	(3.166)	1	10	42.210	(30.332)	1	100
R&D/sales (in %)	1.302	(3.014)	0	21	6.345	(8.108)	0	37.5
Employment (FTEs)	653.428	(570.319)	1	2230.500	1157.243	(991.276)	21.75	3875
Having product innovation	0.956	—	0	1	0.709	—	0	1
Having radical innovation	0.044	—	0	1	0.388	—	0	1
Having financial constraint	0.778	—	0	1	0.748	—	0	1
Having local duties constraints	0.311	—	0	1	0.757	—	0	1
Doing R&D continuously	0.733	—	0	1	0.544	—	0	1
R&D performers	0.889	—	0	1	0.757	—	0	1
Having IPR registered innovations	0.444	—	0	1	0.796	—	0	1
Having land access constraints	0.467	—	0	1	0.699	—	0	1
Having municipality registration constraints	0.089	—	0	1	0.680	—	0	1
Having corruption constraints	0.044	—	0	1	0.709	—	0	1
Having patent office delays	0.044	—	0	1	0.689	—	0	1
Number of firms	45				103			

Source: author's surveys.

continuous R&D (firms that do R&D continuously over the period 2001–2004) and R&D performer (firms that do R&D at least once over 2001–2004). For instance, export intensity of exporting firms is much larger in Indian pharmaceutical firms than in Indian counterparts. The competitiveness model will explain why.

7.3.6.1 Econometric model

Let

$$Z_i^* = \ln\left(\frac{y_{1i}^*}{1 - y_{1i}^*}\right)$$

be a latent function that models the incentive to export.[2] Z_i^* is assumed to be a function of endogenous regressors y_{2i}, exogenous regressors x_{1i} and unobserved variables u_i. Formally, the model is written as

$$Z_i^* = y_{2i}\beta + x_{1i}\gamma + u_i \tag{1}$$

$$y_{2i} = x_{1i}\mathbf{\Pi}_1 + x_{2i}\mathbf{\Pi}_2 + v_i \tag{2}$$

where $i = 1,\ldots, N$, x_{2i} is a vector of additional instruments, $\mathbf{\Pi}_1$ and $\mathbf{\Pi}_2$ matrices of reduced-form parameters and v_i denotes unobserved variables that affect y_{2i}.[3] The observed dependent variable (export intensity) is defined as:

$$Z_i = \begin{cases} a & \text{if } z_i^* < a \\ z_i^* & \text{if } a \leq z_i^* \leq b \\ b & \text{if } z_i^* > b^3 \end{cases} \tag{3}$$

In order to estimate the model, we assume that $(u_i, v_i) \circledR N(0, \Sigma)$ where

$$\Sigma = \begin{bmatrix} \sigma_u^2 & \Sigma_{21} \\ \Sigma_{21} & \Sigma_{22} \end{bmatrix}$$

Using the properties of the multivariate normal distribution, we can write $u_i = v_i \alpha + \varepsilon_i$, where $\alpha = \Sigma_{22}^{-1}\Sigma_{22}$; $\varepsilon_i \rightarrow N(0, \sigma_{u/v}^2)$, where $\sigma_{u/v}^2 = \sigma_u^2 - \Sigma_{22}\Sigma_{22}^{-1}\Sigma_{21}$; and ε_i is independent of v_i, y_{2i}, x_{1i} and x_{2i}.

In our application, y_{2i} includes R&D intensity, x_1 includes the variables of Table 7.3 and a country dummy, and the vector of additional instruments x_{2i} includes indicators for R&D performers, continuous R&D, registered IPRs for innovations and constraints with regards to access to land, municipal regulations, official corruption and patent office delays.

7.3.6.2 Estimation results

Table 7.5 presents instrumental variable maximum likelihood estimation results of the tobit model. R&D intensity, employment and having radically new forms of innovation have *ceteris paribus* a positive and significant effect on export intensity. *Ceteris paribus*, Indian pharmaceutical firms have larger export intensity than Bangladeshi counterparts.

7.3.6.3 A comparison of firm level competitiveness

The (conditional) competitiveness index is calculated as the difference between observed export intensity (for export intensity that is strictly positive and strictly smaller than one) and (conditional) expected export intensity. This is the "residual" obtained after fitting the export intensity model.

Table 7.6 shows that Indian pharmaceutical firms are more competitive than their Bangladeshi counterparts. The comparative advantage of India over Bangladesh in terms of competitiveness is attributed to comparative advantage in terms of R&D, number of personnel in employment and nature of innovation (radically new and different forms of innovation). The last factor – *new and radically different forms of innovation* – seems to be the most important one in terms of being competitive. The structural effects, for example, *R&D employment, innovation, and quality of institutional support and local infrastructure* account for almost 50 per cent of the overall differences between India and Bangladesh in the conditional export intensity (15 per cent out of 33 per cent).

This is a key result that supports the assumptions of institutional capacity made in the theoretical framework of this book and applied throughout.

Table 7.5 Maximum likelihood estimates of the tobit model

Variable	*Coefficient*	*(Std Error)*
Export intensity		
R&D/sales (in %)	0.201**	(0.058)
Employment (in log (FTEs))	0.280*	(0.133)
Having product innovation	0.045	(0.427)
Having radical innovation	0.851*	(0.370)
Having financial constraint	−0.276	(0.375)
Having local duties constraints	−0.335	(0.374)
Intercept	−4.031**	(1.072)
Number of firms	148	
Log-likelihood	−635.49	

Source: author's surveys.

Note
Significance levels: † 10%; * 5%; ** 1%.

Table 7.6 Inter-country differences in the ability to export and compete

	R&D effects	Employment effects	Innovation effects	Institution and infrastructure effects	Sum of structural effects	Expected export intensity	Observed export intensity	Conditional competitiveness
Bangladesh	0.119	0.165	0.575	−0.361	0.498	13.794	4.542	−9.252
India	0.151	0.210	0.627	−0.460	0.572	29.230	37.233	8.003

Source: author's surveys.

7.4 Lead sectors can have system-wide dynamics

Strikingly, the country case studies in Part II reveal that countries that have built capacity for health innovation are curiously those that rank low on knowledge and institutional capacity (the very latecomers) than others that perform better than them (the latecomers).[4] This is somewhat counter intuitive. Figures 7.12 and 7.13 present a comparison of the six countries in this book (split regionally into Asia and Africa) using the World Bank's Knowledge Economy Index methodology. As part of the methodology, three key variables serve as proxies for each Knowledge Economy pillar: economic incentive and institutional regime, education, innovation and ICT, plus two variables for the overall economic and social performance. Knowledge index is the simple average of the normalized country scores on the key variables in three pillars – education, innovation and ICT. Knowledge Economy Index measures performance on all four pillars (World Bank KAM Database 2009).

The performance of Bangladesh and Vietnam over countries that rank above them such as Kenya and Nigeria reconfirms the lead sector hypothesis that Gerschenkron (1962) explicitly raised. Despite their overall shortcomings, these

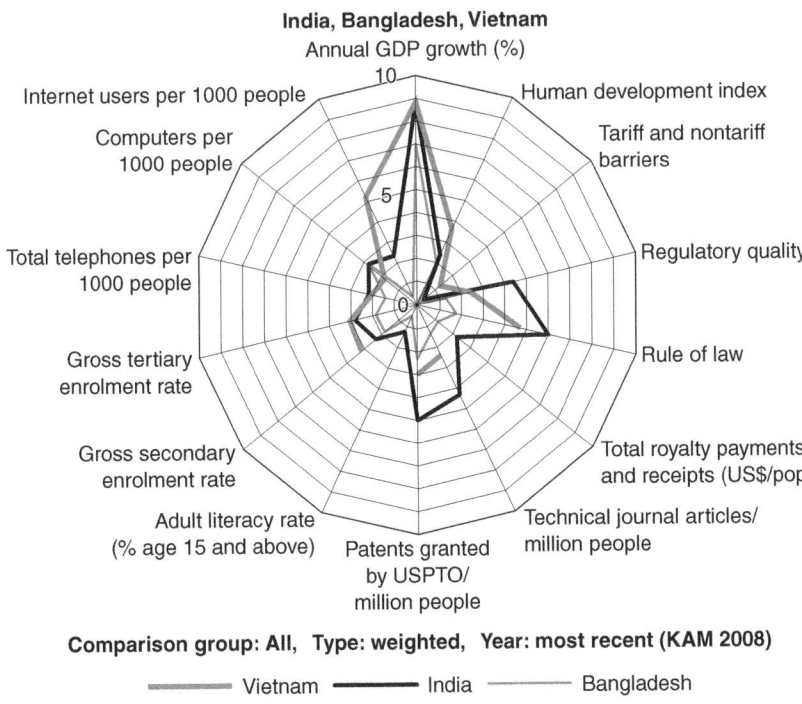

Figure 7.12 KAM scorecard for India, Bangladesh and Vietnam (source: World Bank, 2009).

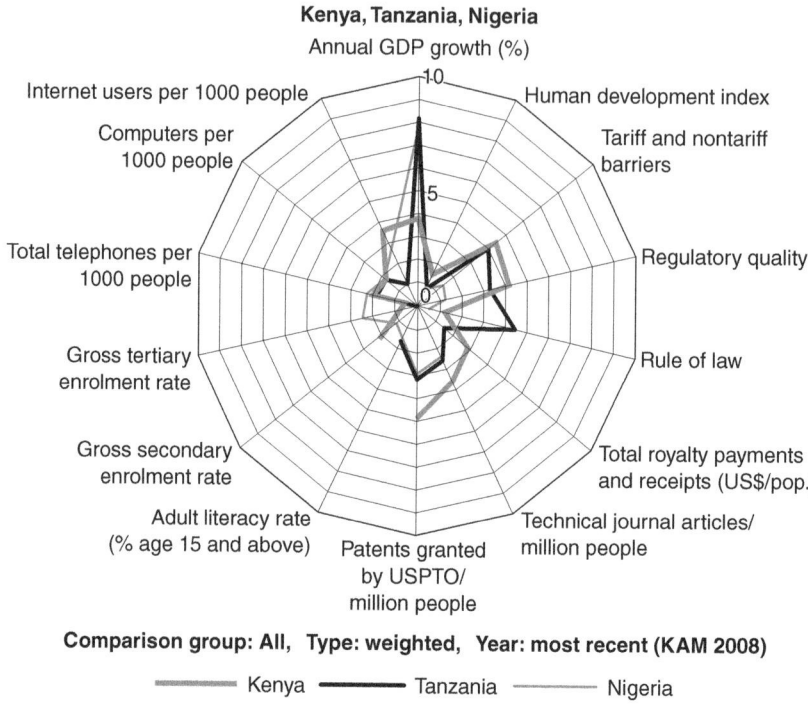

Figure 7.13 KAM scorecard for Kenya, Tanzania and Nigeria (source: World Bank, 2009)

countries have invested in building sectoral infrastructure for health that supersedes what is available in terms of institutions and incentives in the other countries. As a result, although Kenya and Nigeria could have theoretically a better institutional infrastructure for health innovation, Bangladesh and Vietnam have managed to turn these into lead sectors whose knowledge spillovers may be key in building system-wide dynamics. This is why, in the previous section, Bangladesh performs so much better than Kenya in competitiveness, although it may still lag behind India in the quality of the institutional framework and provision of physical and knowledge infrastructure.

Comparative insights further reveal that health innovation systems in latecomer countries are extremely resilient and have the tendency to respond to local demand in specific ways, as already highlighted in the previous section. In the case of both Nigeria and Tanzania, the isolated product development successes that are observed no doubt pose the question of how such sporadic successes can be steered into a well-functioning sectoral system for health innovation, it also points to the fact that much can be achieved if collaborative learning and product development is fostered.

7.5 Promoting global and local access to medicines

Issues of access to medicines are increasingly being explained in the context of weak health care systems in latecomer countries and the inequities being fortified through the TRIPS Agreement. Health care systems notwithstanding, the TRIPS Agreement contributes to weaker access to medicines in two essential ways: by way of diminished research incentives into diseases of the developing world, and high prices of patented drugs and restriction of generic competition. Health innovation in latecomers is important from several perspectives for access to medicines. First, its impact on global market structure as a means of competitive pricing (as the case of India has historically shown), stable supply and innovation, is evidently very relevant. This enhances global consumer welfare. Second, firms and organizations with strengths in low cost, high skilled aspects of health innovation are increasingly becoming highly important partners in global PDPs. Finally, firms from latecomer countries with good health innovation capabilities, such as India and China, have the potential to restructure global health innovation such that the product emphasis shifts at least in certain disease segments to low cost, high economies of scale products such as the case of ARV fixed-dose and paediatric ARVs discussed in Chapter 3 has shown.

7.5.1 Health innovation capacity and global access to medicines

Of the countries analysed in this book, Indian firms play a key role in promoting global access to medicines, since they are actively engaged in the production of drugs for HIV/AIDS, Malaria, TB and other opportunistic infections. Bangladesh and Vietnam seem well poised to play a role (since both are least developed countries according to UN classification and have relatively promising health innovation capabilities). However, the battle is far from being won. WHO estimates that by the end of 2007, there were an estimated 33.2 million people infected with HIV worldwide of which about two-thirds live in sub-Saharan Africa (WHO, 2008b). Only three million people in low and middle income settings received treatment as of December 2007[5] and of all HIV-infected people in need of ARVs in Africa, only 31 per cent were receiving treatments as of 2007 (Global Fund, 2007; WHO, 2008b).

Therefore, the most important question is whether the incentives can be preserved for global competition and to ensure the emergence of an equally competitive market for second-line ARV drugs for local consumption and export. This is a very important issue for global access to medicines because almost all ARV drugs that have received prequalification under the WHO's prequalification programme for essential medicines as of 1 February 2008 are manufactured by Indian firms apart from the South Africa's Aspen Pharmacare and China's Zhejiang Pharmaceutical Co. (the latter has a prequalification only for Nevaripine) (see also Tables 3.6 and 3.7).

7.5.1.1 HIV/AIDS

As Chapter 3 has shown, Indian firms play a key role in the production of drugs for HIV/AIDS globally. Specifically in the area of drugs of importance to public health, it is well acknowledged that price competition offered by Indian firms for first line ARV drugs induced drastic reductions in the prices of drugs and made them widely accessible (see for example, MSF, 2008). According to the Global Price Reporting Mechanism database, generic competition amongst first-line suppliers has brought down the median price of the most commonly prescribed fixed dose combination in first-line regimen (d4T 30 mg + 3TC 150 mg + NVP 200 mg) by 40 per cent from US\$153 (2004) to US\$92 (2007) in low income countries and from US\$154 (2004) to US\$91 (2007) in middle income countries (WHO, 2008a). Their involvement has brought about similar price reductions (as were observed in the case of first-line ARV therapies) in some second-line drugs, although second-line treatments remain very expensive when compared to first-line treatments in low income countries, according to the WHO (2008b).[6]

In the second-line ARVs segment, the introduction of Lopinavir/Ritonaavir by Indian firms like Cipla saw reductions in Abbott's prices for Kaletra in the Indian market by a significant margin (field interviews). Abcavir's median price has reduced from US\$887 (2004) to US\$426 (2007) in low income countries and from US\$887 (2004) to US\$410 (2007) in middle income countries. However, the median price of LPV/r (133/33 mg) has decreased much more in middle income countries than in low income countries and the prices of other second-line drugs remain high.[7] This makes the issue of ensuring adequate price competition through generic firms very critical, especially so because 97 per cent of HIV-infected persons in low income countries are being treated with first-line regimens and will need to shift to second-line regimens sometime in the coming future.

Although there are four Indian firms presently well on their way to producing generic versions of LPV/r and heat-stable LPV/r (Aurobindo, Cipla, Matrix and Emcure), which is expected to make them widely available at cheaper prices, the patent situation of second-line drugs makes it a debatable issue whether Indian firms will be able to continue production (see Gehl Sampath, 2008 for a very detailed discussion). Firms in Bangladesh are presently producing only a few first-line therapies and have not received WHO prequalification status for their products, as a result of which they are not allowed to supply to the GFATM.[8]

7.5.1.2 Malaria

The most common Artemesinin based combination therapy (ACT) for first-line treatment is Coartem, patent holder Novartis, and ASAP, where the patent holder is Sanofi Aventis. There are three Indian firms that produce anti-malarial combination therapies: Cipla, Strides and Ipca, of which all do not have WHO pre-qualification for their first-line ACT, the generic version of Coartem. Ipca has WHO prequalification only for a second-line therapy using Artemesinin; namely, Artemisin Amodiaquine. Strides has developed its own technologies for ACT

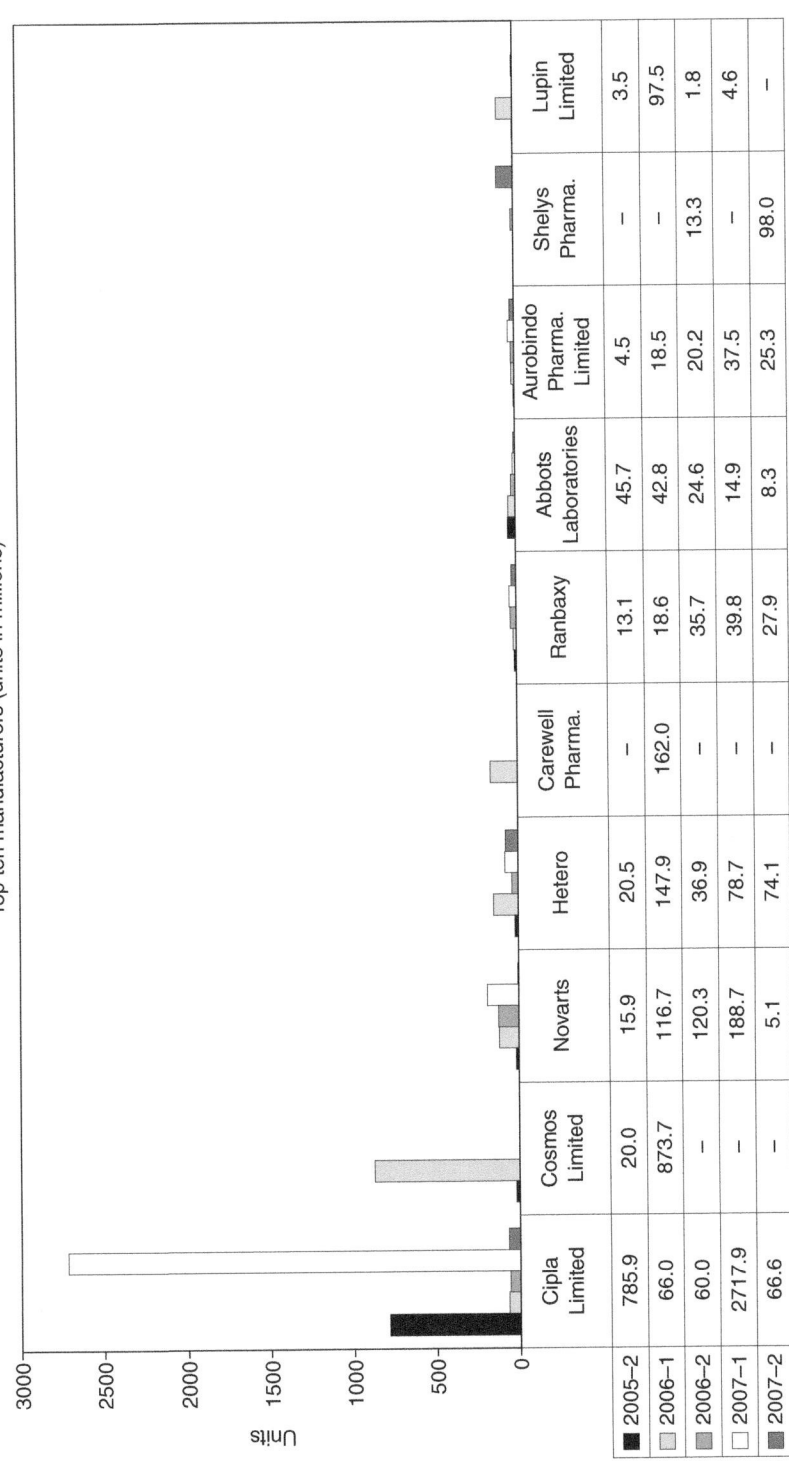

Top ten manufacturers (units in millions)

	Cipla Limited	Cosmos Limited	Novarts	Hetero	Carewell Pharma.	Ranbaxy	Abbots Laboratories	Aurobindo Pharma. Limited	Shelys Pharma.	Lupin Limited
2005–2	785.9	20.0	15.9	20.5	–	13.1	45.7	4.5	–	3.5
2006–1	66.0	873.7	116.7	147.9	162.0	18.6	42.8	18.5	–	97.5
2006–2	60.0	–	120.3	36.9	–	35.7	24.6	20.2	13.3	1.8
2007–1	2717.9	–	188.7	78.7	–	39.8	14.9	37.5	–	4.6
2007–2	66.6	–	5.1	74.1	–	27.9	8.3	25.3	98.0	–

Figure 7.14 Top ten suppliers of pharmaceutical and health products to global fund grant recipients (source: Grace and Gehl Sampath, 2008).

combinations and presently produces several of them. The company has considerable acreage of Artemesinin (the plant that is used to produce ACT drugs) in Vietnam. Ranbaxy's joint collaboration with MMV for the development of an anti-malarial drug has been discontinued recently, despite which Ranbaxy has proceeded with the development of the drug. According to the field interview with the company in April 2008, the drug is presently in clinical trials, and is a substitute for the Artemesinin combination therapy recommended by the WHO. However, it is not clear whether Daiichi's recent takeover of the company will impact upon this in any way. Cosmos Pharmaceuticals, the Kenyan firm discussed in Chapter 5 is a supplier of anti-malarial therapies to the global fund.

7.5.1.3 Tuberculosis

Two Indian firms, Strides and Lupin are also into the production of anti-tuberculosis drugs, for both MDR and HDR Tuberculosis. Strides is the largest producer of first-line TB drugs, for which it has developed the technologies in an alliance with Sandoz. Strides however, expressed scepticism to enter into production of second-line MDR TB drugs. Lupin remains the sole API manufacturer within India for this segment.

7.5.1.4 Other public health drugs

As opposed to widely available drugs to treat opportunistic infections such as Ciprofloxacin and Flucanozole, there are drugs for treating opportunistic infections, such as Valgancyclovir and Valacyclovir that are not available for use in resource-poor settings due to their high prices. The Indian patent situation and the ongoing dispute on Roche's Valcyte (Valgancyclovir) could pave the way for cheaper substitutes of such drugs. In the case of Valgancyclovir, Ranbaxy has recently received market approval for the generic version of Valcyte, and Cipla plans to enter the market with its own version of the drug in July 2008. There are huge price differences between the originator firm's price (which is somewhere between 900 and 1000 rupees for a 450 mg tablet, about US$20–25) and Cipla's price, which is estimated to be around 240 rupees (US$6). Several public health agencies, such as CHAI are keen to promote more widespread use of drugs such as Valgancyclovir in developing and least developed countries[9] and Indian firms will potentially play a large role in this endeavour. The flexible patent interpretations could also pave the way for cheaper generics of other important drugs to treat opportunistic infections, which are presently being manufactured only by the patent holder firm, such as Rifabutin, Famcyclovir and Valacyclovir.[10]

7.5.2 Local access to medicines

Although promoting local health has been a primary motivation amongst latecomers in enacting policy frameworks for health innovation, there is little or no link between cheaper production of drugs and health systems equity. This calls for a rethink on how building capabilities in the latecomer context can contribute to pro-poor innovation and health system equity issues. Health system aspects figure very marginally and often do not figure at all in frameworks that need to be considered and expanded given the extensive inter-linkages between technological innovation and social and organizational innovations in this sector. India and Bangladesh's ability to produce cheap drugs has not permeated into their health systems in ways, which could be expected. A key reason for this is the limitations observed in the health system aspects of these countries. The analysis conducted in this book indicates that health innovation is an organic process, within which delivery and use of useful public health products that are of local significance should form a key part of the capacity building process.

Another important result on this point is that latecomers not only have to catch up on the technologies related to innovation of drugs but also on innovation in delivery systems, which is badly needed if the full benefits of innovation in diagnostics, therapeutics and devices are to be achieved. Health care systems in latecomer countries have particularly not evolved enough to accommodate the complexities posed by technology and service delivery on the one hand, and their own expansion and needs on the other.

7.6 State capacity to enact rules: key results

The vision to achieve self-sufficiency in production of drugs has been the main driver of health innovation in most countries, although the latecomer countries that have achieved it are now following it up with advanced policy initiatives that target new technologies such as genomics and systems biology. In the African countries that have been analysed in this book, it is precisely the lack of state vision that accounts for the lagging institutional infrastructure to support health innovation. In Nigeria and Kenya, the state (in terms of supportive regulatory capacity) has not been able to drive the innovation process through to build further on isolated cases of success (as discussed in Section 7.2) and the positive outcomes of international collaborations (see Chapter 5 on Kenya). This manifests in activities in several ways across many sectors, including health innovation, such as:[11]

a   duplication of results across agencies set out to perform various institutional mandates;

b   duplication of research efforts and wastage of scarce resources available for innovation;

c   a lack of suitable reward structures that promote performance, and hence a resulting "market for lemons" (Akerlof, 1970), where researchers who are interested in serious R&D are forced to leave the country and over a period of time only second-best graduates are available for recruitment in national agencies for research and management;

d   the poor policy convergence between innovation investment and local disease challenges.

The six countries have vast divergences in the way states had put in place different incentive regimes including those dealing with intellectual property and trade related issues for health innovation and access to medicines.

It is precisely state vision and policy capacity that comes to the fore when the experience of India is compared to the rest of the countries, where state capacity is constantly being used to circumvent the negative impacts of the TRIPS Agreement on the local pharmaceutical firms and access (in terms of affordable prices) to drugs locally. Bangladesh, in this sense, reflects immense lost potential. The extensive state capacity that is obvious in the actions of the 1970s and the 1980s have been diluted by a series of unconnected actions and a degenerating institutional support apparatus that is retarding the capacity of the sector. The need for the state to create a *level playing field through supportive regulatory frameworks that complement the market mechanism*, where it works in tandem with all other actors in the system, is nowhere more obvious and urgent than in the case of health innovation. In the main, the state has to achieve the following.

7.6.1 States have to oversee and champion technology choices for the sector that take into account local needs

State vision and state policy play a key role in being able to manage the threat and opportunities presented by the international rules and regulations by coordinating an overarching framework for innovation in health. The results on intellectual property and state capacity discussed in this chapter help to stress this point further. The failure of markets to provide knowledge inputs such as extension services for standards setting, testing, metrology, quality and information, intellectual property, vocational, technical and skill training, and scientific and technological laboratories that could be private or public research organizations all need to be augmented through institutional mechanisms created to bridge these gaps. Table 7.7 contains the innovation policy tool kit for health innovation, with details of all primary and secondary instruments that are necessary for a supportive institutional framework.

7.6.2 States have to proxy as innovators in early stages of health innovation

State proxies in the early stages as an innovator: whether it is the case of India, Bangladesh, China or Vietnam (or several other countries that have not been discussed in this book), state owned enterprises have played a critical role in jump-starting the innovation process. In fact, in all these countries, the enterprise sector was an offshoot of the state's intervention. Both India and Bangladesh (and the case of China briefly presented in Chapter 3 also supports this point) set up state owned pharmaceutical production companies and also fostered public–private interactions at later stages through technology transfer and other incentives.

Table 7.7 An innovation policy tool kit for health innovation

Policy tool	Examples
Direct financial support	Grants, subsidies, loans, provision of equipment or services, loan guarantees
Indirect financial support	Schemes encouraging investment in innovation, venture capital
Information	Information networks, adviser centres, consultancy services, specialist libraries, databases, liaison services
Scientific and technical infrastructure	Public research laboratories, research association, learned societies, research grants
Educational infrastructure	General education system, universities and polytechnics, technical education system, apprenticeship schemes, retraining system
Public procurement	Central or local government purchasing and contracts, R&D contracts
Taxation	Company, personal, indirect and payroll taxation, tax allowances
Regulation	Patents, regulations (e.g. in environmental control), inspectorates, monopoly and anti-trust legislation
Public enterprise	Innovation by public owned industries, use of these as pioneering facilities, establishment of new industries
Political	Planning, regional policies, honours and awards for innovation, encouragement of mergers or joint ventures
Public services	Procurement, maintenance, supervision and innovation in public services, such as telecommunications, transport and health care
Trade	Trade agreements, tariffs and currency regulations

Source: adapted from Oyeyinka and Gehl Sampath (2009b).

This is not trivial and is an important lesson for African latecomer countries that have been discussed in this book, and calls for more rigorous interventions on part of the African state to support health innovation systems. As Johnson (1982, p. 41) states:

> One of the things a state committed to development must do is develop a market system and it does this to the extent that its policies reduce the uncertainties or risks faced by entrepreneurs, generate and disseminate information about investment and sales opportunities, and instil an expansionist psychology in the people. Once a market system has begun to function, the state must be prepared to be surprised by the opportunities that open up to it, ones that it never imagined but that entrepreneurs have discovered.

Such an active role by the state can already be witnessed by some emerging collaborations in African countries, the most notable of which is the recent Quality Chemicals–Cipla Pharmaceuticals venture in Uganda. Supported extensively by the Ugandan government, Quality Chemicals has been set up as a production facility for anti-retroviral and anti-malarial medicines. As part of the joint venture, Cipla Pharmaceuticals is currently providing the tacit know-how, licences for the drugs being produced as well as key expertise in the plant. The plant is expected to produce WHO–GMP pre-qualified drugs for the Ugandan local market and for the East African regional market.

7.6.3   The state to balance external pressures rests on its ability to identify its own strategic interests, and this requires not only innovation policy, but organizational competence

Whether it is in the case of IPRs, data exclusivity or other prevailing concerns, the countries that manage to create a conducive learning environment are those that not only know the needs of the sector, but have competent organizational leadership to implement state vision on a routine basis. Taking a capability view of the organization means that learning efficiency that improves performance will tend to display durability (learning should endure) and appropriability (the ability of a firm to profit from learning).

While most organizations and actors necessary in the health sector are in place, for example, in the research, infrastructure, demand and entrepreneurs domains, it is the organizational competence that is missing. In other words, there is a lack of relevant human skills to steer the organizations into their respective mandates, and to enable them to coordinate their work well in this area. Apart from the latecomer malady of duplicating research efforts across all public research institutes despite the limited resources available, there have been other instances of explicit waste of research results due to a lack of coordination. This can only be eliminated by efforts to build skilled manpower and incentives that seek to retain them in the country.

7.6.4   Informal institutions play a major role in learning and state policy needs to be inclusive enough to incorporate local considerations in a fundamental way

This calls for a more nuanced understanding of the institutions for innovation in a latecomer context with a *greater focus on the informal domain*. The imperative is on initiatives that understand the local barriers to innovation capacity and enact incentives that seek to change entrenched modes of socially disruptive behaviour into more collectively efficient patterns. Such change, by nature, can only be induced at the margin and will require sustained efforts to bear results. Moreover, it calls for rigorous stocktaking of the nature of innovation in any latecomer context including empirical studies that inform patterns of actor behaviour over time. Dynamism indicates the flexibility of the system to shift boundaries according to its gradual transition from one stage of the catch-up process to another. At a more abstract level, it calls for state capacity to foresee and constantly intervene in providing new technological opportunities for actors in the system.

7.7 Impact of IPRs on access to knowledge and the issue of state capacity

The impact of patent protection on biomedical innovation has been a controversial issue. Although a "medical anti-commons" has been predicted due to a proliferation of patents on upstream technologies, evidence to test these concerns is only now emerging. However, most industrial surveys that shed light on this issue are mainly from frontier countries, making it very difficult to predict the impact of patenting on biomedical innovation in developing and least developed countries. Three main issues seem to be of utmost importance for latecomer countries. (a) Can accumulated IPR positions by firms in developed countries that have a lead technological advantage be used to prevent serious competition from industries in latecomer countries in innovative activities at the frontier? (b) What sort of bargaining anomalies could result from monopolistic positions, information issues and transaction costs when one talks of licensing arrangements between firms across the globe? (c) How important are the restrictions placed by such IPRs when compared to other factors that affect firm level decisions on taking up new innovation projects?

In this respect, the data and comparative insights generated by this book provide interesting results. First, IPRs are only important when firms/sectors are in a relatively advanced stage of moving from manufacturing to incremental innovations, where reverse engineering and copying for export begin to play a critical role. Box 7.3 maps the various levels at which access to knowledge issues impact upon health innovation.

Box 7.3 Institutions and access to knowledge for health innovation

Accessibility of knowledge can manifest at several stages in the capabilities building process (Malerba and Orsenigo, 2000). To begin with, firms may require opportunities to access knowledge that are external to their enterprise, to the sector or even to the country. Knowledge is cumulative and does not diffuse easily at the firm level and requires interventions in terms of policy and other institutional support structures (Malerba, 2004) at each and every level. It is precisely this that represents a very interesting set of challenges in terms of how scientific and technological knowledge relate to the economic development process and how institutions can mitigate difficulties in accessing knowledge. Thus, institutional support for access to knowledge is multi-faceted and the problematic needs to be framed at several levels:

1   At a very fundamental level, firms and institutions do not have complete information on all the technological alternatives that might exist, and the skills and infrastructure that they may require (Archibugi and Pietrobelli, 2003) and the states of the world that may materialize in terms of further opportunities and gains. It is the role of institutions to foresee this and to enable these opportunities to materialize in the first place.

2   It entails creation of incentives for diffusion of knowledge at the firm level that are as important as any other variable for innovation, otherwise search and information costs are incurred by firms.

3   It involves regular stocktaking of what the state-of-the-art of innovation activities is within firms and organizations in key sectors and their difficulties in accessing knowledge.

4   It involves a consideration of how international rules on IPRs might affect learning trajectories (which may have specific sectoral dimensions) and how these impacts could be mitigated through local institutions.

5   It involves considerations of access to technologies and the transaction costs that local firms may have to incur (especially those trying to reach agreements with international partners in commercial agreements) and how these could be mitigated though legal certainty and cheaper access to court procedures in case of need.

6   It involves effective approaches that allow for the management and sharing of already existing evidence on health systems research, through initiatives that promote ICT approaches based on open source software for medical publishing and health communications.

Source: author

Within the six stages of access to knowledge described in Box 7.3, the issue of IPRs becomes significant from stage 3 onwards if, and only if, the level of capabilities in the sector are in the stage of accumulating reverse engineering capabilities or more.

8   Bridging the health divide

Institutional capacity in latecomers

Health is a fundamental prerequisite for sustainable economic development; the divide in resources, technology and nature of disease is becoming an increasing hurdle for countries to surmount. A new global political economy of health innovation is required that builds on the result of the book, taking into account that even countries labelled generally as latecomers, that lag behind enormously on general economic indicators, can build capacity in various aspects of health innovation, depending on the policy emphasis in the country over time. A fundamental reason for this lies in the fact that growth and development in latecomer countries is more dependent on structural change, of which technological change forms a part only, as the experience of the industrialized countries indicates (Ocampo and Vos, 2007). In the initial stages of development in countries, small investments in infrastructure and knowledge capacity can often bear huge results, depending on the dynamics of sectors and actors in real time. This book has provided key insights into the state of health innovation in latecomer countries, as well as evidence on several pressing issues that confront them, such as what is the state of higher education and research in these African and Asian countries under consideration? Why do we see so few cases of product development in the latecomer countries, and what explains the successes? What is the role of brain-drain and the missing human resources for health? What is the impact of intellectual property rights on promoting technological change in the pharmaceutical sector in latecomers and access to medicines? – these are some of the topics discussed. The key results of the book that are of relevance to policy are summarized here.

8.1 Translating research to the market

The context specific nature of the process (level of technology and the quality of scientific and technological infrastructure) as well as the nature of institutions (the scientific culture and support systems) means that the factors that foster or hinder the translation of research into innovation differ not only in frontier and latecomer economies, but also can have further variations within latecomer contexts.

In other words, in what ways have institutions shaped the emergence of scientific research and its observed path to the market in health innovation? Why have there been so few successes in taking inventions to the market (in the form of commercial innovations) in Africa whereas in Asia, even countries with significant lags in policy initiation of capacity programmes such as Vietnam, show greater results? In this book, the sectoral systems framework has been applied to test the hypothesis that the institutionally predetermined policy processes have impacted significantly on the ways inventive activities travel, or do not travel, from the laboratory to the market and thus account for varying levels of innovation capacity. On the surface, all latecomer countries have public sector research institutions with some level of endowments dedicated to health innovation as well as some firm level activities, but as the sectoral investigations in Part II show, it is the differences that matter.

8.1.1 Institutional capacity and health innovation

Several key results accrue from the individual country experiences and the comparative insights on the issue of institutional capacity. These are important because they are related to specific policy and institutional framework issues in latecomer countries.

> Result: regulatory and institutional strengthening is required to create the appropriate mix of knowledge and physical infrastructure that can foster innovation.

What tends to separate two latecomer countries more than any other factors that foster development is the intensity and depth of investment in human and non-human resources. Knowledge infrastructure is required at the most basic level of education (training scientists and engineers), as well as at the level of public scientific research and development. State based institutions, mainly the universities and PRIs, fulfil these roles. One of the fundamental functions of these institutions is R&D based learning that creates the absorptive capacity of nations (Teubal, 1999).[1] The state has historically played a leading role in both the early "industrializers", having recognized and used the institutions of universities and PRIs as a vehicle of catch-up in respective periods, although the roles of the institutions expectedly differ/evolve with the stage of development. "Institutional differentiation" is required to generate the right kinds of knowledge and skills in an economy, by which Mowery (2005) means the mix of tertiary but non-university establishments such as polytechnics, community colleges and other forms of technical institutes, depending on the level of capacity in the country in general or the sector in particular. This mix of institutional structures and the variety of funding arrangements that support them have contributed to the successful response of the system to labour market demands for skills and knowledge in the developed countries.

Countries such as India and Vietnam have been relatively consistent in creating the balance between the various institutional infrastructure elements, in terms of creating a "policy package" that caters to both demand and supply aspects of innovation. Countries that are lagging behind, including Nigeria, Vietnam and Kenya, have failed at this juncture. Bangladesh is an example of a country that has demonstrated partial success, but is held back by difficulties in expanding its innovation capacity (in terms of not making a dynamic transition from manufacturing drugs to more knowledge intensive reverse engineering processes) once again due to the lack of appropriate policy initiatives for skills creation and lack of provision of common scientific infrastructure (such as the long-debated common API park).

> Result: the knowledge bases required to promote innovative activity even within established sectors such as health innovation, could be different for latecomers from what we assume them to be while analysing technological change in industrialized countries.

While the literature on health innovation and biotechnology from the experiences of the frontier countries is replete with the kinds of secondary dedicated instruments that support the growth of the sector, the data collected across all the six countries point unanimously towards common denominators of collaboration and learning in latecomer contexts. The results of Table 7.1 show that the factors that play a critical role in promoting collaboration are the availability of skilled scientific manpower and quality of local infrastructure (physical and scientific), and venture capital availability. Skilled manpower, quality of infrastructure and venture capital availability are three factors significantly associated with the probability of establishing local collaboration. All these three factors are critical in the build up towards innovative activities of firms and organizations in health innovation amongst latecomers, in the absence of which, firms do not have sufficient incentives to collaborate. Other factors could begin to play a role as incentives for collaboration and innovation as countries progress. For example, IPRs play a major role only in India (see Table 7.1) since the firms in the Indian context are at a much more advanced stage of innovation capacity when compared to the other two countries.

> Result: secondary policy instruments begin to play a significant role in shaping capacity once there is quality infrastructure, presence of skilled manpower and some level of financial support for enterprise.

A fundamental flaw of latecomers has been to focus extensively on the creation of supply-side organizations in keeping with the linear model of S&T policy, overlooking the importance of balancing system-wide actor configurations. Despite the huge investments on public research institutes, they are often ranked low as sources of information in all countries empirically investigated for this book. Studies on the topic even within industrialized countries shows that often only a third or even less of the firms found the importance of government laboratories to be either moderate or very significant and it is not unusual to find that firms rate the information from universities or government laboratories as not an important input to the innovation process. The absence of a private sector that could uptake and steer research into productive and innovative frontiers is a major hindrance to latecomer capacity in health. This book also shows that the presence of a local enterprise sector has played a major role in those countries that have managed to build significant capacity. Clearly, the absence of one or the other major set of actors of innovation cannot be done away with.

> Result: health innovation systems in latecomer countries are resilient and adaptable.

The country case studies presented in the book make a clear case for considering building capacity, at least in key aspects of health innovation, in latecomer contexts. The limited capacity that exists in the countries under consideration has been the basis for extensive product development even in extremely hostile environments, as the examples of sickle cell research and Typhoid vaccine development in Nigeria and LLINs in Tanzania shows. This is a key finding of relevance to policy.

> Result: although local need has been a precursor to the capacity building exercise, there is little or no link between innovation capacity and health systems' equity.

Latecomers fail in the most essential aspect of bridging the divide between production of health services and products and delivering them to the neediest parts of their population. Local needs play a critical role as the initiator of policies that have led to building capacity (as in the case of India and Bangladesh, and, more recently Vietnam), or have brought together system forces in remarkably novel ways to find solutions (as in the case of the sporadic success of Nigerian product innovation in PRIs). However, policy efforts in latecomers have failed to create the substantive linkages between technological innovation and health system equity. This should assume importance in the efforts of other latecomers seeking to build capacity, for example, Uganda, so that capacity serves the needs of equity first and foremost. The framework on health innovation elaborated in this book helps to bridge these issues, although the case studies could only highlight these inter-linkages in a limited way.

> Result: IPRs are not significant to countries at low levels of capacity in health innovation.

While the results show that IPRs are not significant to countries at low levels of health innovation capacity, the result needs to be understood in a nuanced way. IPRs are currently not significant to those latecomer countries that have low levels of health innovation capacity because they are not involved in knowledge intensive activities or are unable to reverse engineer. As mentioned earlier in the book, technological backwardness of latecomers is the best form of protection to frontier countries. This is not to diminish its importance, but rather to point out that even in these latecomer countries IPRs will begin to play a very important limiting role once the countries begin to accumulate some technological capabilities of relevance to innovation. This paradox needs to be dealt with, while addressing the limitations of the TRIPS Agreement in accommodating countries' individual catch-up possibilities in health innovation.

> Result: newer modes of cooperation and capacity building are beginning to emerge as a result of the emergence of India, China, Brazil and other developing countries.

Divergences amongst the latecomers that have become an intense subject of study for policy (Oyeyinka and Gehl Sampath, 2009a) have in several ways also begun to restructure the notion of technological transfer. A broader, southern perspective that focuses much more on knowledge sharing and capacity building is beginning to emerge. This new paradigm of south–south partnership calls for a greater institutional response from those other latecomer countries that are the recipients. Not only should there be more active participation in structuring partnerships with countries such as India and China, but also there is a greater need for viewing south–south collaborations as a means to reinforcing the developmental needs and priorities of latecomer countries.

> Result: Access to existing and new technologies through new forms of technology transfer initiatives are both integral to the expansion of health innovation capacity in latecomers.

The relative importance and scope of technology in the catch-up process has changed. Experiences of the newly industrializing countries and industrialized countries point towards a pattern of capabilities accumulation, wherein learning trajectories of firms and other actors in the innovation system almost always proceed in a progression from reverse engineering and adaptation to incremental innovation to an R&D based approach. In the early literature, however, incremental innovation is not usually recognized as being part of the R&D process, because it may overlap with development and is not formalized as a clear category of activity (see Rosenberg, 1982). Despite this, incremental innovation is a very important stage in capacity building processes at the firm level, thus affirming the ability of the enterprise to adapt existing knowledge and create commercially viable products. Such a product, although not new to the world or science at large, is a significant step towards the creation of independent local enterprise in latecomer countries, a backbone of industrial activity. While these distinctions are important, technological progress and catch-up in health innovation in latecomers may not necessarily follow the same path as witnessed earlier in other countries due to several new limitations to reverse engineering and imitation of technologies under the WTO regime, especially as part of the TRIPS Agreement.

For these very reasons, technology transfer is becoming an intensely debated area in political negotiations. Recognizing technology's ubiquitous role in health innovation calls for more active approaches to engage in technology transfer to latecomer countries. These approaches need to balance the need for greater access to knowledge with the growing proliferation of intellectual property rights.

8.2 The role of the state

The six-country comparison shows that states and the policy framework as provided by the state are pivotal to learning and innovation process, both on the technological innovation side and on the health systems aspects. As already discussed in Chapter 2, the state catalyses the key actors and configurations through what can be called "market-stimulating technology policies" (Lall and Teubal, 1998, p. 1382). The following main roles can be demarcated.

8.2.1 The state is the champion of health innovation, and its policy vision and organizational competence is the key for success

The developmental state plays an important catalytic role in alleviating the binding constraints to technological learning so that these advantages of openness can be realized. This process involves explicit public policies to support learning to take place both in firms and in the wider innovation context within the country. However, mere physical accumulation of technology is evidently not sufficient. Within the newer paradigm for knowledge and technology, the state plays a key role in mobilizing domestic resources for technological progress.

The state needs to prioritize and enact rules and institutions to support the sector; either through sectoral policy or through specific sectoral initiatives that support/augment the existing the national innovation policy framework in the country. This is the only sustainable way through which isolated product development successes can be channelled into successful sectoral systems of health. Three sets of policy relevant recommendations – regulatory framework, innovation capacity and provision of state based common services – are relevant.

1   Policy assistance that seeks to enhance the competitiveness of the sector needs to focus on:

    a   an integrated innovations approach that promotes human skills development of relevance to the sector, as well as improved coordination between the various components (especially public research and industry) of the domestic knowledge system;

b   reducing the dependencies (which are also the cause for major ineffi-
      ciencies) between medical practice, research and product commerciali-
      zation in the pharmaceutical sector (that presently extend well into the
      performance of the health sector);

c   developing concrete innovation incentives for the sector that could
      work hand-in-hand with IPRs to reduce their potential negative impacts
      on access to technologies for the sector;

d   enhancing capacity of the local intellectual property office, in order to
      be able to document data on patent applications and grants transparently
      and accountably and also to ensure that patent applications serve as
      essential tools of diffusion of information on which the patents are
      granted;

e   forging liaisons between local organizations (including firms) and
      foreign organizations that focus on technological upgrading and innov-
      ative capacity of the sector.

2   Policy assistance on the regulatory framework should focus on:

a   setting standards for good manufacturing and bioequivalence;
b   enhancing the capacity and performance of the Drug Directorates;
c   evolving a system of price control and price setting to enhance access
      to medicines in the local market;
d   setting up education apparatus that match the needs of the sector along
      with rigorous university accreditation and design of courses appropriate
      for the sector;
e   separating the pharmaceutical sector regulations from the Ministry of
      Health.

3   Policy assistance to set up common industry infrastructure. This includes
     provision of common knowledge services that can be used by public and
     private sector actors alike and includes initiatives such as an API park. A
     series of pay-and-go industry facilities can be created for the sector, wherein
     firms face difficulties of raising individual capital for infrastructure expan-
     sion. Such facilities have been a core component of industrial sector policies
     in several countries, including India, China, South Korea and Taiwan. A
     central bioequivalence laboratory for firms wanting to branch out their
     exports to regulated and semi-regulated markets, API parks, technology
     transfer and brokerage services are all part of such common industry
     infrastructure.

8.2.2 *States need to proxy as innovators and strengthen entrepreneurship by providing incentives for collaboration and support*

States not only proxy in the early stages as an innovator, but also provide a
framework within which coordination risks of actors in the health innovation

system are minimized. Whether it is the case of India, Bangladesh, China or Vietnam (or several other countries that have not been discussed in this book), state owned enterprises have played a critical role in jump-starting the innovation process. This is not trivial and is an important lesson for African latecomer countries that have been discussed in this book.

The local enterprise sector will require technological and financial assistance. While technological assistance will depend on improved knowledge infrastructure in the public sector institutions, financing that bolsters small enterprise development through innovative finance schemes and venture capital is required. Health innovation experiences from other latecomer countries reveal significant state investment in setting up enterprises, promoting technology acquisition and sharing, and in standard setting. Such schemes could also be risk-sharing finance schemes that envisage a state investment that matches the private sector in order to make more resources available for innovative activities (such as those being implemented in other developing countries to promote health biotechnology, such as India and China).

Dedicated policy instruments that signal state support need to provide three sets of services, in the absence of thriving enterprise sectors, in ways that mimic the market.

1   Facilitating university research and "spin-off" scientists.
2   Reducing the risk of innovative activities through finance. Support models to help agents overcome financial constraints and engage in innovation include government-support soft loans, R&D subsidies, public risk capital funds, public support for private enterprise through grants, subsidies, private equity, venture capital and buy-out investments. Policies that could promote these (from a review of literature) include: seed-financing programmes, business angels networks, enterprise subsidy programmes (for setting up new biotechnology start-ups), common placement funds for innovation and research tax credit programmes.
3   Providing business support to fledgling ventures. State agencies need to assist entrepreneurs on issues related to IPP (what is protected, what not, how to obtain licences), marketing and demand assessment, advertising and reaching consumers, among many others. These call for policies that provide technology incubation facilities, science and technology parks, competence centres that provide expertise such as legal affairs and marketing.

8.2.3 *The state has to enact rules, laws and institutions to deal with international pull institutions*

As the previous analysis shows, both local and global institutions are germane to capacity building processes of countries in health innovation. While local institutions are critical to give the push factors (like focus on local demand), global factors may or may not be positive in the short or mid-term, and their impact will depend on how their interface with local innovation systems are facilitated.

There are interactive linkages between global and local institutions, and these need to be viewed from a local perspective, and persistent state vision is required to facilitate this.

Whether it is in the case of IPRs, data exclusivity or other prevailing concerns, creating a conducive learning environment calls for competent organizational leadership to implement state vision on a routine basis. Taking a capability view of the organization means that learning efficiency that improves performance will tend to display durability (learning should endure), and appropriability (the ability of a firm to profit from learning). Policy learning and technical assistance on various aspects of health innovation is required to balance local interests in a harmonious way.

8.2.4 The state needs to be dynamically engaged in facilitating the evolution of capabilities

Dynamism indicates the flexibility of the system to shift boundaries according to its gradual transition from one stage of the catch-up process to another. At a more abstract level, it calls for state capacity to foresee and constantly intervene in providing new technological opportunities for actors in the system. What firms need at a very low level of technological change is largely related to infrastructure. As firms progress to more knowledge intensive activities, different forms of policy incentives and access to technologies need to be facilitated.

8.2.5 Informal institutions play a major role in learning and state policy needs to be inclusive enough to incorporate local considerations in a fundamental way

This calls for a more nuanced understanding of the institutions for innovation in a latecomer context with a *greater focus on the informal domain*. The imperative is on initiatives that understand the local barriers to innovation capacity and enact incentives that seek to change entrenched modes of socially disruptive behaviour into more collectively efficient patterns. Such change, by nature, can only be induced at the margin and will require sustained efforts to bear results. Moreover, it calls for rigorous stocktaking of the nature of innovation in any latecomer context including empirical studies that inform patterns of actor behaviour over time.

Pursuing the options in a latecomer context will require paying substantial heed to informal institutions that are centrepiece of a sector's innovative performance due to their extent of embeddedness. Informal norms are entrenched in actors' code of conduct and are difficult to eliminate through simply dictating new rules of interaction. This is a very important result for donors and international agencies who are active in changing capacity for health innovation in latecomer countries.

In practical terms, this calls for far more controlled and reflexive policies, which as Rodrik (2004) suggests, could include the following elements:

- Incentives should be provided only to activities which are new to the national economy (that is, pioneer activities) and which foster diversification.
- There should be clear benchmarks/criteria of success and failure, and winners should be rewarded and losers abandoned. This should be closely monitored.
- There must be a built-in sunset clause; thus, public support will be withdrawn after an appropriate amount of time has elapsed.
- Public support should target activities (such as learning design and engineering skills), not sectors. Although these activities may be sector specific, they should be cross-cutting as far as possible.
- Any activities that are subsidized must have a clear potential of providing spillovers and demonstration effects.
- Support measures should be designed, implemented and monitored by agencies with demonstrated competence.
- Such agencies should be politically accountable and closely monitored.
- The agencies must maintain clear lines of communication with the private sector.
- Transparency is most important since mistakes will certainly be made and need to be reflected upon.
- Support measures must be adaptable to take account of the evolution of the industries concerned.

In addition to these measures, there should be some measures that are induced to reward those that follow norms and policy measures, in order to restrict agent behaviour to cooperative modes.

8.2.6 *States will need to refocus existing strengths and newer initiatives alike on achieving health systems equity*

This calls for a rethink on how health innovation and health services' delivery interact in latecomer contexts with an enhanced emphasis on delivery. There is ample evidence of states (see Kenyan health voucher scheme in Chapter 5) having embarked on programmes that support PPPs not only for product development but also health services delivery. Such a change in perspective is critical at this juncture, because it ensures the delivery of health services – who gets the products and services and through what modes is integrated within the health innovation framework. There are lessons to be learnt from the evidence on the experience of latecomers in structuring public private partnerships for health care delivery (see for example, Raman and Bjorkman, 2008), which for paucity of scope have not been included here but are relevant.

Notes

1 The global health imperative

1 Innovation consists of all the processes by which firms create new knowledge and master and implement application of existing and new knowledge to goods and services that are new to them, irrespective of whether they are new to their competitors, their countries or the world at large defines innovation.

2 Tait (2007a, p. 1) suggests that regulatory regimes for emerging areas in lifesciences "has in the past led to an increasingly onerous and lengthy regulatory process which ensures that 'only major multinationals can play', eventually stultifying the entire innovation system".

3 Abramowitz (1986) terms the social behaviour and attitudes of societies as their "social capital" and points to the fact that technological backwardness is a result of the inefficient and inappropriate forms of social capital in a technologically backward country at any given point of time.

4 Such regulatory changes include those that help prioritization of new technologies and research thereon as in the case of genomics and biotechnology.

5 The Bayh–Dole Act of the USA has been a subject of considerable controversy, which is not the focus of the discussion here.

6 Patent breadth/scope is defined as "how similar other innovations can be without infringing the original patent". Patent scope determines the strength of protection granted, and therefore also the extent of power vested in the patent holder to limit competition. The broader the patent claims that are allowed, the stronger is the protection that is afforded. Patents that are too broad allow their holders to "pre-empt the future", while patents that are too narrow discourage research that feeds into follow-on inventions.

7 Numerous commentaries on the Agreement on Trade Related Aspects of Intellectual Property Rights (TRIPS) and its negotiation document the dominant lobbying of the big pharmaceutical firms for stronger IPRs. See for example, Drahos, 2002.

8 The Commission on Macroeconomics and Health of the WHO has classified diseases into three main types. Type I diseases are those that are prevalent in both rich and poor countries, such as diabetes, cardiovascular illnesses and heart ailments, type II diseases are those diseases that may be prevalent in both the rich and the poor countries but show undue concentration in terms of disease burden in poor countries such as HIV/AIDS and Tuberculosis and type III diseases are those that occur only in poor countries such as River Blindness, Sleeping Sickness and Malaria. Type II diseases are called neglected diseases and type III diseases are called very neglected diseases commonly.

9 Just before the inception of the TRIPS Agreement, in 1994, only 25 out of 98 countries that signed up for the WTO did not grant patent protection to pharmaceutical products (Primo Braga, 1995, p. 357). Even the rest did not provide the same

standards as required by the Agreement. Several of them provided protection terms that were much shorter than the 20 years mandated by the Agreement, not to mention other limitations such as elimination of the "working" requirement, grant of product patent protection, restrictions on compulsory licensing (Article 31), grant of patents on life forms (Article 27(3)(b)), among others.

10 Least developed countries (LDCs) are a group of 49 countries that have been classified as "least developed" in terms of "[t]heir GDP per capita, their weak human assets and their high degree of economic vulnerability", according to the UNCTAD.

11 Extensively discussed in the literature on TRIPS and development, these include providing exceptions to patent rights on the grounds of social or public health importance (Art. 8(b)), transition arrangements to comply with TRIPS for LDCs, freedom to restrict or allow parallel imports (Art. 6), compulsory licensing (Art. 31) and freedom to define the three criteria for patentability – novelty, utility and inventive step – according to national jurisprudence and needs.

12 In economic theory, a public good is one that is both non-rivalrous (marginal cost of a consumption by an extra person is zero) and non-excludable (costs of excluding one extra person from consuming are very high).

13 A comparative survey that assessed the importance of patents in different industries showed that patents were most important for the development and introduction of products in two industries – the pharmaceutical and chemical industries – where they accounted for over 30 per cent of development activities (Mansfield, 1998, p. 174).

14 Health systems in latecomer countries tend largely to be structured on out-of-pocket payments. A recent IFC study found that across sub-Saharan Africa, an estimated 50 per cent of all health care expenses are covered by out-of-pocket payments – and such practices undermine initiatives to supply access to treatment for HIV/AIDS and other major diseases.

15 Aspen Pharma Care (South Africa) supplies HIV/AIDS drugs and Cosmos Pharmaceuticals (Kenya) supplies Malaria drugs for international drug tenders.

16 UNITAID is an International Drug Purchase Facility.

17 See, for example, Light (2006) for a discussion of practical and moral problems with advance purchase commitments, Gallini and Schotchmer (2002) for problems in structuring prize funds.

18 MMV is a not-for-profit foundation that has been created with the aim to discover, develop and deliver new, affordable anti-malarial drugs through effective public–private partnerships. IAVI stands for the International AIDS Vaccine Initiative that focuses on creating a preventive HIV vaccine, and also on creating institutional infrastructure for distributing the vaccine in the event of its development (Chataway and Smith, 2006).

19 DNDi is an offshoot of the well-known organization, Médicines Sans Frontières (MSF).

20 While these issues were initially sparked off by the flexibilities contained in the TRIPS Agreement that allow countries to compulsorily license drugs for local production in the interests of public health, parallel international discussions on science, technology and innovation issues have tended to focus on innovation capacity in health as well.

21 NIPRISAN is the name of the first medication for sickle cell disorder that was discovered through international collaboration in the country. As of 2008, there were two more alternatives, NICOSAN being one of them – NICOSAN is a phytopharmaceutical extract of a biological herbal mixture for the treatment and management of the disease and is produced from Sorghum (Solomon, 2008).

22 For example, India is in the process of enacting a bill that encourages the commercialization of research results in universities, similar to the US Bayh-Dole Act (Bhattacharjee, 2008). What the precise impact of this will be on public health oriented innovation remains to be seen. In the US, the Bayh-Dole Act of 1980 has sparked off

aggressive litigation by universities and their licensees for patent infringement by product developing firms and even substantial settlements have been awarded (Eisenberg, 2006).

23 The national systems of innovation is defined as "the network of institutions in the public and private sectors whose activities and interactions initiate, import, modify and diffuse new technologies" (Freeman, 1987, p. 1). Lundvall's concept of the national systems of innovation emphasizes the diffusion of "economically useful knowledge" (1992, p. 12).

24 This proposition has been advanced and tested by the author either singularly or in collaborative work with other economics of innovation scholars both at a general level and at the sectoral level in the context of development. See for example, Oyeyinka and Gehl Sampath (2009a, b). Here, it is applied for the first time to health innovation.

25 There are several other recent comparisons on health innovation systems in developing countries that use a case study technique. This book presents for the very first time qualitiative and quantitative data on organizations in health innovation in several latecomer countries from Asia and Africa.

2 Sectoral systems for health innovation and development

1 However, the thesis clearly forms the core of the IPRs approach, although attention has been focused on the negative impacts of excessive proliferation of rights on information and related access to knowledge issues in recent times (see for example, Jaffe and Lerner 2004; Bessen and Meurer, 2008).

2 According to Cohen and Levinthal (1990), the absorptive capacity of a firm is its ability to tap external knowledge. It comprises the abilities to "recognize the value of new information, assimilate it, and apply it to commercial ends" (p. 128).

3 The first use of the term "national system of innovation" was by Freeman in 1987, while conducting an analysis of Japan's economic performance and growth. For example, Nelson (1993) compares institutions and mechanisms that support technological innovation in 15 different countries.

4 The concept of technological opportunity is dealt with in greater detail in the next section on sectoral systems definitions. Technological opportunity refers to the likelihood of innovation outcomes in return for investment in a given sector of industrial activity.

5 This section is based on Oyeyinka and Gehl Sampath, 2009.

6 Some other authors who have tried to map learning include Dahlman *et al.*, 1987; Lall 1987; Kim 1997; Hobday 1995.

7 Amongst the exceptions, see Oyeyinka and Gehl Sampath (2009b) and Oyeyinka and Rasiah (2009).

8 These have been analysed by the author in many other contexts, see for example, Gehl Sampath (2010), Oyeyinka and Gehl Sampath (2009a, b).

9 "Organizations" as mentioned in Chapter 1 are agencies set up in order to perform particular functions under the institutional mandates.

10 North (1990) succinctly explains the same in terms of the negative institutions of a mafia.

11 Innovation consists of all the processes by which firms create new knowledge and master and implement application of existing and new knowledge to goods and services that are new to them, irrespective of whether they are new to their competitors, their countries or the world at large defines innovation.

12 Several authors have focused on the complimentary nature of the innovation process for example between traditional drug research and biotechnology based innovation; see for example, Madhok and Osegowitsch, 2000; Nightingale and Mahdi, 2006, among others.

13 These are very important to assess which technologies will provide high quality care, with effectiveness, safety, equity and are reasonably priced to suit the affordability constraints of consumers in latecomer countries.

14 In such a context, one could even argue that the term "losers" does not befit the firms that fall out of competition, because innovation induced through competition is ideally desirable and efficient and these losers do not violate *pareto* criterion (Scherer, 2001).

15 There is still substantial ambiguity in the literature as to whether greater technological change in a sector induces firms to increase or reduce vertical integration and how this can be studied; see Chiarli *et al.*, 2008.

16   For instance, in the 15 years from 1980, investors, largely small science based firms in the USA, invested over US$60 billion into biotechnology (by 1993) in order to appropriate the fruits of what in the main is public sector and university based research. This is because the cost of drug development is extremely high and the process research intensive costing between $100 and $300 per product (Powell, 1996).

17 Fifteen European Union (EU) countries spend over €83 billion yearly (approximately 1 per cent of EU GDP), on measurement and standardization (Wagner and Leydesdorff, 2005).

18 Bhagwati and Virgin (2004) define institutional capacity somewhat differently to mean the functions that institutions should have for the ability to perform, the resources (human, technical and financial) and structures they need towards that end (p. 3).

19 This distinction is based on a theoretical framework for innovation, knowledge and development developed by the author with a colleague in another book, Oyeyinka and Gehl Sampath, 2009a.

20 Decades of debate on S&T policy in developing countries focused mainly on supply-side factors (production of doctors, engineers, scientists and setting up of R&D institutions) inspired by the linear model of science promotion.

21 "TRIPS-Plus" denotes provisions in free trade agreements between countries or stand-alone agreements that recognize IPR protection of levels greater than what is envisaged in the TRIPS Agreement. See, for example, Roffe (2004).

22 See Note 1. Recent years have seen a certain consensus emerging amongst scholars questioning the importance of IPRs as an innovation incentive even in the frontier countries with the "state-of-the-art" technologies. Especially in health innovation, see Heller and Eisenberg (1998), Barton (1998), on issues such as patent thickets, royalty stacking and the medical anti-commons. There is also substantial scepticism as to whether IPRs do encourage and promote collaborative research in emerging areas such as systems biology (Eisenberg 2000).

23 Deardorff (1992) shows that at an individual level, the welfare of the inventing country clearly rises and the welfare of the non-inventing country falls with the extension of IPP; on a global scale, the deadweight losses of extending protection to the entire south in terms of prevention of competition and R&D growth might outweigh the worldwide benefits of getting more inventions. Especially, the extension of patent protection to more and more countries around the world seems to have a negative effect on global welfare according to this analysis.

24 The same applies in the case of agriculture and food security, among others.

25 There is a clear distinction between keeping information secret (data protection) and doing approvals and clinical work "relying" exclusively on the original patent holder's data submitted to obtain regulatory approval for the patented product (data exclusivity).

26 The issue of state capacity and its importance to development has been elaborated in detail in Oyeyinka and Gehl Sampath (2009a) and also Stiglitz Chapter (2010). This section here only contains a summary of the issue as far as it applies to health innovation.

3 India's advanced capacity in health innovation

1 Industry Forecast: Health Care and Pharmaceuticals India, Economist Intelligence Unit, 2007, p. 9 (hereafter referred to in this study as Economist Intelligence Unit Forecast, 2007).

2 KPMG, The Indian Pharmaceutical Industry: Collaboration for Growth, 2006 (hereafter referred to in this study as KPMG, 2006).

3 India Brand Equity Foundation (IBEF), "India: Pharmaceuticals", report by Ernst and Young for IBEF, 2006.

4 This is a decrease of only 5 per cent of the position held by the Indian companies in the fiscal year 2003, where they had a market share of 75 per cent. See IBEF, "India: Pharmaceuticals", report prepared by the India Brand Equity Foundation and Ernst and Young, 2004, p. 8.

5 Economist Intelligence Unit Forecast, 2007.

6 These are the most important sector specific industrial organizations in the country.

7 These are the two most popular, indigenous systems of medicine in the country.

8 India's compliance with the TRIPS Agreement was done in three stages: a 1999 reform followed by one in 2002 and a final Patent Amendments Act that was passed in 2005.

9 Department of Commerce and Industry figures and the Economist Intelligence Unit Forecast, 2007. Prior to this, sector growth has been relatively steady at approximately 22.5 per cent annually over the past few years (National Pharmaceutical Policy 2006) (KPMG, 2006, p. 6).

10 Compiled by author using annual reports of the top ten pharmaceutical firms. Figures on the y-axis represent Rs millions.

11 This may not amount to many countries in reality, since most least developed countries are TRIPS compliant as a result of several bilateral free trade agreements (see Chapter 4, Least Developed Countries Report of UNCTAD, Geneva, 2007).

12 In the USA, when an abbreviated new drug application is submitted for marketing a generic drug, the generic company is required to submit a certification regarding the patents for the drug in a so-called "orange book". One of the ways to do so is to make a Para IV application. When a generic company wins a Para IV application, it is granted a 180 days exclusivity to market the drug in the US market.

13 Approximately US$100 billion worth of drugs will lose patent status in the USA by 2008, and products that went off-patent in 2006 itself generated US$21 billion in sales. See Loefgren (2007).

14 This is somewhat contrary to the expectations and initial strategies of firms just a couple of years ago. In a similar firm level survey of the top 100 firms in 2005, most of the large Indian firms were very keen on focusing exclusively on the regulated markets, since the profit margins of success in these markets were very huge (Gehl Sampath, 2005). Three years on, there seems to a consensus on the importance of diversification so long as their product portfolios are in demand in other unregulated markets, in order to insulate from shocks of focusing extensively on regulated markets.

15 KPMG, 2006, p. 21.

16 Personal Communication, Dilip Shah, President, IPA.

17 KPMG, 2006, p. 17.

18 Deepti Ramesh, "Actavis to Buy Indian API Business", *Chemical Week*, 14–21 February 2007, p. 23.

19 David Ho, Hovid's managing director, believes that Hovid will be able to produce many more drugs in India due to its flexible interpretations of the TRIPS Agreement. See Deepti Ramesh, "Malaysian Firm to Establish Plant in India", *Chemical Week*, 14–21 February 2007, p. 23.

20 KPMG, 2006.

21 Some of the firms have been really innovative in discovering and exploring new niche activities. For example, Avaant Pharmaceuticals' main focus is to secure drug development licences for compounds that were discovered by global pharmaceutical firms, but subsequently ignored due to research difficulties, change in R&D focus or management changes in the company. Avaant presently has licences for drug development from several big companies, like Bayer (G.S. Krishnan, "Avaant Pharmaceuticals: The Contrarian", Cover Story, *Businessworld*, 13–19 June 2006).

22 Directory of Clinical Research Companies in India – November 2005, Cygnus India.

23 KPMG, 2006.

24 A 1986 cross-country comparison of several developing countries including Brazil, Mexico, Philippines, Thailand and India ranked in the top category of government spenders for health research within developing countries (CHRD, 1990, p. 49).

25 Economist Intelligence Unit Forecast, 2007, p. 11.

26 Given that generics are less risky than proprietary R&D, they take only about two to four years and result almost always in a new product. Proprietary R&D, on the other hand, is capital intensive, can take up to 15 years and a marketable product is not a certain outcome. Indian investors are used to a generics mode of investment: short-term (two years on average) with assured returns and marketable products. Firms operating within this model find it increasingly difficult to raise finances for their proprietary R&D activities; hence separating the operations and potential investors makes it easier for them to operate.

27 Field interviews with officials of the Department of Chemicals and Petrochemicals, government of India.

28 A similar survey of the sector in 2005 showed the lack of collaborative linkages amongst the various actors in the system.

29 The EIU forecasts that health care spending (in rupee terms) will rise by 9 per cent between 2008 and 2013. The Indian government has also committed to enhance its health care expenditure to 6 per cent and more in the coming years.

30 The Economist Intelligence Unit forecasts a growth in consumption of pharmaceuticals to slow slightly in 2008–2012 to an annual average of 4 per cent in local currency terms, from 6.2 per cent in 2002–2006 and the health care spending is predicted to have an average annual growth of about 9 per cent in rupee terms between 2008 and 2013 (see Economist Intelligence Unit Report, 2007, pp. 8–10).

31 Amongst the top 15 firms, only four (Ranbaxy, Cipla, Aurobindo and Hetero) manufacture first and second line ARVs. The other firms that produce ARV products – Matrix, Emcure, Strides and Micro Labs – are not amongst the top 15 in the market, but all ARV-manufacturing firms were interviewed in detail during the survey. Of these Ranbaxy, Aurobindo and Matrix Laboratories all began to produce ARVs due to the commercial incentives provided by the President's Emergency Plan for HIV/AIDS Relief Initiative that was launched in 2004.

32 DAT Overview, Clinton HIV and AIDS Initiative, 11 April 2008.

33 *Novartis AG* v. *Union of India et al.*, W.P. No. 24754 of 2006 (Mad. High Ct.) (19 May 2006). Online, available at: www.lawyerscollective.org/ (accessed 18 May 2008).

34 I.A 642/2008 IN CS (OS) 89/2008, reserved on 31 January 2008, date of decision: 19 March 2008.

35 In the High Court of Delhi at New Delhi, FAO (OS) 188/2008, date of decision: 24 April 2009.

36 The report defines "new chemical entity" for purposes of data protection as: "a chemical compound which contains an active ingredient or formulation of such an ingredient *that has not been previously approved in India* irrespective of its registration or use in any other country" (emphasis added).

37 See Lanjouw (2002) and Gehl Sampath (2005).

38 This point has been analysed at length by the author elsewhere, see Oyeyinka and Gehl Sampath, 2009a.

4 Health innovation systems in Bangladesh and Vietnam

1 Personal Communication, Dr Habibur Rahman, Director, Drugs Administration, 11 April 2007.
2 Square Pharmaceuticals is currently engaged in manufacturing eight drugs that are part of several ARV combinations that are expected to be available in the market later this year. Personal Communication, Parvez Hashim, Executive Director Operations, Muhammadul Haque, Director Marketing, and Md Nawabur Rahman, Assistant General Manager, Square Pharmaceuticals, 9 April 2007.
3 Personal Communication, Parvez Hashim, Executive Director Operations, Muhammadul Haque, Director Marketing, and Md Nawabur Rahman, Assistant General Manager, Square Pharmaceuticals, 9 April 2007; Amanullah Chowdhury, Executive Vice President and Habibur Rahman, Vice-President and Director, Rangs Pharma, 16 April 2007.
4 Square Annual Reports, 2006–2007.
5 Beximco Pharmaceuticals could not be interviewed personally for the study due to political circumstances in the country and the firm's management at the time of the survey. However, the company participated in the survey and was later interviewed in 2008.
6 As mentioned earlier, on an unofficial basis, Dhaka University is rated to be the best on grounds of its historical importance as well as the fact that it receives maximum support from governmental initiatives (field interviews) but how Dhaka University as well as other universities fare in relative and absolute terms as far as the quality of education in pharmaceutical sciences is concerned is unclear.
7 According to the office of the Drug Directorate, around eight drug firms have WHO-prequalified facilities for manufacturing, and another six are presently in the process of acquiring WHO prequalification, which could not be corroborated by the survey. Personal Communication, Dr Habibur Rahman, Director, Drugs Administration, 11 April 2007.
8 Several factors prevent cheap access to medicines in the local market within Bangladesh, especially in the public sector health institutions. For a detailed analysis see Gehl Sampath (2007b).
9 "National Guidelines on Medical Biotechnology", Ministry of Health and Family Welfare, Government of Bangladesh, Dhaka, 2005.
10 The Directorate of Drug Administration has only two laboratory facilities (in Dhaka and Chittagong) that can test about 3500 samples of medicines a year. About 12,000 samples of different brands of medicines remain without test every year, although the regulations require that medicines are tested for quality and efficacy twice every year (Bumpas, 2007).
11 The government policy and institution variables are not present in the hospital questionnaire.
12 If Bangladesh manages to transition to the "developing countries" group before 2016, this transition deadline will no longer hold.
13 Article 1(c) of the treaty specifies that IPRs includes rights with respect to copyrights, and related patents, trademarks, trade names, industrial designs, trade secrets and know-how, and goodwill.
14 Section 7 reads:

> After the acceptance of an application and until the date of sealing a patent in respect thereof, or the expiration of the time for sealing, the applicant shall have the like privileges and rights as if a patent for the invention has been sealed on the date of the acceptance of the application.

Section 15(a)(1) on "Patents of Addition" provides that:

> Where a patent for an invention has been applied for or granted, and the applicant or the patentee, as the case may be, applies for a further patent in respect of any

improvement in or modification of the invention, he may in his application for the further patent request that the term limited in the original patent or so much of that as is unexpired, and if he does so, a patent (herein after, referred to as a patent of addition) may be granted for such term as aforesaid.

15 The first largest firm in the market, Square Pharmaceuticals, is reported to be exporting only 3 per cent of its total production, and Beximco, another firm in the top five, exports only 2.7 per cent.

16 According to World Bank Indicators (2007), Bangladesh reported a population of 141.8 million in 2005.

5 Kenya's health innovation capacity

1 This second survey was conducted as part of a different UNU-MERIT project that looked at biotechnology sectors of innovation in countries across Asia and Africa, see Oyeyinka and Gehl Sampath, 2009b.

2 We note here that in the Nigerian context, the education level of the researchers is not the main reason impeding progress into other more challenging biotechnologies, whereas in the Kenyan case, this is an important reason.

3 The Export Processing Zones Authority (2005) estimates that the market for pharmaceutical products in Kenya is Kshs8 billion, and that the government, through the Kenya Medical Supplies Agency is the leading buyer of these products.

4 Kenya is not a least developed country and is obliged to implement the TRIPS Agreement.

6 Nigeria and Tanzania's incipient health innovation capacity

1 The author wishes to acknowledge that both projects that contributed to the Nigerian survey and this chapter were conducted with a colleague, Professor Banji Oyeyinka. This chapter is based on several papers that were written together.

2 For general information on Nigeria's economy, see the government of Nigeria's website, online, available at: www.nigeria.gov.ng and the Federal Ministry of Finance's website, online, available at: www.fmf.gov.ng.

3 Significant financial support was provided by the International Development Research Center, Ottawa, Canada.

4 See Oyeyinka and Gehl Sampath (2009b), for a detailed review of agricultural biotechnology system of innovation in Nigeria.

5 See Oyeyinka and Gehl Sampath, 2009a.

6 This section is based on: Mboera *et al.*, 2004, which was prepared as part of a project coordinated by the author.

7 Health innovation and latecomer development

1 These are the same terms that were used in the survey questionnaires.

2 The original export intensity variable lies in the unit interval. We take a logit transformation to make it lie in the set of all real numbers.

3 In the application, only R&D intensity is assumed to be endogenous.

4 See Oyeyinka and Gehl Sampath (2009a) for a ranking of countries according to their knowledge and institutional capacity in order to derive a framework on how institutional capacity links to economic development.

5 As of December 2006, only 2.2 million people were receiving treatments, and this figure had gone up to about 3 million (2,700,000–3,280,000 people) at the end of 2007 in low and middle income countries, nearly 950,000 more compared with the end of 2006. See WHO (2008a, 2008b); Global Fund, 2007.

6 WHO, 2008b.
7 A Summary Report by the Global Price Reporting Mechanism on Antiretroviral Medicines, February 2008.
8 The Global Fund to Fight HIV/AIDS, Tuberculosis and Malaria was established in 2001 as a financing body, raising and disbursing resources to combat infection, illness and death resulting from the three pandemics. To date, the Global Fund has committed $10 billion to over 520 programmes in 136 developing countries, and it is estimated that between 35 and 49 per cent of the funding is budgeted for the purchase of medicines, essential health products and commodities.
9 Grace and Gehl Sampath, Potential Market Impact of In-Kind Donations to the Global Fund, A Report to the Global Fund to Fight TB, AIDS and Malaria, Draft, 14 July 2008.
10 Same as above.
11 See Oyeyinka and Gehl Sampath (2009) where the same results accrue in the case of agricultural biotechnology comparisons across countries.

8 Bridging the health divide

1 Teubal considers two mutually reinforcing phases, namely inter-firm learning about R&D (applicable largely to the early innovation phase such as searching for markets and technical information, identifying and generating new projects, learning to screen, evaluate and choose new projects, and learning to manage the process), and collective learning, which in addition to inter-firm learning, includes managerial and marketing functions that are crucial to the innovation process.

References

Abdulla, S., J.R. Schellenberg, R. Nathan, O. Mukasa, T. Marchant, T. Smith, M. Tanner and C. Lengeler, "Impact on Malaria Morbidity of a Programme Supplying Insecticide Treated Nets in Children Aged Under 2 Years in Tanzania: Community Cross Sectional Study", *British Medical Journal*, vol. 322, no. 7281, 2001, pp. 270–273.

Abramovitz, M., "Catching up, Forging Ahead and Falling Behind", *Journal of Economic History*, vol. 46, no. 2, 1986, pp. 385–406.

Abrol, D., "The Reality of Chasing Global Innovation Leadership: Lessons from CSIR, India", Presentation at the fourth Globelics Conference, Saratov, 10–14 September 2007.

Agbo. E.C., S. Agwale, C.O. Ezeugwu, B. Semete, H. Swai, A. Ikeme, R.I. Somiari, "Biotechnology Innovation in Africa", *Science*, Vol. 321, no. 5879, 26 September 2008, p. 1778.

Akerlof, George, A., "The Market for 'Lemons': Quality Uncertainty and the Market Mechanism", *Quarterly Journal of Economics*, vol. 84, no. 3, August 1970, pp. 488–500.

Allansdottir, A. *et al.*, "Innovation and Competitiveness in European Biotechnology", Enterprise Papers No. 7, European Commission, 2002.

Amsden, A.H., *Asia's Next Giant: South Korea and Late Industrialization*, Oxford University Press, Oxford, 1989.

Amsden, A.H. and W.W. Chu, *Beyond Late Development Taiwan's Upgrading Policies*, MIT Press, Cambridge, 2003.

Andersson, M. and O. Ejermo, "How does Accessibility to Knowledge Sources affect the Innovativeness of Corporations? – Evidence from Sweden", Working Paper series in Economics and Institutions of Innovation 3, 2004.

Archibugi, D., " 'Pavitt' Taxonomy Sixteen Years On: A Review Article", *Economics of Innovation and New Technology*, vol. 10, no. 5, 2001, pp. 415–425.

Archibugi, D. and K. Bizzari, "Committing to Vaccine R&D: A Global Science Policy Priority", *Research Policy*, vol. 33, no. 10, 2004, pp. 175–194.

Archibugi, D. and J. Michie, "Technological Globalisation or National Systems of Innovation?" *Futures: The Journal of Forecasting, Planning and Policy*, vol. 29, no. 2, 1997, pp. 121–137.

Archibugi, D. and C. Pietrobelli, "The Globalization of Technology and its Implications for Developing Countries: Windows of Opportunity or Further Burden?" *Technological Forecasting and Social Change*, vol. 70, no. 9, 2003, pp. 861–883.

Arora, A., "Licensing Tacit Knowledge: Intellectual Property Rights and the Market for Know-how", *Economic Innovation of New Technologies*, vol. 4, no. 1, 1995, pp. 41–59.

Arora, A. and R.P. Merges, "Specialized Supply Firms, Property Rights and Firm Boundaries", *Industrial and Corporate Change*, vol. 13, no. 3, 2004, pp. 451–475.

Arrow, K.J., "Economic Welfare and the Allocation of Resources for Invention", in K.J. Arrow (ed.) *The Rate and Direction of Inventive Activity*, Princeton University Press, Princeton NJ, 1962, pp. 609–625.

Arundel, A., "The Relative Effectiveness of Patents and Secrecy for Appropriation", *Research Policy*, vol. 30, no. 4, 2001, pp. 611–624.

Attaran, A., "How Do Patents and Economic Policies Affect Access to Essential Medicines in Developing Countries", *Health Affairs*, vol. 23, no. 5, 2004, p. 281.

Bain and Co., "The Indian Opportunity in Pharmaceuticals and Manufacturing", Presented at the Annual Meeting of the World Economic Forum, 2008.

Bartholomew, S., "National Systems of Biotechnology Innovation: Complex Interdependence in the Global System", *Journal of International Business Studies*, vol. 28, no. 2, 1997, pp. 241–266.

Barton, J.H., "The Impact of Contemporary Patent Law on Plant Biotechnology Research", DAFFE/CLP Competition Policy and Intellectual Property Rights, OECD, vol. 18, no. 458, 1998, pp. 305–321.

Bell, M., "Time And Technological Learning In Industrialising Countries: How Long Does It Take? How Fast Is It Moving (If At All)?" *International Journal of Technology Management*, vol. 36, no. 1–3, 2006, pp. 25–39.

Bell, R. and Pavitt, K., "Technological Accumulation and Industrial Growth: Contrasts Between Development and Developing Countries", *Industrial and Corporate Change*, vol. 2, no. 2, 1993, pp. 157–210.

Belsey, M.J., L.M. Harris, R.R Das and J. Chertkow, "Biosimilars: Initial Excitement Gives Way to Reality", *Drug Discovery*, vol. 5, no. 7, July 2006, pp. 525–536.

Bercowitz, J. and M. Feldman, "Technology Transfer and the Academic Department: Who Participates and Why?" Rotman School of Management, Mimeo, University of Toronto, 2003.

Besen, S.M. and L.J. Raskind, "An Introduction to the Law and Economics of Intellectual Property", *Journal of Economic Perspectives*, vol. 5, no. 1, 1991, pp. 3–27.

Bessen, J. and E. Maskin, "Sequential Innovation, Patents, and Imitation," Working Paper 00-01, MIT Department of Economics, Cambridge, MA, 2000.

Bessen, J. and S. Maurer, *Patent Failure: How Judges, Bureaucrats and Lawyers put Innovators at Risk*, Princeton University Press, Princeton NJ, 2008.

Bhattacharjee, Y., "Indian Government hopes Bill will Stimulate Innovation", *Science*, vol. 319, 1 February 2008, p. 566. Online, available at: www.sciencemag.org (accessed 11 January 2009).

Bostanci, A. and J. Calvert, "Invisible Genomes; The Genomics Revolution and Patenting Practice", *Studies in History and Philosophy of Biological and Biomedical Sciences*, vol. 39, no. 1, 2008, pp. 109–119.

Bottazzi, G., G. Dosi, M. Lippi, F. Pammolli and M. Riccaboni, "Innovation and Corporate Growth in the Evolution of the Drug Industry", Paper presented at the DRUID Conference, June 2000.

Branstetter, L.G., R. Fisman and C.F. Foley, "Do Stronger Intellectual Property Rights Increase International Technology Transfer? Empirical Evidence from U.S. Firm-Level Panel Data", *Quarterly Journal of Economics*, vol. 121, 2004, pp. 321–349.

Breschi, S. and F. Malerba, "Sectoral Innovation Systems: Technological Regimes, Schumpeterian Dynamics, and Spatial Boundaries", in C. Edquist (ed.) *Systems of Innovation: Technologies, Institutions and Organizations*, Pinter Publishers, London/ Washington, 1997, pp. 130–156.

Brusoni, S. and A. Principe, "Unpacking the Black Box of Modularity: Technology, Products, and Organisations", *Industrial and Corporate Change*, vol. 10, no. 1, 2001, pp. 179–205.

Budworth, D., *Finance and Innovation*, International Thompson Business Press, London, 1996.

Bühler, F., C.M. Tang, P. Shah, M. Leuchtenberger, K.-C. Lin and P.D.N. Pissarra, "The Preeminence of Clusters in Biotechnology", *Nature Biotechnology*, vol. 25, no. 11, 2007, pp. 1207–1209.

Bumpas, J., "Private Sector Approaches to Improving Bangladesh Drug Quality", Discussion Paper, 2007, Draft on file with author.

Cao Minh Quang, *Vietnam Pharmaceuticals Industry: Opportunities and Challenges*. General Department of Pharmaceuticals Management. Hanoi, 2006.

Carlsson, B., ed., *Technological Systems and Economic Performance: The Case of Factory Automation*, Kluwer Academic Publishers, Dordrecht, 1995.

Castellacci, F., "Evolutionary and New Growth Theories: Are They Converging?" *Journal of Economic Surveys*, vol. 21, no. 3, 2007, pp. 585–627.

Castellacci, F., "Technology Clubs, Technology Gaps and Growth Trajectories", *Structural Change and Economic Dynamics*, vol. 19, no. 4, 2008, pp. 301–314.

Castellacci, F. and D. Archibugi, "The Technology Clubs: The Distribution of Knowledge Across Nations", *Research Policy*, vol. 37, no. 10, 2008, p. 1659–1673.

Champenois, C., "Co-localization of Innovative Firms as Non-choice: The Example of German Biotechnology Industry", *Geographie Economie Societe*, vol. 10, no. 1, 2008, pp. 61–85.

Champenois, C., D. Engel, and O. Heneric, "What Kind of German Biotechnology Start-ups do Venture Capital Companies and Corporate Investors Prefer for Equity Investments?" *Applied Economics*, vol. 38, no. 5, 2006, pp. 505–518.

Chang, H.J., *The Rebel Within*, Wimbledon Publishing Company, London, 2001.

Chang, H.J., *Kicking Away the Ladder; Development Strategy in Historical Perspective*, London: Anthem Press, 2002.

Chang, H.J., *Globalization, Economic Development and the Role of the State*, Zed Press, London, 2003.

Chataway, J. and R. Hanlin, "Sustainable (vaccine) Development: The International AIDS Vaccine Initiative (IAVI) and Capacity Building", *Health Partnerships Review*, 2008, pp. 43–45.

Chataway, J. and J. Smith, "The International Aids Vaccine Initiative (IAVI): Is it Getting New Science and Technology to the World's Neglected Majority?" *World Development*, vol. 34, no. 1, 2006, pp. 16–30.

Chataway, J., J. Smith and D. Wield, "Shaping Scientific Excellence In Agricultural Research", *Journal of International Biotechnology*, vol. 9, no. 2, 2007, pp. 172–187.

Chataway, J., S. Brusconi, E. Caccitori, R. Hanlin and L. Orsenigo, "The International AIDS Vaccine Initiative (IAVI) in a Changing Landscape of Vaccine Development: A Public/Private Partnership as Knowledge Broker and Integrator", *European Journal of Development Research*, vol. 19, no. 1, 2007, pp. 100–117.

Chaudhuri, S., "Is Product Patent Protection Necessary in Developing Countries for Innovation? R&D by the Indian Pharmaceutical Companies After TRIPS", Working Paper series of the Indian Institute of Management, Calcutta, No. 614, September 2007.

Chen, Y. and T. Puttitanun, "Intellectual Property Rights and Innovation in Developing Countries", *Journal of Development Economics*, vol. 78, no. 2, 2005, pp. 474–493.

Chen, Z., H.-G. Wang, Z.-J. Wen and Y. Wang, "Lifesciences and Biotechnology in China", *Philosophical Transactions of the Royal Society*, 2007, vol. 362, no. 1482, pp. 947–957.

Chesbrough, H., *Open Innovation: The New Imperative for Creating and Profiting from Technology*, Harvard Business School Press, Boston MA, 2003.

Chesbrough, H., *Open Business Models: How to Thrive in the New Innovation Landscape*, Harvard Business School Press, Boston MA, 2006.

Chesbrough, H.W. and D.J. Teece, "When is Virtual Virtuous: Organizing for Innovation", *Harvard Business Review*, vol. 74, no. 1, 1996, pp. 65–73.

Chiaroni, D., V. Chiesa, A. De Massis and F. Frattini, "The Knowledge Bridging Role of Technical and Scientific Services in Knowledge Intensive Industries", *International Journal of Technology Management*, vol. 41, nos 3–4, 2008, pp. 249–272.

Chin, J.C. and G.M. Grossman, "Intellectual Property Rights and North–South Trade", NBER Working Papers Series No. 69, National Bureau of Economic Research, Cambridge MA, 1991.

Chin, J.C. and G.M. Grossman, "Intellectual Property Rights and North–South Trade", NBER Working Paper Series No. 2769, National Bureau of Economic Research, Cambridge MA, 1988.

Chowdhury, F., S. Gurinder, S. Raihanuddin and S. Hasan Nasir, "A Strategy for Establishing the API Park", Interim Report, Ministry of Industry, Bangladesh, 2006.

Ciarli, T., R. Leoncini, S. Montresor and M. Valente, "Technological Change and the Vertical Organization of Industries", *Journal of Evolutionary Economics*, vol. 18, nos 3–4, 2008, pp. 367–387.

Clark, C., J. Mugabe and J. Smith, *Governing Agricultural Biotechnology in Africa: Building Public Confidence and Capacity for Policy-Making*, ACTS Press, Nairobi, 2005.

Cockburn, I., "The Changing Structure of the Pharmaceutical Industry", *Health Affairs*, vol. 23, no. 1, 2004, pp. 10–22.

Cohen, W.M. and D.A. Levinthal, "Absorptive Capacity: A New Perspective on Learning and Innovation", *Administrative Science Quarterly*, vol. 35, no. 1, 1990, pp. 128–152.

Cohen, W.M., R.R. Nelson and J.P. Walsh, "Protecting Their Intellectual Assets: Appropriability Conditions and Why US Manufacturing Firms Patent or Not", NBER Working Paper No. 7552, Cambridge MA, 2000.

Cohen, W.M., R. Florida, L. Randazzese and J. Walsh, "Industry And The Academy: Uneasy Partners In The Cause Of Technological Advance" The Brookings Institution, Washington, 1998.

Commission on Health Research for Development (CHRD), *Health Research: Essential Link to Equity in Development*, New York, 1990.

Commission on Intellectual Property Rights, Innovation and Public Health (CIPIH), *Report of the Commission on Intellectual Property Rights, Innovation and Public Health, Public Health, Innovation and Intellectual Property Rights*, World Health Organization, Geneva, 2006.

Commission on Social Determinants of Health, *Closing the Gap in a Generation: Health Equity through Action on the Social Determinants of Health*, World Health Organization, Geneva, 2008.

Correa, C.M., "Intellectual Property after Doha: Can Countries Move Forward Their Agenda on Biodiversity and Traditional Knowledge?" *UNU-INTECH Technology Policy Brief*, vol. 3, no. 2, 2004, Maastrict.

Correa, C.M., *Protection of Data Submitted for the Registration of Pharmaceuticals: Implementing the Standards of the TRIPs Agreement*, Geneva: South Centre. 2002.

Correa, C.M., "Intellectual Property in Less Developed Countries: Strategies for Enhancing Technology Transfer and Dissemination", Background Paper No. 4 for the LDC report on Knowledge, Technological Learning and Innovation for Development, 2007.

Curtis, C.F., J. Myamba and T.J. Wilkes, "Comparison of Different Insecticide and Fabrics for Anti-mosquito Bednets and Curtains", *Medical and Veterinary Entomology*, vol. 10, no. 1, 1996, pp. 1–11.

Daar, A.S., K. Berndtson, D.L. Persad and P.A. Singer, "How Can Developing Countries Harness Biotechnology to Improve Health?" *BMC Public Health*, vol. 3, no. 7, 2007, p. 346.

Dahlman, C.J., B. Ross-Larson and L.E. Westphal, "Managing Technological Development: Lessons from Newly Industrializing Countries", *World Development*, vol. 15, no. 6, 1987, pp. 759–775.

Deardorff, A.V., "Welfare Effects of Global Patent Protection", *Economica*, vol. 59, no. 233, 1992, pp. 35–51.

Dionisio D. and D. Messeri, "Impending Flop for Brand Antiretrovirals in the Emerging Markets?" *Open AIDS Journal*, vol. 2, 2008, pp. 68–71.

Dosi, G. and M. Mazzucato (eds), *Knowledge Accumulation and Industry Evolution: The Case of Pharma-Biotech*, Cambridge University Press, Cambridge, 2006.

Dosi, G., D. Levinthal and L. Marengo, "The Uneasy Organizational Matching Between Distribution of Knowledge, Division of Labor and Incentive Governance", LEM Papers Series, No. 26, 2002.

Dosi, G., A. Gambardella, M. Grazzi and L. Orsenigo, "Technological Revolutions and the Evolution of Industrial Structures: Assessing the Impact of New Technologies upon Size, Pattern of Growth and Boundaries of the Firms", LEM Papers Series No. 12, 2007.

Dosi, G., C. Freeman, R.R. Nelson, G. Silverberg and L. Soete, *Technica Change And Economic Theory*, Pinter Publishers, London, 1988.

Dowlah, C.A.F., "Bangladesh", in M.D. Ingco (ed.) *Agriculture, Trade and the WTO in South Asia*, Washington DC: World Bank, 2003.

Drahos, P., "Biotechnology Patents, Markets and Morality", *European Intellectual Property Law Review*, vol. 21, no. 9, 1999, pp. 441–449.

Drahos, P., "Developing Countries and International Intellectual Property Standard-Setting", *Journal of World Intellectual Property*, vol. 5, no. 5, 2002, pp. 765–789.

Dumont, B. and P. Holmes, "The Scope of Intellectual Property Rights and their Interface with Competition Law and Policy: Divergent Paths to the Same Goal?" *Economics of Innovation and New Technology*, vol. 11, no. 2, 2002, pp. 149–162.

Economist Intelligence Unit, "Industry Forecast: Health Care and Pharmaceuticals India", EIU, London, November 2007.

Edquist, C., "Systems of Innovation Approaches: Their Emergence and Characteristics", in C. Edquist (Ed.) *Systems Of Innovations: Technologies, Institutions And Organizations*, Pinter Publishers, London, 1997, pp. 1–29.

Eicher, C.K., K. Maredia and I. Sithole-Niang, "Crop Biotechnology and the African farmer", *Food Policy*, vol. 31, no. 6, 2006, pp. 504–552.

Eisenberg, R., "Public Research and Private Development: Patents and Technology Transfer in Government-Sponsored Research", *Virginia Law Review*, vol. 82, no. 8, 1996, pp. 1663–1727.

Eisenberg, R., "Re-examining the Role of Patents in Appropriating the Value of DNA Sequences", *Emory Law Journal*, vol. 49, no. 3, 2000, 783–799.

Eisenberg, R., "Bargaining over the Transfer of Proprietary Research Tools: Is This Market Failing or Emerging?" in R.C. Dreyfuss, D.L. Zimmerman and H. First (eds) *Expanding the Boundaries of IP: Innovation Policy for the Knowledge Society*, Oxford University Press, Oxford, 2001, pp. 223–249.

Eisenberg, R., "Patents and Data-Sharing in Public Science." *Industrial and Corporate Change*, vol. 15, no. 6, 2006, p. 1013–1031.

Elias, C.J., "Can We Ensure Health is Within Reach for Everyone?" *Lancet*, vol. 368, 2006, pp. S40–S41.

Enzing, C., A. van der Giessen, and S. van der Molen, "Dynamics in Biotechnology Policy-Making in Europe in the Period 1994–2006", *International Journal of Biotechnology*, vol. 10, no. 4, 2008, pp. 283–302.

Enzing, C.M., T. Reiss, T Gronning, E. Cantarella, M. Braennback, G. Blankenfeld-Enkvist, R. von Soederlund, *et al.*, *Innovation in Pharmaceutical Biotechnology; Comparing National Innovation Systems at the Sectoral Level*, OECD, Paris, 2006.

Ernst, D. "Limits to Modularity: Reflections on Recent Developments in Chip Design", *Industry and Innovation*, vol. 12, no. 3, 2005, pp. 303–335.

Evans, P. *Embedded Autonomy: States and Industrial Transformation*, Princeton University Press, Princeton NJ, 1995.

Export Processing Zones Authority, "Kenya's Pharmaceutical Industry 2005", EPZ, Nairobi, 2005.

Export Promotion Bureau, "Statistical Data", Export Promotion Bureau, Bangladesh, 2006.

Fennell, M., "The New Medical Technologies and the Organizations of Medical Science and Treatment", *Health Services Research*, vol. 43, no. 1, 2008, pp. 1–9.

Fink, C., "How Stronger Patent Protection in India might affect the Behavior or Transnational Pharmaceutical Industries", World Bank Working Paper no. 2352, World Bank, Washington DC, 2000.

Fink, C. and P. Reichenmiller, "The Tightening TRIPS: The Intellectual Property Provisions of Recent US Free Trade Agreements", Trade Note, The World Bank Group, February 2005.

Foray, D., "Knowledge Distribution and the Institutional Infrastructure: The Role of Intellectual Property Rights", in Horst Albach and Stephanie Rosenkranz (eds) *Intellectual Property Rights and Global Competition: Towards a New Synthesis*, WZB Publications, Berlin, 1995, pp. 77–118.

Foray, D., *The Economics of Knowledge*, MIT Press, Cambridge MA, 2004.

Fraser-Hurt, N., I. Felger, D. Edoh, S. Steiger, M. Mashaka, H. Masanja, T. Smith, F. Mbena and H.P. Beck, "Effect of Insecticide-treated Bednets on Haemoglobin Values, Prevalence of Multiplicity of Infection with *Plasmodium falciparum* in a Randomised Controlled Trial in Tanzania", *Transactions of the Royal Society of Tropical Medicine and Hygiene*, vol. 93 (suppl. 1), 1999, pp. 47–51.

Freeman, C., *Unemployment and Technical Innovation: A Study of Long Waves and Economic Development*, Greenwood Press, Westport CT, 1982.

Freeman, C. *Technology Policy and Economic Performance: Lessons from Japan. London*, Pinter Publishers, London, 1987.

Freeman, C., "Japan: A New National System of Innovation?" in G. Dosi, C. Freeman, R.R. Nelson and L. Soete (eds) *Technical Change and Economic Theory*, Pinter Publishers, London, 1988, pp. 331–348.

Frew, S.E., S.M. Sammut, A.F. Shore, J.K. Ramjist, S. Al-Bader, R. Rezaie, A.S. Daar and P.A. Singer, "Chinese Health Biotech and the Billion Patient Market", *Nature Biotechnology*, vol. 26, no. 1, January 2008, pp. 37–53.

Frost and Sullivan, "Frost and Sullivan Study on Contract Research and Manufacturing", Health Care Practice Frost and Sullivan, 2006. Online, available at: www.icis.com/ICISCONNECT/files/folders/155/download.aspx (accessed 7 March 2008).

Gallini, N. and S. Schotchmer, "Intellectual Property: When is it the Best Incentive System?" in A.B. Jaffe, J. Lerner and S. Stern (eds) *Innovation Policy and the Economy* Vol. 2, MIT Press, Cambridge MA, 2002, pp. 51–78.

Gambardella, A., *Science and Innovation*, Cambridge University Press, Cambridge, 1995.

Gehl Sampath, P., *Economic Aspects of Medicines after 2005: Product Patent Protection and Emerging Firm Strategies in the Indian Pharmaceutical Industry, A study for the CIPIH*, World Health Organization, Geneva, 2005.

Gehl Sampath, P., "India's Product Patent Regime: Less or More of 'Pills for the Poor'", *Journal of World Intellectual Property*, vol. 9, no. 6, 2006, pp. 694–726.

Gehl Sampath, P., "Breaking the Fence: Can Patent Rights Deter Biomedical Innovation in 'Technology Followers'", *Journal of Technology Assessment and Strategic Management*, Special No. on the Indian Pharmaceutical Industry edited By David Wield, Joanna Chataway and Dinar Kale, September 2007a.

Gehl Sampath, P., "Intellectual Property and Innovation in Least Developed Countries: Pharmaceuticals, Agro- Processing and Textiles and RMG in Bangladesh", Background Paper No. 9 for the Least Developed Countries report 2007 on Knowledge, Technological Learning and Innovation for Development, UNCTAD, Geneva, 2007b.

Gehl Sampath, P., "Innovation and Competitiveness in Bangladesh's Pharmaceutical Sector", UNU_MERIT Working Paper No. 31, Maastricht, 2007c.

Gehl Sampath, P. "India's Product Patent Compliance: Emerging Strategies for Global and Local Access to Medicines", a study for the DFID, UK, 2008.

Gehl Sampath, P., "Enabling Institutional Responses to Innovation in Developing Countries", in European Commission, Directorate-General for Research (ed.) *The External Dimension of the European Research Area: EU International Science and Technology Cooperation in a Globalised World*, Edward Elgar, London, September 2010.

Gehl Sampath, P. and B. Oyeyinka, "Interfacing Health Care and Innovation: Traditional Medicinal Knowledge in Nigeria", *International Journal of Technology Management and Sustainable Development*, vol. 6, no. 2, 2007, pp. 103–121.

Gehl Sampath, P. and B. Oyeyinka, "Rough Road to the Market: Constrained Biotechnology Innovation and Entrepreneurship in Nigeria and Ghana", *Journal of International Development*, vol. 2, no. 3, 2008, pp. 173–192.

Gerschenkron, A., *Economic Backwardness in Historical Perspective*, Harvard University Press, Cambridge MA, 1962.

Gichuki, S.T., "Current Status of Agricultural Biotechnology Application in Kenya", KARI Biotechnology Centre, Kenyan Agriculture Resources Institute, Kenya.

Gittelman, M., "National Institutions, Public–Private Knowledge Flows, and Innovation Performance: A Comparative Study of the Biotechnology Industry in the United States and France", *Research Policy*, vol. 35, no. 7, 2006, pp. 1052–1068.

Glass, A.J. and K. Saggi, "Intellectual Property Rights and Foreign Direct Investment", *Journal of International Economics*, vol. 56, no. 2, 2002, pp. 387–410.

Global Fund, The Global Fund ARV Fact Sheet, Geneva, 1 December 2007.

Grabowski, H., "Patents and New Product Development in the Pharmaceutical and Biotechnology Industries", Working paper, Duke University, Durham NC, 2002.

Grace, C., "The Effect of Changing Intellectual Property on Pharmaceutical Industry Prospects in India and China: Considerations for Access to Medicines", DFID Health Systems Resource Centre, London, 2004.

Grace, C., "Update on India and China and Access to Medicines", Briefing paper for DFID Health Resource Centre, London, 2005.

Grace, C. and P. Gehl Sampath, "Global Fund In-Kind Donations: Assessing the Potential for Market Impact", a study for the Global Fund, August 2008.

Grandstand, O., *The Economics and Management of Intellectual Property*, Edward Elgar, London, 2000.

Hanushek, E.A, "Interpreting Recent Research on Schooling in Developing Countries", *World Bank Research Observer*, vol. 10, no. 2, 1995, pp. 227–246.

Health Biotechnology, "Innovation in Developing Countries", *Nature Biotechnology*, vol. 22, Supplement, December 2004.

Heller, M.A. and R.S. Eisenberg, "Can Patents Deter Innovation? The Anticommons in Biomedical Research", *Science*, vol. 280, no. 5364, 1998, pp. 698–701.

Helpman, E., "Innovation, Imitation, and Intellectual Property Rights", *Econometrica*, vol. 61, no. 6, 1993, pp. 1247–1280.

Hobday, M., "East Asian Latecomer Firms: Learning the Technology of Electronics", *World Development*, vol. 23, no. 7, 1995, pp. 1171–1193.

Hoen, E.T., *The Global Politics of Pharmaceutical Monopoly Power*, AMB Publishers, the Netherlands, 2009.

Hollis, A., "The Health Impact Fund: A Useful Supplement to the Patent System", *Public Health Ethics*, vol. 1, no. 2, 2008, pp. 124–133.

Hossain, M.A. and N.D. Karunarathne, "Export Response to the Reduction of Anti-export Bias: Empirics from Bangladesh", Discussion Paper No. 303, School of Economics of the University of Queensland, Brisbane, 2002.

Huggett, B., "Big Pharma Swallows Biotech Pride", *Nature Biotechnology*, vol. 26, 2008, pp. 955–956.

India Brand Equity Foundation (IBEF), "India: Pharmaceuticals", a report by Ernst and Young for IBEF, 2006.

Institute of Mathematical Statistics (IMS), *Annual Statistics*, IMS, 2006.

IFC, "The Business of Health in Africa: Partnering with the Private Sector to Improve People's Lives", International Finance Corporation, World Bank, 2008.

"Is the Indian Drug Controller Participating in the ACTA Negotiations", Managing Intellectual Property, 19 June 2008 Online, available at: http://spicyipindia.blogspot.com/2008/06/is-indian-drug-controller-participating.html (accessed 13 July 2010).

Jaffe, A.B. and J. Lerner, *Innovations and Its Discontents: How Our Broken Patent System is Endangering Innovation and Progress, and What to Do About It*, Princeton University Press, Princeton NJ, 2004.

Johnson, B. and B.-Å. Lundvall, "Promoting Innovation Systems as a Response to the Globalizing Learning Economy", in J.E. Cassiolato, H.M.M. Lastres and M.L. Maciel (eds) *Systems of Innovation and Development*, Edward Elgar, Cheltenham, UK, 2003, pp. 143–172.

Johnson, B. and B.-Å. Lundvall, "National Systems of Innovation and Economic Development", in M. Mazzucato and G. Dosi (eds) *Knowledge Accumulation and Industry Evolution: The Case of Pharma Biotech*, Cambridge University Press, Cambridge, 2006, pp. 79–101.

Johnson, C., *MITI and the Japanese Miracle: The Growth of Industrial Policy 1925–1975*, Stanford University Press, Stanford CA, 1982.

Johnson, J.A., "FDA Regulation of Follow-On Biologics", CRS Report For Congress, Congressional Research Service, USA, 2007.

Kaiser, R. and H. Prange, "Managing Diversity in a System Multi-level Governance: the Open Method of Coordination in Innovation Policy", *European Public Policy*, vol. 11, no. 2, 2004, pp. 249–266.

Kanwar, S. and R.E. Evenson, "Does Intellectual Property Protection spur Technological Change?" Center Discussion Paper 831, Economic Growth Center, Yale University, New Haven CT, 2001.

Kaplan, W., *Priority Medicines for Europe and the World, A Public Health Approach to Innovation: Priority Setting*, WHO, Geneva, 2004.

Katz, M.L. and H.S. Rosen, *Microeconomics*, 3rd edn, Irwin, McGraw Hill, Boston MA, 1998.

Kim, L, *Imitation to Innovation: The Dynamics of Korea's Technological Learning*, Harvard Business School Press, Boston MA, 1997.

Kirea, S., V.O. Awuor and S.S. Atsali, "Biotechnology Research and Development in Kenya: Policy Background Study Report on Product development Partnerships", Discussion Paper No. 9, ISNAR, 2003.

KPMG, "The Indian Pharmaceutical Industry: Collaboration for Growth", 2006.

Kremer, D.M., "Creating Markets for New Vaccines Part II: Design Nos", NBER Working Papers 7717, National Bureau of Economic Research, Cambridge MA, 2000.

Kreps, D.M., *A Course in Microeconomic Theory*, Princeton University Press, Princeton NJ, 1995.

Krishnan, G.S., "Avaant Pharmaceuticals: The Contrarian", cover story, *Businessworld*, 13–19 June 2006.

N.K. Kumar, U. Quach, H. Thorsteinsdóttir, H. Somsekhar, A.S. Daar and P.A. Singer "Indian Biotechnology – Rapidly Evolving and Industry Led", *Nature Biotechnology* vol. 22, no. 12 Supp., 2004, pp. DC31–DC36.

Kumra, G., P. Mitra and P. Chandrika, *Indian Pharma 2015: Unlocking the Potential of the Indian Pharmaceuticals Market*, Mckinsey and Company, 2007

Lai, E.L.C., "International Intellectual Property Rights Protection and the Rate of Product Innovation", *Journal of Development Economics*, vol. 55, no.1, 1998, pp. 133–153.

Lai, E.L.C., "Would Global Patent Protection be too Weak Without International Coordination?" Discussion Paper series 226, Research Institute for Economics and Business Administration, Kobe University, Japan, 2005, revised August 2008.

Lall, S., *Learning to Industrialize: The Acquisition of Technological Capacity in India*, Macmillan, London, 1987.

Lall, S. and Teubal, M., "Market-Stimulating" Technology Policies in Developing Countries: A Framework with Examples from East Asia", *World Development*, vol. 26, No. 8, 1998, pp. 1369–1385.

Langlois, R.N., "Transaction Cost Economics in Real Time", *Industrial and Corporate Change*, vol. 1, no. 1, 1992, pp. 99–127.

Lanjouw, J.O., "The Introduction of Pharmaceutical Product Patents in India: Heartless Exploitation of the Poor and Suffering?" Economic Growth Center, Yale University, New Haven CT, and NBER Working Paper no. 6366, January 1998.

Lanjouw, J.O., "Intellectual Property and the Availability of Pharmaceuticals in Poor Countries", *Innovation Policy and the Economy*, Vol. 3, 2002, pp. 91–130.

Lanjouw, J.O., "Patents, Price Controls and Access to New Drugs: How Policy Affects Global Market Entry", a study commissioned by the CIPIH, Geneva, World Health Organization, 2005.

Lanjouw, J.O. and I. Cockburn, "Do Patents Matter? Empirical Evidence after GATT", NBER Working Papers 7495, Cambridge MA, 2000.

Lederman, D. and L. Saenz, "Innovation and Development around the World, 1960–2000", Policy Research Working Paper series 3774, World Bank, 2005.

Lerner, J., "Patent Protection and Innovation Over 150 Years", NBER Working Papers 8977, National Bureau of Economic Research, Cambridge MA, 2002.

Light, D.W., "Basic Research Funds to Discover Important New Drugs: Who Contributes How Much?" in M.A. Burke (ed.) *Monitoring the Financial Flows for Health Research 2005: Behind the Global Numbers*, Global Forum for Health Research, Geneva, 2006, pp. 27–43.

Lines, J.D., J. Myamba, and C.F. Curtis, "Experimental Hut Trials of Permethrin-impregnated Mosquito Nets and Eave Curtains against Malaria Vectors in Tanzania", *Medical and Veterinary Entomology*, vol. 1, no. 1, 1987, pp. 37–51.

Loefgren, H., "The Global Biopharma Industry and the Rise of Indian Drug Multinationals: Implications for Australian Generics Policy", Australian and New Zealand Health Policy, June 2007.

Lundvall, B.Å. *Product Innovation and User-Producer Interaction*, Aalborg University Press, Aalborg, Denmark, 1985.

Lundvall, B.Å. "Innovations as an Interactive Process: From User–Producer Interaction to the National System of Innovation", in G. Dosi (ed.) *Technical Change and Economic Theory*, Pinter, London, 1988, pp. 349–369.

Lundvall, B.Å. *National Systems of Innovation: Towards a Theory of Innovation and Interactive Learning*, Pinter, London, 1992.

McKelvey, M., "Using Evolutionary Theory to Define Systems of Innovation", in C. Edquist (ed.) *Systems Of Innovation: Technologies, Institutions And Organizations*, Pinter Publishers, London, 1997, pp. 200–222.

McMillan, G.S. and R.D. Hamilton, "Using Bibliometrics to Measure Firm Knowledge: An Analysis of the U.S. Pharmaceutical Industry", *Technology Analysis and Strategic Management*, vol. 12, no. 4, 2000, pp. 465–475.

Madhok, A. and T. Osegowitsch, "The International Biotechnology Industry: A Dynamic Capabilities Perspective", *Journal of International Business Studies*, vol. 31, no. 2, 2000, pp. 325–335.

Magesa, S.M., T.J. Wilkes, A.E. Mnzava, K.J. Njunwa, J. Myamba, M.D. Kivuyo, N. Hill, J.D. Lines and C.F. Curtis, "Trial of Pyrthroid Impregnated bednets in an Area of Tanzania Holoendemic for Malaria. Part 2: Effects on the Malaria Vector opulation", *Acta Tropica*, vol. 49, no. 2, 1991, pp. 97–108.

Mahoney, R.T. and C.M. Morel, "A Global Health Innovation System (GHIS)", *Innovation Strategy Today*, vol. 2, no. 1, 2006, pp. 1–12.

Makemba, A.M., P.J. Winch, V.M. Makame, G.L. Mehl, Z. Premji, J.N. Minjas and C.J. Shiff, *Treatment Practices for Degedege, a Locally Recognised Febrile Illness, and Implications for Strategies to Decrease Mortality from Severe Malaria in Bagamoyo District*, Tanzania, 1996.

Malerba, F., "Sectoral Systems of Innovation and Production", *Research Policy*, vol. 31, no. 2, 2002, pp. 247–264.

Malerba, F., "Sectoral Systems of Innovation: Basic Concepts", in F. Malerba (ed.) *Sectoral Systems of Innovation: Concepts, Issues and Analyses of Six Major Sectors in Europe*, Cambridge University Press, Cambridge, 2004, pp. 9–41.

Malerba, F., "Sectoral Systems: How and Why Innovation Differs across Sectors", in J. Fagerberg, D.C. Mowery and R.R. Nelson (eds) *The Oxford Handbook of Innovation*, Oxford University Press, Oxford, 2005, pp. 381–405.

Malerba, F., "Innovation and the Evolution of Industries", *Journal of Evolutionary Economics*, vol. 16, no. 1, 2006, pp. 3–23.

Malerba, F. and L. Orsenigo, "Towards a History Friendly Model of Innovation, Market Structure and Regulation in the Dynamics of the Pharmaceutical Industry: The Age of Random Screening", KiteS Working Papers 124, KITeS, Centre for Knowledge, Internationalization and Technology Studies, Universita' Bocconi, Milano, Italy, 2000.

Malerba, F., R. Nelson, L. Orsenigo and S. Winter, "Competition and Industrial Policies in a 'History Friendly' Model of the Evolution of the Computer Industry", *International Journal of Industrial Organization*, vol. 19, no. 5, 2001, pp. 635–664.

Mansfield, E., "Intellectual Property Protection, Foreign Direct Investment, and Technology Transfer", International Finance Corporation Discussion Paper No. 19, 1994.

Mansfield, E., "Academic Research and Industrial Innovation: An Update of Empirical Findings", *Research Policy*, vol. 26, no. 7–8, 1998, pp. 773–776.

Marchant, T., J.A. Schellenberg, T. Edgar, R. Nathan, S. Abdulla, O. Mukasa, H. Mponda and C. Lengeler, "Socially Marketed Insecticide-treated Nets Improve Malaria and Anaemia in Pregnancy in Southern Tanzania", *Tropical Medicine and International Health*, vol. 7, no. 2, 2002, pp. 149–158.

Marsili, O. and B. Verspagen, "Technology and the Dynamics of Industrial Structures: An Empirical Mapping of Dutch Manufacturing", *Industrial and Corporate Change*, vol. 11, no. 4, 2002, pp. 791–815.

Mashelkar, R.A., "Nation Building through Science and Technology: A Developing World Perspective", *Innovation Strategy Today*, vol. 1, 2005, pp. 16–32.

Maskus, K., *Intellectual Property Rights in the Global Economy*, Institute for International Economics, Washington DC, 2000.

Maskus, K. and J.H. Reichman, "The Globalization of Private Knowledge Goods and the Privatization of Global Public Goods", *Journal of International Economic Law*, vol. 7, no. 2, June 2004, pp. 279–320.

Matsoso, P., M. Auton, S. Banoo, H. Fomundam, H. Leng and S. Noazin, "How does the Regulatory Framework Affect Incentives for Research and Development", A Proposal for a Regulatory Framework to Improve Regulatory Capacity and Introduce Incentives for Research and Development in Areas of Public Health Importance, Draft on file with author, 2004.

Maxwell, C.A., J. Myamba, K.J. Njunwa, B.M. Greenwood and C.F. Curtis, "Comparison of Bednets Impregnated with Different Pyrethroids for their Impacts on Mosquitoes and on Re-infection with Malaria Fever after Clearance of Pre-existing Infections with Chlorproguanil-dapsone", *Transactions of the Royal Society of Tropical Medicine and Hygiene*, vol. 93, 1999, pp. 4–11.

Mboera, L.E.G., B. Diyamett, E. Shayo, S.F. Rumisha, and J.E. Mghamba, "Health Innovation Systems in Tanzania", Preliminary Report, November 2004

Menghaney, L., "HIV/AIDS Treatment Legal and Political Choices for India", *Journal of Creative Communications*, 2006, vol. 1, no. 2, pp. 195–202.

Merges, R., "Intellectual Property Rights and Bargaining Breakdown: The Case of Blocking Patents", *Tennessee Law Review*, vol. 62, no. 1, 1994, pp. 74–106.

Metcalfe, J.S., "Evolution, Technology Policy and Technology Management", *Prometheus*, vol. 12, no. 1, 1994, pp. 29–35.

Metcalfe, J.S., A. James and A. Mina, "Emergent Innovation Systems and the Delivery of Clinical Services: The Case of Intra-ocular Lenses", *Research Policy*, vol. 34, no. 9, 2005, pp. 1283–1304.

Metcalfe, J.S., J. Foster and R. Ramlogan, "Adaptive Economic Growth", *Cambridge Journal of Economics*, vol. 30, no. 1, 2006, pp. 7–32.

Milgrom P.J. and J.D. Roberts, *Economics, Organization and Management*, Prentice Hall, Upper Saddle River NJ, 1996.

Miller, J.E., A. Buriyo, A. Karugila and J.D. Lines, "A New Strategy for Treating Nets. Part 1: Formulation and Dosage", *Tropical Medicine and International Health*, vol. 4, no. 3, 1999a, pp. 160–166.

Miller, J.E., C.O. Jones, S. Ndunguru, V. Curtis and J. Lines, "A New Strategy for Treating Nets. Part 2: Users' Perceptions for Insecticide Dosage", *Tropical Medicine and International Health*, vol. 4, no. 3, 1999b, pp. 167–174.

Ministry of Science and Technology (MOST), "Review of the Biotechnology Development in Vietnam", Report of conference, Hanoi, 2003.

Mokyr, J., "Long-term Economic Growth and the History of Technology", in P. Aghion and S. Durlauf (eds) *Handbook of Economic Growth*, Elsevier, Amsterdam, 2003, pp. 15–21.

Morel C., *et al.*, "Health Innovation in Developing Countries to Address Diseases of the Poor", *Innovation Strategy Today*, vol. 1, no. 1, 2005, pp. 1–15.

Mowery, D., "The Role of Knowledge-based Public Goods", Industrial Development Report Background Paper series, UNIDO, 2005.

Mowery, D. and A.A. Ziedonis, "Market Magic or Market Failure? Structural Change in the U.S. National Innovation System", *STI Review*, vol. 22, no. 1, 1998, pp. 101–136.

MSF, "Untangling the Web of Price Reductions: A Pricing Guide for the Purchase of ARV for Developing Countries", Geneva, 2008.

Muchie, M., P. Gammeltoft and B.-Å. Lundvall (eds), *Putting Africa First: The Making of African Innovation Systems*, Aalborg University Press, Aalborg, Denmark, 2003.

National Science Foundation (NSF), *Science Indicators*, Arlington, VA, 2006.

Nelson, R., "The Simple Economics of Basic Scientific Research", *Journal of Political Economy*, vol. 67, no. 3, 1959, pp. 297–306.

Nelson, R.R., 1986. "Explaining Technical Change", *Journal of Economic Behavior and Organization*, vol. 7, no. 3, 1986, pp. 336–339.

Nelson, R., *National Innovation Systems: A Comparative Analysis*, Oxford University Press, New York and Oxford, 1993.

Nelson, R.R., "Economic Development from the Perspective of Evolutionary Economic Theory", *Oxford Development Studies*, vol. 36, no. 1, 2008, pp. 9–21.

Nelson, R.R., "Capitalism as an Engine of Progress", *Research Policy*, vol. 19, no. 3, 1990, pp. 193–214.

Nelson, R.R., "The Changing Institutional Requirements for Technological and Economic Catch Up", *International Journal Of Technological Learning, Innovation And Development*, vol. 1, no. 1, 2007, pp. 4–12.

Nelson, R.R., and N. Rosenberg, "Technical Innovation and National Systems", in R.R. Nelson (ed.) *National Innovation Systems: A Comparative Analysis*, Oxford University Press, Oxford, 1993, pp. 3–22.

Nightingale, P. and S. Mahdi, *"The Evolution of Pharmaceutical Innovation"*, in G. Dosi and M. Mazzucato (eds) *Knowledge Accumulation and Industry Evolution: The Case of Pharma-Biotech*, Cambridge University Press, Cambridge, 2006, pp. 73–111.

NISTPASS, "Biotechnology Innovation System in Viet Nam", Background Study prepared for the UNU-MERIT Project on Comparative Systems of Biotechnology in Asia and Africa, 2007, file on draft with author.

Njunwa, K.J., J.D. Lines, S.M. Magesa, A.E. Mnzava, T.J. Wilkes, M. Alilio, K. Kivumbi, and C.F. Curtis, "Trial of Pyrthroid Impregnated Bednets in an Area of Tanzania Holoendemic for Malaria. Part 1: Operational Methods and Acceptability. *Acta Tropica*, vol. 49, no. 2, 1991, pp. 87–96.

Nooman, A. and J. Stiglitz, "Africa Task Force Meeting: Background, Themes and Agenda", Background Paper, IPD Dialogue Series 1, Columbia University, New York, 2007.

North, D.C., *Institutions, Institutional Change and Economic Performance*, Cambridge University Press, Cambridge, 1990.

North, D.C., "The New Institutional Economics and Development", Economic History 9309002, EconWPA, 1993.

North, D.C., *Economic Performance through Time: Empirical Studies in Institutional Change*, Cambridge University Press, Cambridge, 1996.

Nguyen Thanh Tung, "Guidance for SMEs in Technology Innovation", working paper, NISTPASS, Hanoi, 2004.

Ocampo, J. A. and R. Vos, *Uneven Economic Development*, Zed Books, London, 2007.

Odame, H., "Thinking about Local Set-ups: Making Sense of Biotechnology in Kenyan Agriculture", Paper presented at the Workshop on the Globalization of Agricultural Biotechnology: Multi-disciplinary views from the South, Centre for the Study of Globalization and Regionalization at the University of Warwick, UK, 11–13 March 2005.

Odame, H., P. Kameri-Mbote and D. Wafula, "Innovation and Policy Process: Case of Transgenic Sweet Potato in Kenya", *Economic and Political Weekly*, vol. 37, no. 27, 6 July 2002, pp. 2727–2777.

OECD, *National Innovation Systems*, Organization for Economic Cooperation and Development, Paris, 1997.

OECD, *The Emerging Digital Economy*, Organization for Economic Cooperation and Development, Paris, 1998.

OECD, *Innovative Clusters: Drivers of National Innovation Systems*, Organization for Economic Cooperation and Development, Paris, 2000.

OECD, *Sectoral Case Studies in Innovation: Pharmaceutical Biotechnology*, Organization for Economic Cooperation and Development, Paris, 2006.

OECD, *Bioeconomy to 2030*, Organization for Economic Cooperation and Development, Paris, 2008.

Ohba, M. and P. Figueiredo, "Collaboration to Compete: A Search into Capabilities and Strategic Alliances in the Pharmaceutical Industry", *Journal of Technology Management and Innovation*, vol. 2, no. 2, 2007, pp. 18–30.

Orbinski, J. and B. Burciul, "Moving Beyond Charity for R&D for Neglected Diseases", in J.C. Cohen, P. Illingworth and U. Schüklenk (eds) *The Power of Pills*, Pluto Press, London, 2006, pp. 117–124.

Organisation of Pharmaceutical Producers in India (OPPI), *35th Annual Report*, Mumbai, OPPI, 2000.

Osman, F.A., *A Study of the Health Policy Process: Policy Making in Bangladesh*. A H Development Publishing House, Dhaka, Bangladesh, 2004.

Oyeyinka, B., *Learning to Compete in African Industry*, Ashgate Publishing Limited, Aldershot, 2006.

Oyeyinka, B. and P. Gehl Sampath, "Learning Through Interorganizational Interactions: Public Research Institutes in the Nigerian (Bio)pharmaceutical System of Innovation", *European Journal of Development Research*, Special Issue on "Promoting Innovation, Productivity and Industrial Growth and Reducing Industrial Poverty: Bridging the Policy Gap", vol. 19, no. 1, March 2007, pp. 174–193.

Oyeyinka, B. and P. Gehl Sampath, *Latecomer Development: Innovation, Knowledge and Economic Growth*, Routledge, Oxford, 2009a.

Oyeyinka, B. and P. Gehl Sampath, *The Gene Revolution and Global Food Security: Biotechnology Innovation in Latecomers*, Palgrave Macmillan, London, 2009b.

Oyeyinka, B. and R. Rasiah, *Uneven Economic Development*, Edwar Elgar, London, 2009.

Oyeyinka, B., L.K. Mytelka and P. Gehl Sampath, *Study on the Biopharmaceutical System of Innovation in Nigeria*, UNU-INTECH/ NABDA Study for the IDRC, November 2004.

Pakes, A. and Z. Griliches, "Patents and R and D at the Firm Level: A First Look", NBER Working Papers 0561, National Bureau of Economic Research, Cambridge MA, 1980.

Pakes, A. and Z. sGriliches, "Patents and R&D at the Firm Level: A First Look", in Z, Griliches, Z. (ed.) *R&D, Patents, and Productivity*, University of Chicago Press, Chicago, IL, 1984, pp. 55–72.

Pavitt, K., "Sectoral Patterns of Technical Change: Towards a Taxonomy and a Theory", *Research Policy*, vol. 13, no. 6, 1984, pp. 343–373.

Pavitt, K., "On the Nature of Technology", Inaugural Lecture at University of Sussex, Brighton, UK, 1987.

Pavitt, K., "Viewpoint: Internationalisation of Technological Innovation", *Science and Public Policy*, vol. 19, no. 2, 1992, pp. 119–123.

Popovici, I., "Impact of Intellectual Property Rights Reforms on the Diffusion of Knowledge through FDI", NBER Working Paper 0602, 2006.

Powell, W., "Inter-Organizational Collaborations in the Biotechnology Industry", *Journal of Institutional and Theoretical Economics*, vol. 152, no. 1, 1996, pp. 197–215.

Primo Braga, C.A., "Trade-related Intellectual Property Issues: The Uruguay Round Agreement and its Economic Implications", in W. Martin and L.A. Winter (eds) *The Uruguay Round and the Developing Countries*, World Bank discussion paper 307, World Bank, Washington DC, 1995, pp. 381–411.

Pugatch, M.P., "Intellectual Property and Pharmaceutical Data Exclusivity in the Context of Innovation and Market Access', Paper Presented at the UNCTAD-ICTSD Dialogue on Ensuring Policy Options for Affordable Access to Essential medicines, Bellagio, 12–16 October 2004.

Raffetry, M.A., "Managing Change in Biotech: Setbacks and Failures", *Nature Biotechnology*, Vol. 25, No. 9, 2007, p. 1059.

Raman, A. and J.W. Bjorkman, *Public Private Partnerships for Health Care Delivery in India*, Routledge, Oxford, 2008.

Ramesh, D., "Actavis to Buy Indian API Business", *Chemical Week*, 14–21 February 2007, p. 23.

Robertson, P.L. and R.N. Langlois, "Innovation, Networks, and Vertical Integration", *Research Policy*, vol. 24, no. 4, 1995, pp. 543–562.

Rodrik, D., *In Search of Prosperity: Analytic Narratives on Economic Growth*, Princeton University Press, Princeton NJ, 2003.

Rodrik, D., "Industrial Policy for the Twenty-First Century", CEPR Discussion Papers 4767, 2004.

Roffe, P., "Bilateral Agreements and a TRIPS-plus World: The Chile–USA Free Trade Agreement", TRIPS Issue Papers No. 4, Quakers International Affairs Programme, Ottawa, 2004.

Rosenberg, N., *Inside the Black Box: Technology and Economics*, Cambridge University Press, Cambridge, 1982.

Sakakibara, M. and L. Branstetter, "Do Stronger Patents Induce More Innovation? Evidence from the Japanese 1988 Patent Reforms", *RAND Journal of Economics*, vol. 32, no. 1, 2001, pp. 77–100.

Schellenberg, J.A., S. Abdulla, R. Nathan, O. Mukasa, T.J. Marchant, N. KIkumbih, A.K. Mushi, H. Mponda, H. Minja, H. Mshinda, M. Tanner and C. Lengeler, "Effect of Large-scale Social Marketing of Insecticide Treated Nets on Child Survival in Rural Tanzania", *Lancet*, vol. 357, no. 9264, 2001, pp. 1241–1247.

Scherer, F.M., "The Innovation Lottery", in R. Dreyfuss, D.L. Zimmerman and H. First (eds) *Expanding the Boundaries of Intellectual Property*, Oxford University Press, Oxford, 2001, pp. 3–21.

Scherer, F.M. and S. Weisburst, "Economic Effects of Strengthening Pharmaceutical Patent Protection in Italy", International Review of Industrial Property and Copyright Law, 1995. p. 1009.

Schmiedchen, F. and C. Spenneman, "Intellectual Property Rights and Public Health", VDW Policy Papers, No. 1, 2008, Berlin.

Scotchmer, S., "Standing on the Shoulders of Giants: Cumulative Research and the Patent Law", *Journal of Economic Perspectives, American Economic Association*, vol. 5, no. 1, 1991, pp. 29–41.

Seigel, D.S., D. Waldman and A. Link, "Assessing the Impact of Organizational Practices on the Productivity of Technology Transfer offices: An Exploratory Study", NBER Working Paper series 7256, 1999.

Siegel, D.S., D.A. Waldman and A.N. Link, "Assessing the Impact of Organizational Practices on the Productivity of University Technology Transfer Offices: An Exploratory Study", *Research Policy*, vol. 32, no. 1, 2003, pp. 27–48.

Siegel, D.S., D.A. Waldman, L.E. Atwater and A.N. Link, "Toward a Model of the Effective Transfer of Scientific Knowledge from Academicians to Practitioners: Qualitative Evidence from the Commercialization of University Technologies", *Journal of Engineering and Technology Management*, vol. 21, no. 1–2, 2004, pp. 115–142.

Simoens, S., "International Comparison of Generic Medicine Prices", *Current Medical Research and Opinion*, 2007 Online, available at: www.redorbit.com/news/health/1195638/international_comparison_of_generic_medicine_prices/index.html (accessed 5 April 2008).

Singer, P.A., E.B. Court, A. Bhatt, S.E. Frew, H. Greenwood, D.L. Persad, F. Salamanca-Buentello, B. Séguin, A.D. Taylor, H.T. Daer and A.S. Daar, "Applying Genomics-related Technologies for Africa's Health Needs", *African Journal of Medicine and Medical Sciences*, vol. 36, 2007, pp. 7–14.

Smith, K., "Measuring Innovation", in J. Fagerberg, D.C. Mowery and R.R. Nelson (eds) *The Oxford Handbook of Innovation*, Oxford University Press, Oxford, 2005, pp. 148–177.

Smits, R.E.H.M. and W.P.C. Boon, "The Role of Users in the Pharmaceutical Industry", *Drug Discovery Today*, vol. 13, No. 7–8, April 2008, pp. 353–359.

Solomon, B.O., "Sorghum Activities in Nigeria as they Relate to ABS", a presentation by the Nigerian National Biotechnology Development Agency, 20 September 2008, on file with author.

Srinivasan, R., "Sources, Characteristics and Effects of Emerging Technologies: Research Opportunities in Innovation", *Industrial Marketing Management*, vol. 37, no. 6, 2008, pp. 633–640.

Stiglitz, J.E., "On the Market for Principles of Economics Textbooks: Innovation and Product Differentiation", *Journal of Economic Education*, vol. 19, no. 2, 1988, pp. 171–177.

Stiglitz, J.E., "Public Policy for a Knowledge Economy", Department for Trade and Industry and Centre for Economic Policy Research, London, 1999.

Stiglitz, J.E. and B.C. Greenwald, "Externalities in Economics with Imperfect Information and Incomplete Markets", *Quarterly Journal of Economics*, vol. 101, no. 2, 1986, pp. 229–264.

Teubal, M., "Towards an R&D Strategy for Israel", *Economic Quarterly*, vol. 46, no. 2, 1999, pp. 359–383.

Thumm, N., *Intellectual Property Rights: National Systems and Harmonisation in Europe*, Contributions to Economics, Physica-Verlag (Springer), Heidelberg, Germany, 2000.

Tait, J., "Governing Synthetic Biology: Processes and Outcomes", Draft, on file with the author, 2007a.

Tait, J., "Systemic Interactions in Lifescience Innovation", *Technology Analysis and Strategic Management*, vol. 19, no. 3, May 2007b, pp. 257–277.

Tait, J., J. Chataway and D. Wield, "The Case for Smart Regulation", Appropriate Governance of the Lifesciences – 2, Innogen Policy Brief, 2007.

Tait, J., D. Wield, J. Chataway and A. Bruce, "Health Biotechnology to 2030", report to OECD International Futures Project, "The Bio-Economy to 2030: Designing a Policy Agenda", OECD, Paris, 2008, p. 51. Online, available at: www.oecd.org/dataoecd/12/10/40922867.pdf (accessed 14 July 2009).

Tami, A., G. Mubyazi, A. Talbert, H. Mshinda, S. Duchon and C. Lengeler, "Evaluation of Olyset Insecticide Treated Nets Distributed Seven Year Previously in Tanzania", *Malaria Journal*, vol. 3, 2004, p. 19.

Towse, A., "Industrial Policy and the Pharmaceutical Industry", Office of Health and Economics, London, 1995.

Ullah, A. and H.S. Muhammad, *Unani Chikitsha Bigyaner Itihash* (History of Unani Medicine), Bangladesh Board of Unani and Ayurvedic Systems of Medicine, Dhaka, 2002.

UNAIDS, "AIDS Epidemic Update: Special Report on HIV/AIDS", UNAIDS/WHO, Geneva, Switzerland, 2006.

UNCTAD, *World Investment Report*, UNCTAD, Geneva, 2006a.

UNCTAD, *Developing Productive Capacities: Least Developed Countries Report*, United Nations, New York and Geneva, 2006b.

UNCTAD, *Knowledge, Technological Learning and Innovation for Development: The Least Developed Countries Report*, UNCTAD, Geneva, 2007.

Vidotti, C.C.F., L.L.C. Castro and S.S. Calil, "New Drugs in Brazil: Do They Meet Brazilian Public Health Needs?" *Rev Panam Salud Publica*, vol. 24, no. 1, 2008, pp. 36–45.

Wafula, J.S. and C. Falconi, "Agricultural Biotechnology Research Indicators", Kenya Discussion Paper No. 98–9, The Hague, ISNAR, September 1998.

Wagner, C. and L. Leydesdorff, "Mapping Global Science Using International Co-Authorships: A Comparison of 1990 and 2000", *International Journal of Technology and Globalization*, Vol. 3, 2005.

Waning, B. and C. Cashin, "Development of a Simulation Model to Measure Potential Cost Savings from Reducing Treatment Costs for Antiretroviral Medicines", Draft for the DFID, 25 March 2008, on file with the author.

WHO, "Demand Forecast for Antiretroviral Drugs in Low and Middle Income Countries 2007–2008", prepared by the WHO, UNAIDS, Clinton Foundation and the Mexican Institute for Public Health, November 2007.

WHO, "A Summary Report by the Global Price Reporting Mechanism on Antiretroviral Medicines", World Health Organization, Geneva, February 2008a.

WHO, "Towards Universal Access: Scaling Up Priority HIV/AIDS Interventions in the Health Sector", Progress Report, World Health Organization, Geneva, 2008b.

Williamson, O.E., "Transation Cost Economics: The Governance of Contractual Relations", *Journal of Law and Economics*, vol. 22, no. 2, 1979, pp. 233–261.

Woodcock, J., *et al.*, "The FDA's Assessment of Follow-On Protein Products: A Historical Perspective", *Nature Reviews Drug Discovery*, vol. 6, no. 6, 2007, pp. 437–442.

Woo-Cumings, M., "Chalmers Johnson and the Politics of Nationalism and Development", in M. Woo-Cumings (ed.) *The Developmental State*, Cornell University Press, Ithaca NY, 1999, pp. 1–31.

World Bank, "Revitalizing the Agricultural Technology System in Bangladesh", Bangladesh Development Series, paper No. 7, The World Bank Office, Dhaka, 2005a.

World Bank, "Promoting the Rural Non-Farm Sector in Bangladesh", University Press Limited, Dhaka, 2005b.

World Health Report, *Working Together for Health*, World Health Organization, Geneva, 2006.

Zeng, M. and P.J. Williamson, *Dragons at your Door: How Chinese Cost Innovation is Disrupting Global Competition*, Harvard Business Press, Boston MA, 2007.

Index